T0339531

ORGANIZING CHRISTMAS

Organizing Christmas is an exploration of the organizational character of Christmas. Taking as its starting point the view that Christmas initially achieved popularity due to its potential to promote social cohesion and political stability, this book both charts and scrutinizes its global emergence as the year's preeminent economic and organizational event.

Combining historical narrative, original interviews, and social scientific research and theories, it tells the story of how Christmas came to dominate the festival landscape and how it emerged as an integral component of the global evolution of contemporary social and economic relations. From the pre-Christian celebrations and politics of the turning of the calendar year, through the power games of Elizabethan England and the wily reinvention of the season by industrious Victorians, to today's vast economic and logistical exercise that relies on everything from global supply chains to the domestic division of labour, *Organizing Christmas* demonstrates how the season exemplifies the spirit and practices of industrial, and now post-industrial, modernity.

As well as documenting this fact, however, *Organizing Christmas* also critically interrogates what has become a vast festive-industrial complex. From low-paid factory workers in Yiwu to Santa Claus performers in Kingston, readers are given a chance to consider what the cost of this global festival might be and whether it is a price worth paying. Drawing on intellectual resources ranging from Adorno and Horkheimer's classic critique of the culture industry, through Böhme's analysis of the sociomaterial production of atmospheres, to Bloch's 'principle of hope', it paints a picture of Christmas as a profoundly important, if deeply contested historical, cultural and, most significantly, organizational phenomenon.

Aimed at students and academics in Organization Studies, Cultural Studies, and the Sociology of Work and Employment, as well as the general reader interested in the festive season, *Organizing Christmas* offers a differing perspective on a subject so familiar and yet so often overlooked.

Philip Hancock is Professor of Work and Organization at the University of Essex. He is a member of the Centre for Work Organization and Society, and his work on organizational aesthetics, spatiality, and the challenges of working at Christmas has been widely published in international journals and edited collections.

ORGANIZING CHRISTMAS

Philip Hancock

Routledge
Taylor & Francis Group

NEW YORK AND LONDON

Cover image: © D3signAllTheThings

First published 2024
by Routledge
605 Third Avenue, New York, NY 10158

and by Routledge
4 Park Square, Milton Park, Abingdon, Oxon, OX14 4RN

Routledge is an imprint of the Taylor & Francis Group, an informa business

© 2024 Taylor & Francis

Library of Congress Cataloging-in-Publication Data
Names: Hancock, Philip, 1965– author.
Title: Organizing Christmas / Philip Hancock.
Description: New York, NY : Routledge, 2024. |
Includes bibliographical references and index.
Identifiers: LCCN 2023010514 | ISBN 9781138638150 (hardback) |
ISBN 9781032552705 (paperback) | ISBN 9781315637969 (ebook)
Subjects: LCSH: Christmas–Social aspects–History. |
Christmas–Economic aspects–History. | Organization.
Classification: LCC GT4985 .H2725 2024 |
DDC 394.2663–dc23/eng/20230508
LC record available at https://lccn.loc.gov/2023010514

ISBN: 978-1-138-63815-0 (hbk)
ISBN: 978-1-032-55270-5 (pbk)
ISBN: 978-1-315-63796-9 (ebk)

DOI: 10.4324/9781315637969

Typeset in Times New Roman
by Newgen Publishing UK

CONTENTS

PREFACE

Christmas, or so we are told, is the most wonderful time of the year: A time when treetops glisten and children listen, and when it may well be cold outside but at least war is over (if you want it). It is a season that many people, especially children, often look forward to with unbridled anticipation. They tick the months, weeks, and days off the calendar until December comes around once more, and the festivities can begin. For many others, of course, Christmas is something that is at best tolerated if not, at worst, something they would rather ignore or avoid altogether. Nonetheless, whether one loves, hates, or is ambivalent about Christmas, from Tokyo to Chaguanas, Minsk to Colombo, the fact is that it has become a global phenomenon that is nigh on 'inescapable' (Bowler, 2005: viii).

My own attitude towards Christmas has probably reflected all of these perspectives at one time or another. As a very young child, it was, without doubt, the highlight of the year despite the strange reluctance of the adults around me to always embrace the festive spirit. As I grew, I realized, however, that the spirit of Christmas could go either way at home. As such, I viewed it with an increasing sense of ambivalence, especially as I entered my teenage years. It was not until my early 30s and the opportunity to start my own family that, once again, Christmas became something more than a few bleak days to be endured but rather a time to be truly enjoyed.

Nevertheless, despite my somewhat uneven relationship with the season, it is one that fascinated me for many years, if not decades. In particular, what really struck me was the apparent contradiction between all the talk of Christmas as a magical time in which one could relax and let peace and goodwill flow, and the reality of all the work and stress that I saw going on around me, both at home and in the wider world. Having then eventually become an academic in a business school with a particular interest in work and its organization, it was not long before I started to try and order my thoughts on this matter more systematically.

In 2008, as I describe in the book, these thoughts led to the idea of putting together a short symposium of like-minded colleagues to discuss the relationship between Christmas, work, and its organization. Prior to this, with a few notable exceptions (Rosen, 1988; Thompson and Hickey, 1989; Bartunek, 2006), the idea of Christmas had featured little in the academic field of organization studies, and I, along with my co-organizer Alf Rehn, had really no idea how it would go down. Nonetheless, despite our concerns, the event proved to be an enjoyably fruitful couple of days resulting in not only a special 2011 Christmas edition of the scholarly journal *Organization* that featured papers from the symposium but also a small research grant with which I was able to start the work that eventually culminated in this book.

Given its origins in the first decade of the century, you will notice, however, that it has taken me many more years than I care to remember to finish actually writing it. At some point along the way, I discovered that I am not an enthusiastic writer and that I am far too easily distracted by other responsibilities and the immediate gratification derived from pleasurable trivialities. And it is due to this extended gestation period that I have somewhat lost track of all the people who have helped me in its production and kindly provided me with all sorts of not only insights into their own experiences of Christmas but also news reports, random festive statistics, and even seasonal photographs, not to mention stimulating and thought-provoking discussions.

Despite this, there are several individuals that I would like to express my thanks to. Firstly, Alf Rehn deserves special recognition for being audacious enough to assist me in organizing the two-day symposium on *Organizing Christmas* which, as I mentioned above, ultimately led to the writing of this book. Additionally, I want to express my appreciation to all those who participated in that event and who approached the entire affair with much more seriousness than I really anticipated. Although I believe I can remember everyone, if I have inadvertently left anyone out, I apologize, and if you were not in attendance, I hope that mentioning your name does not cause any offense or harm to your career. Therefore, I extend my thanks to Jean Bartunek, Jo Brewis, Gibson Burrell, Martin Corbet, Karen Dale, Peter Fleming, Gavin Jack, Jeanette Lemmergaard, Damian O'Doherty, Sara Louise Muhr, Martin Parker, Ann Rippin, and Andre Spicer. Thank you!

Next, there are those who have invited me to numerous academic and public discussions about my work, mainly, it should be said, in December. Alas, I can't remember them all, but Simon Lilley, Frank Worthington, and David Collins all come to mind as having provided opportunities for me to discuss and defend my work. I would also like to thank the British Academy, which funded my initial research through the award of a small research grant (SG54347), James Scott, who undertook some of the interviews for me, and the business schools of the University of Warwick and the University of Essex, both of which supported me as the work developed.

Perhaps the most exciting opportunity to discuss many of the ideas contained in this book, as well as collect invaluable data, came from the chance to visit the University of Lapland in Rovaniemi, Finland, firstly as a visiting professor in 2015, and then as a contributor to their postgraduate Christmas Experience Academy in 2018. And no, I am not making it up. There really is a University of Lapland. Look it up, it is a great institution. As such, I would like to extend my thanks to all those whom I have met and worked with there, not least of all José-Carlos García-Rosell who arranged both these particular visits and whose shared academic interest in Christmas has made him not only a valid collaborator but also a friend.

As well as academic colleagues, I also would like to extend my deepest gratitude to all those working in the various Christmas industries and beyond who, over the years, gave up their time to speak with me and share their experiences and ideas about the organization of Christmas. From company directors to Santa Claus performers, and from musicians and actors to homemakers, amongst many others, their openness and insight brought the book's subject matter to life and made much of its preparation a joy. Finally, in extending my thanks, I would also like to give a special mention to the organizers of, and participants in, the World Santa Claus Congress in Bakken Amusement Park near Copenhagen, whose willingness to let me take part in their event and generally hang out with more Santas than one could shake the proverbial candy cane at was invaluable.

On a personal note, I want to thank Veronica, Michael, and Jeremy, even though they are no longer with me, and my sister Abbigayle, who most certainly is, all of whom and in different ways, made Christmas special over the years.

In particular, I would like to express my love and gratitude to my children, Ellis and William, who helped me rediscover the joys of Christmas and reignited my love for it. Despite its imperfections, they helped me again see the fun, happiness, and magic of the season through their eyes. As they enter adulthood, I hope they cherish the memories we shared and continue to embrace the possibilities of Christmas.

Last, but anything but least, I would like to thank Melissa, who shared my first Christmas away from my parental home and has been with me ever since. While I have been working on this book, she has been a constant source of support, inspiration, and information. And while I must admit this book has disrupted our Christmas preparations on more than one occasion, she has unflinchingly backed my efforts to complete it, and for that, and so much more, I am eternally grateful.

References

Bartunek, J. (2006) 'The Christmas Gift: A Story of Dialectics'. *Organization Studies* 27(12): 1875–1894.

Bowler, G. (2005) *Santa Claus: A Biography*. Toronto: McClelland and Stewart Ltd.

Rosen, M. (1988) 'You Asked for It: Christmas at the Bosses' Expense'. *Journal of Management Studies* 25(5): 463–480.

Thompson, W.E. and Hickey, J.V. (1989) 'Myth, Identity, and Social Interaction: Encountering Santa Claus at the Mall'. *Qualitative Sociology* 12(4): 371–389.

INTRODUCTION

Introduction

This book offers a critical analysis of the relationship between organization and Christmas. It explores how various practices, values, and organizational logics contribute to the creation and shaping of Christmas, from the manufacturing of presents and decorations to household preparations for a successful Christmas dinner. It also investigates how Christmas impacts and organizes different aspects of society, including nation-states, economies, and family and individual identities, delving into the historical development of Christmas, from its roots in the Christian church to its commercialization by film studios and record labels. In doing so, the narrative challenges the notion of Christmas as merely a carefree and festive occasion, highlighting instead the immense organizational resources, both human and material, that are required to make it happen, as well as the social and economic interests it serves.

Not that this should imply this is a book simply about, or a critique of, the role of organizations in the commercialization of the season. Rather, as I shall explain later in this introduction, the concept of organization that underpins it is not restricted to the activities of businesses, big or small, or indeed even other formal organizations such as governments or religious foundations. Nevertheless, considering the importance of Christmas to business, alongside the impact business organizations have not only on Christmas and its customs but also on many people's everyday lives, commerce remains an important and guiding thread throughout the book. After all, across the year, the global production and distribution of many goods are organized with an eye on them being consumed mainly at and for Christmas. At the same time, Christmas also

DOI: 10.4324/9781315637969-1

functions as a barometer of business performance and a driver of investment as companies make organizational decisions about, say, levels of staff recruitment based on the buoyancy of their seasonal performance.

Furthermore, for many people, business organizations are also often at the heart of creating Christmas. For not only has celebrating Christmas become closely identified with obviously commercial activities such as shopping, many of the events and attractions that are today closely associated with 'doing' Christmas, from attending shows, visiting Santa Claus, and experiencing Christmas parades and fairs are themselves conceived, sponsored, and organized by business organizations. In promoting such events and activities, these organizations are not only setting out to create a festive environment that might encourage additional consumption at that point in space and time, however. It is deeper than this in that they contribute to the mass formation and production of what is a suitably festive subject; an individual who, as I shall argue, invests themselves in the pursuit of the perfect Christmas unconstrained by many of the usual everyday concerns of life, particularly that of affordability.

Nevertheless, as I have said, there is more than commerce and business organizations to this book. From its earliest role as a focus of social solidarity in the face of extreme environmental challenges to, more latterly, the part it plays in sustaining established ideas surrounding the supremacy of the family as a unit of social reproduction and the gendered division of labour that consistently underpins it, Christmas also plays an important role in helping to organize many of those material and discursive practices that constitute contemporary social relations. Moreover, it is a season that is deeply enmeshed in the ways and means by which the prevailing values and practices of Western cultures have been sustained and often exported. As such, in bringing together ideas and material from a range of sources, this book seeks to contribute to a way of thinking critically about Christmas that is willing to move beyond certain fixed identities and often established categories in respect of the season; exploring and questioning common sense assumptions and expectations that surround what it is to both study and celebrate Christmas.

Why (Organizing) Christmas?

Before I go any further with introducing the content of the book, however, I feel that it is probably incumbent on me to say a little about why I have chosen to write about Christmas at all, especially from an organizational perspective. Today, as a professor of work and organization at a UK research university, my fascination with the season has raised more than the occasional quizzical eyebrow amongst colleagues frequently drawing the question, 'so, just why are you interested in Christmas?'. To this, my somewhat perfunctory answer usually goes along the lines of 'well, it's something a bit different, isn't it?'. Or, if I am pushed a little harder, it might also take the supplemental form of 'and I just don't feel that it is an area of economic and organizational activity that is taken seriously enough', and, more often than not, either or both of these responses will usually suffice.

Although, to be honest, these two relatively stock answers are not as disingenuous as they might first appear. Firstly, having started my academic career in sociology departments before moving to a business school, I still sometimes find it challenging to engage with many of the research topics that, quite understandably, interest my colleagues. As such, Christmas has provided a somewhat welcome distraction and is indeed, therefore, 'something a bit different'. Secondly, and perhaps more importantly, given that Christmas is now one of the most economically and organizationally significant events of the year, I genuinely believe that it does not receive the scholarly attention it deserves, especially from academics working in UK business schools.

Furthermore, in addition to the above, I also have a more critical interest in the season. Christmas is often presented as a 'holiday', an escape from the drudgery of work that befits its ancient origins as a celebration of the lull in the annual productive cycle. However, the truth is that for lots of people who celebrate it, and those who do not, this is not their lived experience. For many, if not the majority of people, Christmas is, in fact, a time that demands a significant amount of hard work and organization from them, both in private and in public. It drains energy and financial resources and is often the source of much worry and trepidation. Yet somehow, despite this, Christmas seems to thrive and grow as a promised mid-winter break from the demands of labour and the worries and pressures of everyday life, however unlikely we know this to be.

It is this particular tension, and the urge to explore and understand it at the various points at which these seemingly antithetical expectations collide that has perhaps, more than anything else, continued to draw me back to the topic despite my frequent efforts to leave it behind. As a consequence of this, in this book, I set out to explore not only the organizational dynamics of Christmas but also those practices and beliefs that appear to both often obscure and sustain this apparent contradiction, measuring Christmas against its ability to foster what Aristotle (2004) traditionally termed the good life. What I mean by this is that at various junctures throughout the book, I ask to what extent our contemporary Christmas, and how it is organized, actually supports human flourishing and makes life somehow better as it so often claims to do. In particular, I consider whether it helps us recognize our mutual obligations and responsibilities both to and for others or, rather, despite its themes of family and togetherness, serves to isolate us from one another, increasing somewhat un-Christmas-like competitiveness and division.

The Magic Key – An Organizational Parable

One encounter that particularly inspired my interest in Christmas and its relationship to work and organization I would like to recount here if only to try and set the scene more clearly was, perhaps not unsurprisingly for an academic, with a book. However, this was no academic tome, but rather a story written for preschool and early years children. Entitled *Christmas Adventure* (Hunt and Brychta, 1994), I originally acquired it to read to my then preschool son in the build-up to the season. Part of a series of illustrated early years readers featuring a group of children called *Kipper, Biff, Chip, Wilf*, and *Wilma*, that tell of their adventures with a 'magic key' that can transport them off to faraway places, *Christmas Adventure* opens during a busy Christmas Eve at home where 'mum and dad' are in the kitchen desperately trying to prepare the family Christmas meal.

Visible behind the parents is a list of all the Christmas chores still to be done while, in the foreground, Dad is identified as being particularly 'cross', lamenting the fact that 'Christmas is hard work' and trying in vain to encourage the children to contribute to the domestic economy by putting up the decorations. Suddenly, however, the children are rescued from their household obligations by the key activating, which carries them away to what is described as the 'land of Father Christmas'. Yet, on arrival, the children find not some ethereal landscape of elves and candy canes as they might have expected, but rather a business complex called 'Father Christmas Ltd'. Somewhat bemused, what they experience are sights that will be familiar to anybody who has visited or worked in such a place, including workshops, portacabins, signs to the post room, offices, a deliveries depot, and even a list of international subsidiaries, including 'Santa Claus Inc.' and 'St Nicholas Plc'. However, despite it being Christmas Eve, the one thing they can't find is any sign of Father Christmas himself. This, it turns out, is because he is fast asleep in his armchair.

Why is this? Quite simply because he is exhausted from the work of preparing for Christmas. The laborious demands of organizing a magical Christmas for children across the world have taken their toll, resulting in Santa being unable to put up his own decorations, go food shopping or, most importantly, load his sleigh and prepare to deliver the seasonal gifts. Needless to say, the children quickly realize that Christmas does not simply happen 'by magic' but that it requires planning and hard work. As such, they decide to divide the various functional tasks that need to be done between them, ensuring that Father Christmas has a decorated house and food for his journey while contributing to the organizational effort necessary for a successful Christmas. This lesson is then taken back home, where the last one sees the children are in the kitchen helping their parents prepare the Christmas meal and asking, 'What else can we *do*?'.

For me, this story represented, and indeed still does, a perfect illustration of the narrative of Christmas that I want to explore in this book. Yes, Christmas is a unique event of a sort, and, for some, it might indeed represent a period of downtime and relaxation. Nonetheless, in most cases underpinning the holiday are numerous organized and organizational activities that simply have to take place, be it putting up the decorations and ensuring the turkey is in the oven, to far more public responsibilities such as making the presents and, in this instance, getting them onto Santa's metaphorical sleigh by the allotted hour. Moreover, the children in the story are themselves also subject to a process of ethical and economic organization. They learn, *through Christmas*, that to contribute to the common good one must accept the need to work hard and adopt the subject position of economically active citizens. While this might not be the kind of seasonal subjectivity I discuss later in the book, nonetheless, it illustrates the way in which Christmas can itself organize individuals and how they relate to the world and others.

This is more than a simple children's fantasy, therefore. It is a story that has both normative and economic content. It presents its young readers with a version of Christmas in which the need to 'pitch in' with its organization is both an ethical responsibility and a means of ensuring an economic reward by ensuring Santa can deliver their presents. Furthermore, the story itself contributes to the Christmas narrative and, at the very least, the discursive production of the season, both as a seasonal artefact and, in its reading, as part of how Christmas is itself both organized and organizing.

Which Christmas?

I am aware that so far, when referring to Christmas, I have done so in a fairly unspecific manner, seeming to assume that all Christmases are the same wherever and whenever they are celebrated. Well, in many respects, this has been my intention. For while Christmas traditions and the extent to which they are observed vary not only around the globe but very often within national and regional borders, it is today increasingly possible to speak of a reasonably particular and increasingly dominant style or form of Christmas. Labelled by anthropologist Daniel Miller (1993: 3) the 'Anglo-American Christmas', this is a Christmas that, while both respectful and celebratory of its origins, is a distinct product of modernity, embodying many of the values, priorities, and indeed contradictions and tensions that characterize the age.

Forged in the fires of the intellectual, urban, and industrial revolutions of the eighteenth and nineteenth centuries, the Anglo-American Christmas is a work of human imagination that responded to an age in which God was found wanting (Nietzsche, 1974) and all that was solid, as Karl Marx and Friedrich Engels (2002) declared, melted into air. Revived and reimagined as a legitimizing narrative for both those who wished to champion those productive and consumptive forces that were tearing old certainties apart, as well as for those who sought to defend or reclaim traditional values and practices in order to erect a new moral order in the industrial age, this was a Christmas that looked both to its past and to its future offering, in the face of those tremendous challenges of modernity – many of which remain with us today – such as alienation (Marx, 1973), anomie (Durkheim, 1951), and disenchantment (Weber, 1946), a new hope of recognition, ethics, and especially re-enchantment in the form of its seasonal magic.

And today it is this Anglo-American Christmas, from here on simply referred to as Christmas apart from when it aids clarity, that is the template for what has become '*the* global festival' (Miller, 1993: 5, *original emphasis*) of our age. Characterized predominantly by a combination of British (although in truth, primarily English), Germanic, and American values and practices, it is a Christmas that is mainly secular in character but which champions stability and civic cohesion through its emphasis on an altruistic but predominantly family-oriented celebration. Focusing on the primacy of children, the importance of gift-giving and charity, and the centrality of the figure known as Santa Claus, it is a socially integrative festival (Etzioni, 2004) but also one that is emblematic of many of the contradictions of the age in which it first emerged and, today, continues to thrive.

While now globally dominant, this is not to say, however, that one should simply overlook many of the characteristics, ambitions, and self-perceptions of those nations from which this Christmas grew. For historians such as John Pimlott (1978) and Mark Connelly (1999), for example, Christmas is synonymous with Englishness, especially its rural traditions. Alternatively, Joe Perry (2010) believes it to be emblematic of contemporary Germanic identity and culture, while for Phillip Snyder (1985) and Karal Ann Marling (2001), it is America's greatest holiday and is deeply embedded in that nation's psyche. Nor does it mean that my argument will be entirely confined to the 1800s and onwards. As I will show, the organizational character of Christmas also extends back to its most ancient origins. As such, throughout many stages of the book, it will also be necessary to give these histories, and indeed its pre-history, due consideration, but more on that in a momment.

Researching Christmas

Having laid out the book's concerns, I hope that it will be of interest not only to academics and students who study work and its organization but also to a more general readership interested in Christmas. Nonetheless, as a book located within the social sciences, I do need to say a little about the methodological and theoretical (as if one can separate the two) approaches I have taken towards my research and subsequent writing. That is, I need to explain how I have gone about collecting evidence or data and what ideas, concepts, and theories I have drawn on to construct what I hope is a plausible interpretation of the festive season.

As I have said, this is a book about how the season or festival of Christmas is organized and is, in its own way, also organizational and organizing. Alternatively, to put it another way, it explores how Christmas is created and made to happen and how, in turn, it also can make other things happen. Its primary focus is the Anglo-American Christmas that emerged during the nineteenth century and which remains globally dominant today. Furthermore, it takes the majority, but not all of its illustrative material from the UK and, to a lesser extent, the US. But, as I have stated above, its origins and history before this are not ignored. Indeed, my argument is that in many respects, Christmas has always been organized and organizational in one form or another. Nonetheless, much of what is written about here will, I suspect, be reasonably familiar to any reader who has celebrated the contemporary season at some point in their life.

The origins of the research underpinning this book are to be found in a symposium I convened with Professor Alf Rehn in 2008, while I was an Associate Professor at the *University of Warwick*. This two-day event focused on Christmas and its organization and brought together European and US participants. It led to the publication of a special issue of the academic journal *Organization* in which many of the symposium papers were featured, as well as a successful *British Academy* grant application on my part that provided enough funding to allow me to meet and interview a significant number of the individuals who have informed aspects of this work. Since then, I have continued collecting everything I could about the festive season and both its organization and organizational impact.

Many of the resources I draw on to make my case in this book are not only somewhat eclectic in origin, therefore, but are deployed in an equally diverse number of ways across the pages before you. Academic books and scholarly papers, newspaper and magazine articles, web blogs, private and government-generated statistics, staff recruitment brochures, the occasional novel, and other works of certified fiction, including songs, films, and television programmes, have all provided sources of insight and information on which this work is built. In some instances, you will find this material used to illustrate an established or at least reasonably plausible observation about the season. In others, it provides empirical evidence to support claims about, for example, the economic significance of Christmas or some other complex organizational process. At other times, I have included it simply because it is interesting or informative, reflecting, as it does, prevalent ideas about the season and why it is so significant to so many people. Finally, where I have made extensive use of my own interview data, observations, and information gleaned from informal conversations, this, once again, is used to either illustrate a broader point I am making or to develop a more substantive, if critical understanding of the day-to-day practices, motivations and lived experiences of those directly involved in the organization of Christmas.

As I have noted, the bulk of the primary and secondary data utilized in the book refers mainly to the celebration of Christmas in the UK and, to a lesser extent, the US. This is not intended as an act of chauvinism, however. Instead, it is both an attempt to focus my argument as well as, it must be admitted, a pragmatic exercise resulting from both the strictures of access and translation and, of course, the advantages to an author of familiarity. And while I hope that this does not give the book too much of a parochial feel, as is apparent when international comparators are used, most of the trends I discuss, particularly in respect of the season's evolution from the nineteenth century onwards, are comparable across many nations; a result of the global reach of this Anglo-American approach to the season and the economic and cultural practices it has carried in its wake. Nonetheless, I accept that there will be significant swathes of materials, stories, and other resources from around the world that, in either my ignorance or my need to ensure that what you have here is of a readable length, I have either missed or omitted.

I also want to briefly acknowledge a couple of other matters while hopefully I still have your attention. Firstly, at times I paint with somewhat broad-brush strokes when presenting the history of Christmas. This is partly because a wealth of historical and interdisciplinary literature has previously been published about the season, much of which I draw upon throughout this book and which already presents intense details about the origins and evolution of Christmas. So as to not simply repeat what has already been written, my aim here, therefore, is to offer a bigger picture that conveys the currents of organization that flow both through and because of Christmas. This is not to say that details and facts are not important; far from it. In many respects, they provide the primary content of many forthcoming chapters. Nonetheless, while attempting to demonstrate the organizational relevance of Christmas and pursuing some critical reflections on it, I have not always sought the level of historical detail one might find elsewhere.

Secondly, I am also aware that in pursuing this way of thinking about the season, I am presenting what, at times, might be considered an unduly functionalist account of Christmas or what organization theorist Gibson Burrell (2013) might describe as a somewhat unreflexive 'will to form'. This is particularly evident in some of the earlier chapters that draw on, for example, sociologist Amitai Etzioni's (2004: 10) largely structural-functionalist approach to understanding holidays as socialization activities. Yet while I do emphasize both the well-documented Victorian emphasis on Christmas as a celebration of 'commence and domesticity' (Johnes, 2016: xiii) as well as its earlier implication in various religious and political struggles over power, legitimacy, and rights, I hope this is not quite the case. Instead, I present Christmas in what I believe are far more dialectical terms (Benson, 1977) in that I recognize that such functions are, in fact, historical products.

What I mean by this is that Christmas and its ideas and practices are often contingent and subject to contestation and change depending on the historical and geospatial context within which they emerge and are enacted. So, while it is possible to speak and write of the Anglo-American Christmas as a historical trend, I still try to maintain sight of those localized differences and distinctions that continue to exist if and when they become relevant to my overall argument. Equally, I aim to be sensitive to the contradictions that frequently define not only the organization of the season but, as I observed in the opening of this chapter, how it is experienced. For however one celebrates Christmas or indeed does not, the sense always seems to be that one is pulled in many different directions at once: between the desire to rest and yet to organize, to spend time with extended family but also withdraw into relative isolation, or to perhaps address spiritual needs while continuing to try and meet the material demands of oneself and others. And it is this sense of tension or contradiction, one of the undeniable characteristics of Christmas, especially today, that will also feature in the pages to come.

Organization and Christmas

As this is a book that is not only about Christmas but organization as well, I also want to say a little more here about what I mean by this and how I will approach the matter in a more critical manner. For anyone unfamiliar with the academic field of organization studies, its contemporary foundations can be traced back to at least the work of German sociologist and historian Max Weber (1910–1914) during the late nineteenth and early twentieth centuries. Weber's reflections on the technical superiority of emerging bureaucratic forms of organization formed a way of understanding them as predominantly rational endeavours geared towards maximizing efficiency and effectiveness in the coordination human affairs, particularly economic and administrative. And while there quickly became only fine lines to be drawn between the study of organizations and their management, the field grew over the decades into a specialist area that focused mainly on how increasingly complex organizations (Etzioni, 1975) might function most effectively within a predominantly market economy (Donaldson, 2003).

Gradually, however, alternative voices also emerged to challenge this increasingly institutionalized orthodoxy and its limited focus on the pursuit of operational efficiency within what were considered to be somewhat abstract systems. New approaches began to ask different questions, including how institutional agents, such as the state, might act to facilitate or constrain organizational practices (Scott, 1995). Others considered how organizations exist primarily as the outcome of intersubjective processes of meaning and sensemaking between people (Silverman, 1970; Weick, 1995) rather than simply as pre-determined, quasi-objective entities. Then, deriving from this latter strain of thought, an even more radical approach eventually developed. For instead of focusing on the functioning of formal and usually business-oriented organizations, it took the broader processes of human organizing as its primary object of analysis (Burrell and Morgan, 1979; Burrell, 1997).

This is illustrated, for example, in the work of organizational sociologists such as Martin Parker (2011, 2013), who has written on everything from circuses to skyscrapers as both organizations in their own right, as well as agents of socio-economic and cultural organization. This reorientation was accompanied by a concern within the field about organization not only as a noun, as a description of a thing or institution, but also with organization in the form of a verb; that is, towards ongoing configurational processes of social coordination, breakdown, and repair, that are while often sited within formal organizations could also refer to everyday acts of, to use a phrase, getting things done or bringing things, including social relations and individual subjects, into being. Such a shift in perspective subsequently led to a broad variation in the application of the term organization, as well as to the study of everyday processes of political, social, and cultural reproduction through a specifically organizational lens, including, for instance, popular culture (Hassard and Holiday, 1998), gender relations (Leonard, 2002), and even everyday practices of the self in respect of say how we dress, eat, and even make love (Hancock and Tyler, 2004).

Now, throughout this book, I am more than happy to move between these meanings of the term organization and how its different usages can lead to a refocusing of one's attention. As such, I explore not only how Christmas and the magic of Christmas can be conceived of both as a driver and outcome of processes of organization but also how, at the same time, it manifests as an integral component of relatively stabilized organizational forms and institutions. My understanding of the relationship between Christmas and organization rests, therefore, on what I consider to be a sociological dialectic akin to, say, Anthony Giddens's (1986) approach to the constitution of social relations or Henri Lefebvre's (1991) model of the production of space, in that while Christmas reproduces the conditions necessary for certain kinds of organization to flourish, such as the marketing and consumption of Christmas gifts, at the same time, it only comes into being through these very same organizational forms and practices.

Take, as a concrete example of this, the matter of Christmas films, something that I discuss at length in Chapter 3. Such films frequently provide a template that organizes how we expect to feel about and act at Christmas. They present the viewer with a seasonal repertoire based on recurring motifs and tendencies (Kracauer, 1995), such as snow, gift-giving, and family gatherings, and are concerned with promoting the virtues we should value at this time of the year, such as generosity, and how we should express our appreciation of them. In doing so, they contribute to producing a particular form of seasonal subjectivity, a human subject that knows how to celebrate the season and whose Christmas dreams and aspirations are also known to those who seek to promote them. At the same time, however, to be culturally and commercially successful, these films both rely on and reproduce a network of pre-existing Christmas institutions, such as Christmas movie channels. They are part of an organizational network that provides the material and ideational framework within which the representation of appropriate affective responses to the season can be identified and played out.

Christmas and Organization Studies

Despite my view that Christmas represents an important and instructive topic, it is yet to generate much interest from others working in organization studies. This is not to say such work does not exist, however, and, as such, I would like to acknowledge some of it here before drawing on it in more depth in the chapters to come. The earliest organizational analysis developed within the context of Christmas is found in a 1988 article by Michael Rosen in the *Journal of Management Studies*. Considering the possible symbolic and organizational functioning of the company Christmas party, Rosen explores how the organization of fun at work (cf. Alferoff and Knights, 2003, Fleming and Sturdy, 2009) and the camaraderie that derives from this serves to reproduce a set of integrated professional and personal identities that help mediate, if not avoid, potential organizational tensions. As he puts it:

> it is a relatively free space in which people can do play, but it is also a space in which 'fun' has been institutionalized. By accepting the informal second-order relationships of play within an organization of free space, a member implies an acceptance of the legitimacy of the first-order relations of bureaucratic action and control.
>
> *(Rosen, 1988: 468)*

This is a theme subsequently taken up by Anna Laura Hidegh (2015) in her doctoral study and subsequent publications (Hidegh and Primecz, 2020) about what she considers to be the controlling or colonizing impetus of such seasonal events. For Hidegh (2015), workplace Christmas parties draw on historical notions of the season as a celebration of collective identity to diffuse legitimate organizational disquiet through a manufactured aura of togetherness and communal celebration.

Such a critique of the normalizing or repressive role of workplace Christmas events is also developed in a series of articles published in the aforementioned Christmas issue of the journal *Organization* published in 2011. These include Ann Rippin's (2011) take on the importance of Christmas headwear at such parties and how it reflects but also trivializes and therefore diffuses established corporate power relations, and Jeanette Lemmergaard and Sara Louise Muhr's (2011) exploration of the practice of exchanging workplace Christmas gifts where they identify how such gifts help sustain social and professional relationships and those hierarchies upon which they depend.

Another area investigated in the current body of organizational studies literature pertaining to Christmas revolves around the unique characteristics of work directly connected to the season. An early and influential example of this is William Thompson and Joseph Hickey's (1989) ethnographic study of men working as Santa Claus and how members of the public responded to them not as employees but as embodied representatives of their seasonal expectations. This is something that subsequent accounts of the work associated with being Santa Claus – including my own – have also observed in that the labour that goes into making Santa a believable presence when appearing, particularly in commercial settings (Hancock, 2013, 2016), is integral to the production of the Christmas experience and, as such, its success (Pretes, 1995; Okleshen et al., 2000; Hall, 2014; Palo et al., 2018; Hancock, 2019). And while concerned with a less obviously seasonal form of work, Ödül Bozkurt's (2015) research into the workplace experiences of fixed-term and part-time supermarket employees at Christmas is equally significant in this respect in that it also demonstrates how the festivities can transform relatively mundane jobs into commercially sensitive roles given the extreme demands placed on employees at Christmas.

Another area of business-orientated research and scholarship that Christmas occasionally features in is the field of marketing and the study of consumer cultures. Russell Belk (1987, 1993), for instance, is a leading marketing academic whose interest in the materiality of consumption has led him to consider the commercial significance of Christmas and how it is entwined with consumer practice. According to (Belk, 1993), the commercialization of Christmas can lead to negative outcomes such as debt and social isolation. However, when viewed as a means rather than an end, it can also be a powerful medium for celebrating family, friends, and community. Furthermore, as he also argues, Christmas is an event during which many of us seek to repair not only social relations but our possibly fractured sense of self through acts of individualized consumption whereby:

As post-shoppers, we are as tempted to buy gifts for ourselves as for others. We increasingly view life and shopping as a series of purchases to patch together a lifestyle from bits and pieces of consumer goods we have seen on television.

(Belk and Bryce, 1993: 293)

Taking a somewhat different tack, Eileen Fischer and Stephen Arnold (1990) observe through their own more sociological research into Christmas consumption that despite other changes to gender relations, particularly in the US and Europe, one constant is that such seasonal shopping remains predominantly identified as 'women's work' that is undertaken on behalf of others. This focus on the prominent role that women play in organizing Christmas consumption, both through shopping and forms of domestic planning and the like, also features in work within organization studies and more sociological explorations of the structuring of gender relations through the mass media. Both Joanna Brewis and Samantha Warren (2011) and Lynne Freeman and Susan Bell (2013), for example, have conducted surveys of historical and contemporary Christmas magazines to unravel the idealized gender relations embedded within such publications, with Freeman and Bell (2013: 337) concluding that 'magazines continue to place the responsibility for putting the "magic" in Christmas firmly at the woman's feet'.

A Critical Book

While the above is simply a brief summary, and this research will be revisited in more depth throughout the book, a concern with how gender roles are often either played out or, as is often the case for women, circumscribed at Christmas, leads me to say something briefly about the fact that in addition to its desire to understand the organizational contours of Christmas, this is a book that is also somewhat critical about much that characterizes the time of the year. What I mean by this is that while I want to explore and understand the organizational character of Christmas, I am also concerned with analysing how such organizational processes also need to be understood as designed to further what are often relatively narrow interests and agendas. In doing so, I often present Christmas as part of what might be termed a broader 'culture industry' (Adorno and Horkheimer, 1973). And while deployed in several ways to describe and understand different, if albeit related phenomena, in the context of this book, the term is used to conceptualize the role that Christmas plays in the organization of a range of socio-economic and cultural relations that again tend to favour particular interests and agendas mainly pertaining to activities of consumption while encouraging a specific form of individual subjectivity suited to appeasing or complying with such interests.

To achieve this aim, I draw much of my inspiration from ideas that emerged from a group of critical philosophers and social scientists associated with the Institute of Social Research based in Frankfurt, Germany. And while individuals associated with this tradition of critical social philosophy appear at different points throughout this book, it is worth outlining some of the guiding tenets of their work and its impact on the field of organization studies. Founded in 1923, the institute is today more commonly referred to as the *Frankfurt School* (Wiggershaus, 2010) and the work that has emerged from it as 'Critical Theory'. While the ideas associated with Critical Theory have evolved over the decades, it has retained several core preoccupations and priorities. Central to these is an approach that rejects both the limitations of established materialist approaches to critically studying society, associated most notably with forms of orthodox Marxism (Adorno and Horkheimer, 1973) and what might be considered a return to a naïve if not reactionary subject centred philosophy associated with phenomenology (Adorno, 2002). Instead, it adopts what Martin Jay (1996) has described as a dialectical imagination that acknowledges the social interdependency of subject and object or, to put it more simply, people and the social relations and institutions in and through which they live their lives.

From a political and philosophical standpoint, Critical Theory aspires to challenge the prevailing influence of instrumental modes of reasoning in society. These modes of thinking, driven by an obsession with efficiency, are believed to overshadow a more normative or substantive form of reason that emphases ethical judgments concerning the essence and calibre of human freedom, as well as the pursuit of societal structures able to achieve such values. The pursuit of efficiency for its own sake takes, therefore, a backseat to these broader objectives (Honneth, 1995). However, it is essential to acknowledge that, despite such continuity, Critical Theory is not a static worldview. Developing over the years with emerging generations of theorists each building on the work of those that inspired and came before them, it now represents a variety of concerns and orientations, albeit united by a drive to expose and often address the irrationalities of contemporary societies, concerns that I will draw on as the book develops.

In referring to this particular school of thought it is not my intention, however, to close down in advance other ways I might think about Christmas, critically or otherwise. Nor does it limit what one might term my methodological approach to the subject, which is somewhat broad anyway. As will become evident below, in seeking to understand the organizational contours of Christmas I have drawn upon a range of theoretical resources in ways that are appropriate to the source material rather than in accord with any pre-determined sampling strategy or methodological master plan. Not that a formalized approach would be particularly congruent with the values of Critical Theory, as I have identified them here. The very idea that a purportedly rigorous methodology can generate a framework for the collection of objective facts about the world is inevitably tinged with assumptions that, as Max Horkheimer (1976), an early critical theorist observed over 60 years ago, underpin what he referred to as a static and conservative form of 'traditional theory' rather than its critical variant. And while this has several implications, an important one here is that to gain the most comprehensive understanding of a phenomenon such as Christmas, I have had to cast my net widely and adopt both an interpretive and critical approach. One that recognizes, as leading Critical Theorist Theodor Adorno (1976: 106) put it, that 'society is full of contradictions and yet determinable; rational and irrational in one, a system and yet fragmented' and, as such, is non-reducible to simple atomistic observations – however important – that overlook a possibly bigger picture that stubbornly seeks to resist capture.

Chapter by Chapter

The rest of this introduction is taken up by a chapter-by-chapter guide to the book's content. Here, I not only indicate the contents of each chapter but also complete the methodological aspect of this introduction by detailing what material I have utilized and how it has been collected and analysed. Chapter 1 is entitled *A Brief Organizational History of Christmas*. It is perhaps the most conventional chapter for a book with Christmas in its title in that it considers the evolution of Christmas from its pre-history up to and including its nineteenth-century emergence as the Anglo-American festival we know today. Drawing on existing scholarly literature, it explores how the organizational evolution of Christmas and its 'pagan' predecessors can be understood as serving, and adapting to, various social and political functions and interests within those cultures in which they were celebrated. The chapter also considers how the festive season has become inexorably entwined with those forms of economic and commercial organization that developed in the wake of the industrial revolutions in Europe and North America.

The Buying and Selling of a Season, the title of Chapter 2, explores how the celebration of Christmas has become a significant economic commodity and commercial exercise in its own right. It commences with the reimagining or reinvention of the season during the 1800s as a unique festival of domestic consumption. It then proceeds to explore the evolution of Christmas as a commercial force by considering, amongst other things, the significance of the arrival of Christmas advertising by leading retailers and the mass production and vast logistical networks that underpin Christmas's global mobility. In doing so, it presents Christmas as a vital contributor to international commerce's organizational practices and relative stability. While again utilizing published academic research, it also moves into the world of current and publicly available information and news sources, including media articles and widely accessible internet sites. Guided by my primary research objectives, this approach enables me to access a rich body of contemporary data and, I hope, provides a keen sense of the intimate relationship between Christmas and commerce.

Chapter 3 explores something less tangible in economic terms, but which is directly related to the issues raised in Chapter 2. Entitled *The Magical Atmospherics of Christmastide*, it considers how Christmas's symbolic and aesthetic dimensions are created and organized in such a way as to make it *feel* like Christmas. From its sights, smells, and sounds, to cultural products such as Christmas movies and music, the season is closely associated with a host of visual and auditory stimuli geared towards evoking feelings that demarcate it as a unique or magical time of the year. In doing so, it is argued that the need to recognize it as a profoundly atmospheric event is central to understanding the organizational qualities of Christmas. That is, one that is brought into being in such a way as to reach beyond our conscious, reflective faculties and play on our emotions, sentiments, and embodied sensations so as to encourage us to adopt a specifically seasonal subjectivity that reproduces both the economic and socio-cultural practices of the season in a wholeheartedly and dedicated manner. Methodologically, this is the first chapter that combines established academic literature and publicly available information with primary ethnographic material and the analysis of particular artefacts and texts. As such, I will discuss the approach taken here and in subsequent chapters to collecting this aspect of the research data.

The 'artefacts and texts' I have described above take many different forms, including musical tracks, films, Christmas merchandise, and even seasonal lighting displays, all of which constitute aspects of Christmas's cultural economy and were selected based on their material capacity to illustrate Christmas processes and activities. The extracts taken from interviews and the more ethnographic conversations that appear in this chapter and throughout the rest of the book not only allow me to present a more phenomenological account of how the people I spoke to both understand and orientate themselves to the work they do at, or for Christmas, but also allow these actions to be understood as dialectically entwined with those structural resources that both facilitate and mirror them. Throughout the book, the individuals I interviewed or spoke with ranged from senior retail managers to homemakers and from professional actors to police officers, each of whom took the time to share, through formal interviews and passing conversations, their experiences of, and reflections on, Christmas.

Much of this research originated in the aforementioned project that was funded by the *British Academy*, and which studied the work of men employed primarily as Santa Claus performers in stores, malls, and other venues over Christmas. Focusing on the aesthetic and emotional tasks associated with performing this particular role, it rapidly expanded, however, into a study of a range of individuals involved in organizing varying aspects of the season, some commercially and some not. Initially, these included owners, managers, and employees of Christmas-focused organizations, such as Christmas grotto management companies, as well as large UK department stores and shopping malls, predominantly in London and the southeast of England. It also involved several international visits, including a visiting fellowship at the *University of Lapland*, Rovaniemi and, in 2012, a visit to the *World Santa Claus Congress* held in *Bakken, Copenhagen*, enabling further discussions with performers and organizers of Christmas events from across Europe and the US.

The bulk of the interview material you will find cited here was collected using semi-structured interviews and informal, unstructured conversations. Even when involved in formal data gathering, my approach to questioning was relatively relaxed, utilizing open-ended questions and becoming more concerned with experiences than the recall of specific facts or events as the interviews developed. The participants were contacted using several approaches. The performers associated with the original study were initially identified by contacting leading theatrical and public relations agencies advertising Santa Claus performers at commercial rates. This was followed up by an advertisement in *The Stage* magazine, the principal UK publication for members of the theatrical profession, which in turn led to a snowballing process relying on word-of-mouth contacts and serendipitous meetings. Informal contacts were used to reach those working in the wider industry, as well as unsolicited calls to geographically accessible organizations deemed relevant to the study, including Christmas lighting companies, large grotto design and management organizations, specialist retail outlets, and individual entrepreneurs. Then, as I started to disseminate my findings through the media and more traditional academic channels, I found myself regularly approached by interested individuals who provided a rich source of knowledge, understanding, and insight into the production of Christmas on a more daily basis.

This formal interview data and many of my notes from informal conversations were analysed through what Mathew Miles and A. Michael Huberman (1994: 10) describe as a three-stage process of qualitative data reduction, data display, and conclusion drawing. Firstly, what is termed a process of open coding was used to organize and categorize my data in line with a combination of theoretically pre-indicated priorities, which, in the instance of this chapter, was the symbolic and aesthetic organization of Christmas activities and the sociomaterial assemblages through which the magic of Christmas might be achieved. For other chapters, this differed somewhat, depending on the issues or phenomena I was exploring. However, one thing that remains consistent throughout the chapters is that given the diversity of the sources, individual participants cited in this article are not identified by either pseudonyms or unique labels but are referred to in respect of their position in an organization or their occupational role. While I realize this does not conform with usual practice in this respect, I hope it makes for an easier and more flowing read during the relevant sections.

Returning to the contents of the remainder of the individual chapters, Chapters 4 and 5 are successively titled *Working at Christmas* and *Here Comes Santa Claus* and are both characterized by a more substantial consideration of the work and experiences of those who, along with those people appearing in Chapter 3, can be considered to be on the frontline of organizing Christmas. Chapter 4 commences with a discussion of the longstanding relationship between the festive season and the organization of work and working practices. It then considers the conditions and experiences, as well as the stories of those employed in various occupations, including factory workers, department store elves, seasonal performers, and live entertainers. In doing so, it places at centre stage the importance of labour at Christmas, a time nominally associated with rest and a withdrawal from the everyday demands of economic productivity and work. Once again, accounts of such activity and the context within which it takes place are drawn from multiple sources, including academic texts, newspaper articles, web blogs, popular literature, first-hand observations, interviews, and conversations. Similar sources are also utilized in Chapter 5 of the book, focusing specifically on the most well-known icon of the contemporary Anglo-American Christmas, Santa Claus, and those performers who, each year, bring him to life.

I have dedicated a whole chapter to the seasonal gift giver for two reasons. Firstly, the history of Santa Claus is not only fascinating in its own right, but once again it highlights how Christmas performs several organizational roles across both society and the economy and how, at the heart of these, there has more often than not been the towering figure of Santa. Secondly, and equally important, one of the unique features of Christmas is that each year the mythical character of Santa Claus is brought to life in a manner incomparable, or so I will argue, with any other such fantastical or magical figure. Returning to the theme of Chapter 4, this chapter explores, therefore, and through first-hand accounts, the creative work and organization that goes into the delivery of the Santa Claus mythos and the encounters both children and adults frequently expect with this living embodiment of the spirit and magic of Christmas. By doing so, it offers a valuable perspective on the distinct challenges faced by individuals working not just during, but also at the forefront of the holiday season. Moreover, it sheds light on the underlying desire for recognition that motivates these individuals to assume such specific responsibilities.

As with several previous chapters, Chapter 6 combines a range of academic, cultural, and first-person narratives and resources. Entitled *Home and the Gendered Organization of Christmas*, it focuses on the often-underappreciated work undertaken to reproduce the season within the private sphere of the home. Traditionally, preparing the house for Christmas, including, for example, the choosing and purchasing of gifts, the preparation of menus and coordinating inter-family get-togethers is perhaps one of the least recognized organizational dimensions of the season and one that largely falls on women to perform. In an age whereby being well organized is considered a cultural, if not indeed a moral good, I explore the contents of those resources, most notably women's lifestyle magazines and professional and semi-professional websites and publications, that exhort women to experience Christmas as a time when they should embrace their purportedly gendered skills to achieve what, they are told continually, must be 'the most magical Christmas ever'. In doing so, I also explore how such resources not only define how women should organize Christmas but also how they play a broader role in organizing gender subjectivities throughout the season and beyond.

Chapter 7, Organizing Christmas: The Wrapping Up, serves as my final and concluding chapter. Here, I begin by revisiting the core themes and objectives explored throughout the book. I reflect upon what has been accomplished and what may still be lacking in terms of providing fresh insights into the world's largest festival. I then take the opportunity to revisit and expand on some of the more critical voices and organizations engaged with the season, exploring a more post-Christmas sensibility, particularly concerning its negative impact on the natural and human environment. In conclusion, and especially given the above, I consider whether we should think about jettisoning Christmas as so much humbug, to evoke a popular critic, or if the possibility of a Christmas worthy of its name lies within our grasp. That is, can we identify a vision of this most utopian of festivals that continues to provide some latent source of hope, re-enchantment, and even the promise of an albeit perhaps temporary taste of the good life, one that remains embedded within the values and ideals of the season, and that might provide an alternative way of thinking not only about how we celebrate, but organize Christmas.

References

Adorno, T. and Horkheimer, M. (1973) *Dialectic of Enlightenment* (trans. J. Cumming). London: Verso.

Adorno, T.W. (1976) 'On the Logic of the Social Sciences'. In, T.W. Adorno et.al. (eds) *The Positivist Dispute in German Sociology* (trans. G. Adey and D. Frisby). Aldershot: Avebury. Pp. 105–122.

Adorno, T.W. (2002) *The Jargon of Authenticity*. London: Routledge.

Alferoff, C. and Knights, D. (2003) 'We're All Partying Here: Target and Games, or Targets as Games in Call Centre Management'. In, A. Carr and P. Hancock (eds) *Art and Aesthetics at Work*. Basingstoke: Palgrave. Pp. 70–92.

Aristotle (2004) *The Nicomachean Ethics* (trans. J.A.K Thomson). London: Penguin.

Belk, R. (1987) 'A Child's Christmas in America: Santa Claus as Deity, Consumption as Religion'. *The Journal of American Culture* 10(1): 87–100.

Belk, R. (1993) 'Materialism and the Making of the Modern American Christmas'. In, D. Miller (ed.) *Unwrapping Christmas*. Oxford: Oxford University Press. Pp. 75–104.

Belk, R. and Bryce, W. (1993) 'Christmas Shopping Scenes: From Modern Miracle to Postmodern Mall'. *International Journal of Research in Marketing* 10(3): 277–296.

Benson, J.K. (1977) 'Organizations: A Dialectical View'. *Administrative Science Quarterly* 22(1): 1–21.

Bozkurt, Ö. (2015) 'The Punctuation of Mundane Jobs with Extreme Work: Christmas at the Supermarket Deli Counter'. *Organization* 22(4): 476–492.

Brewis, J. and Warren, S. (2011) 'Have Yourself a Merry Little Christmas? Organizing Christmas in Women's Magazines Past and Present'. *Organization* 18(6): 747–762.

Burrell, G. (1997) *Pandemonium: Towards a Retro-Organization Theory.* London: Sage.

Burrell, G. (2013) *Styles of Organizing: The Will to Form.* Oxford: Oxford University Press.

Burrell, G. and G. Morgan (1979) *Sociological Paradigms and Organizational Analysis.* London: Heinemann.

Connelly, M. (1999) *Christmas: A Social History.* London: I.B. Tauris.

Donaldson, L. (2003) 'Organizational Theory as a Positive Science'. In, H. Tsoukas and C. Knudsen (eds) *The Oxford Handbook of Organization Theory: Metatheoretical Perspectives.* Oxford: Oxford University Press. Pp. 39–62.

Durkheim, E. (1951) *Suicide: A Study in Sociology.* New York, NY: The Free Press.

Etzioni, A. (1975) *Comparative Analysis of Complex Organizations.* New York, NY: Free Press.

Etzioni, A. (2004) 'Holidays and Rituals: Neglected Seedbeds of Virtue'. In, A. Etzioni and J. Bloom (eds) *We Are What We Celebrate: Understanding Holidays and Rituals.* New York, NY: New York University Press. Pp. 3–40.

Fischer, E. and Arnold, S. (1990) 'More Than a Labor of Love: Gender Roles and Christmas Gift Shopping'. *Journal of Consumer Research* 17(3): 333–345.

Fleming, P. and Sturdy, A. (2009) '"Just be yourself!": Towards Neo-Normative Control in Organisations?'. *Employee Relations* 31(6): 569–583.

Freeman, L. and Bell, S. (2013) 'Women's Magazines as Facilitators of Christmas Rituals'. *Qualitative Market Research: An International Journal* 16(3): 336–354.

Giddens, A. (1986) *The Constitution of Society.* Cambridge: Polity.

Hall, C.M. (2014) 'Will Climate Change Kill Santa Claus? Climate Change and High-Latitude Christmas Place Branding'. *Scandinavian Journal of Hospitality and Tourism* 14(1): 23–40.

Hancock, P. (2013) '"Being Santa Claus": The Pursuit of Recognition in Interactive Service Work'. *Work, Employment & Society* 27(6): 1004–1020.

Hancock, P. (2016) 'Recognition and the Moral Taint of Sexuality: Threat, Masculinity and Santa Claus'. *Human Relations* 69(2): 461–481.

Hancock, P. (2019) 'Organisational Magic and the Making of Christmas: On Glamour, Grottos and Enchantment'. *Organization* 27(6): 797–816.

Hancock, P. and Tyler, M. (2004) '"MOT Your Life": Critical Management Studies and the Management of Everyday Life'. *Human Relations* 57(5): 619–645.

Hassard, J. and Holiday, R. (eds) (1998) *Organization-Representation: Work and Organizations in Popular Culture.* London: Sage.

Hidegh, L.A. (2015) *Critical Human Resource Management: The Reproduction of Symbolic Structures in the Organizational Lifeworld through the Case of the Colonization of Corporate Christmas.* Unpublished PhD Thesis, Corvinus University of Budapest.

Hidegh, L.A. and Primecz, H. (2020) '"Corporate Christmas": Sacred or Profane? The Case of a Hungarian Subsidiary of a Western MNC'. In, J. Mahadevan, H. Primecz and L. Romani (eds) *Cases in Critical Cross-Cultural Management: An Intersectional Approach to Culture.* New York, NY: Routledge. Pp. 46–58.

Honneth, A. (1995) *The Struggle for Recognition: The Moral Grammar of Social Conflicts* (trans. J. Anderson). Cambridge: Polity Press.

Horkheimer, M. (1976) 'Traditional and Critical Theory'. In, P. Connerton (ed.) *Critical Sociology: Selected Readings.* Harmondsworth: Penguin. Pp. 206–224.

Hunt, R. and Brychta, A. (1994) *Christmas Adventure.* Oxford: Oxford University Press.

Jay, M. (1996) *The Dialectical Imagination: A History of the Frankfurt School and the Institute of Social Research, 1923–1950.* London: University of California Press.

Johnes, M. (2016) *Christmas and the British: A Modern History.* London: Bloomsbury.

Kracauer, S. (1995) *The Mass Ornament: Weimar Essays* (trans. T. Levin). Harvard, MA: Harvard University Press.

Lefebvre, H. (1991) *The Production of Space* (trans. D. Nicholson-Smith). Oxford: Blackwell.

Lemmergaard, J. and Muhr, S. (2011) 'Regarding Gifts: On Christmas Gift Exchange and Asymmetrical Business Relations'. *Organization* 18(6): 763–777.

Leonard, P. (2002) 'Organizing Gender? Looking at Metaphors as Frames of Meaning in Gender/Organizational Texts'. *Gender, Work & Organization* 9(1): 60–80.

Marling, K.A. (2001) *Merry Christmas: Celebrating America's Greatest Holiday.* Cambridge, MA: Harvard University Press.

Marx, K, and Engels, F. (2002) *The Communist Manifesto.* London: Penguin.

Marx, K. (1973) *Economic & Philosophic Manuscripts of 1844* (trans. D. Struik). London: Lawrence & Wishart.

Miles, M. B. and Huberman, A.M. (1994) *Qualitative Data Analysis.* Thousand Oaks, CA: Sage.

Miller, D. (1993) 'A Theory of Christmas'. In D. Miller (ed.) *Unwrapping Christmas.* Oxford: Oxford University Press. Pp. 3–37.

Nietzsche, F. (1974) *The Gay Science, with a Prelude in Rhymes and an Appendix of Songs* (trans. W. Kaufmann). New York, NY: Random House.

Okleshen, C., Baker, S.M. and Mittelstaedt, R. (2000) 'Santa Claus Does More Than Deliver Toys: Advertising's Commercialization of the Collective Memory of Americans'. *Consumption Markets & Culture* 4(3): 207–240.

Palo, T., Mason, K. and Roscoe, P. (2018) 'Performing a Myth to Make a Market: The Construction of the "Magical World" of Santa'. *Organization Studies* 41(1): 53–75.

Parker, M. (2011). 'Organizing the Circus: The Engineering of Miracles'. *Organization Studies* 32(4): 555–569.

Parker, M. (2013) 'Vertical Capitalism: Skyscrapers and Organization'. *Culture and Organization* 21(3): 217–234.

Perry, J. (2010) *Christmas in Germany: A Cultural History.* Chapel Hill, NC: University of North Carolina Press.

Pimlott, J.A.R. (1978) *The Englishman's Christmas: A Social History.* Hassocks: The Harvester Press.

Pretes, M. (1995) 'Postmodern Tourism: The Santa Claus Industry. *Annals of Tourism Research* 22(1):1–15.

Rippin, A. (2011) 'Ritualized Christmas Headgear or "Pass Me The Tinsel, Mother: It's the Office Party Tonight"'. *Organization* 18(6): 823–832.

Rosen, M. (1988). 'You Asked for It: Christmas at the Bosses' Expense'. *Journal of Management Studies* 25(5): 463–480.

Scott, R.W. (1995). *Institutions and Organizations*. Thousand Oaks, CA: Sage.

Silverman, D. (1970) *The Theory of Organizations*. London: Heinemann.

Snyder, P. (1985) *December 25th: The Joys of Christmas Past*. New York, NY: Dodd, Mead & Company.

Thompson, W.E. and Hickey, J.V. (1989) 'Myth, Identity, and Social Interaction: Encountering Santa Claus at the Mall'. *Qualitative Sociology* 12(4): 371–389.

Weber, M. (1946) 'Science as a Vocation'. In, H.H. Gerth and C. Wright Mills (eds and trans.) *From Max Weber: Essays in Sociology*. New York, NY: Oxford University Press. Pp. 129–156.

Weick, K (1995) *Sensemaking in Organizations*. Thousand Oaks, CA: Sage.

Wiggershaus, R. (2010) *The Frankfurt School: Its History, Theory and Political Significance*. Cambridge: Polity Press.

1

A BRIEF ORGANIZATIONAL
HISTORY OF CHRISTMAS

Introduction

For anyone taking the time to read this book, the traditional Christmas story is most likely a familiar one. Baby Jesus, flesh incarnate of the God of Israel, is born to the Virgin Mary in a stable in Bethlehem while her divinely cuckolded husband, Joseph, stands by her in reverent awe. Throughout the tale, numerous supporting cast members appear, including a troupe of what are probably Zoroastrian priests, although we tend to refer to these as 'wise men' or 'kings', assorted shepherds, angels, and an assembly of animals, especially, it would seem, donkeys and cows. However, what is generally less well known is that, in reality, the Judeo-Christian Bible has very little to say about this particular event. Details about the nativity are sparse and confined to only a few relatively short passages in the gospels of Matthew and Luke. Much of what we think we know about an event that may or may not have happened was invented over the decades and centuries that followed the story's first appearance in print.

Given such a shaky start, it is perhaps unsurprising that the history of Christmas, the supposed celebration of this miraculous event, is itself something of a contested topic. For example, some scholars, such as Ronald Hutton (1996), consider Christmas to largely be a continuation of mid-winter celebrations that predate not only Christianity but monotheism itself. Alternatively, Joseph Kelly (2004) remains wedded to a predominantly theological account of the season. For him, the Christian nativity is a historical event and the spiritual and intellectual starting point of the Christmas story, even if it was not celebrated until long after the purported birthdate of Christ. Then there are social historians, such as Mark Connelly (1999), who tend to approach the Christmas we celebrate today

DOI: 10.4324/9781315637969-2

as a predominantly secular and relatively contemporary affair, albeit one with a Christian veneer. While acknowledging that the origins of the season are far more ancient than those of organized Christianity, this approach is primarily concerned with how the festival has evolved over more recent centuries while simultaneously retaining a vital kernel of cultural continuity.

Finally, some constitute what one might call the 'reinvention school' of Christmas scholarship. Exemplified in the writings of John Golby and Bill Purdue (2000), this is a view that, while again not denying the season's ancient origins and Christian significance, argues that the Christmas we now embrace is a far more contemporary fabrication. Something that was effectively created by the middle classes of nineteenth-century Europe and America and is, in fact, more of an invented tradition as the historian Eric Hobsbawm (2012) might have it. Hence, while this modern celebration draws upon festive themes and practices, some undoubtedly Christian, that can be traced back to previous centuries, what we celebrate today should be considered a mainly Victorian innovation.

Now, as I argued in the introduction, I have much sympathy with the view that the Christmas celebrated most widely today, the Anglo-American Christmas, is, if not necessarily an invention of, then a response to, the socio-economic and cultural context within which it emerged. More important to this book, however, is the view that whatever version of Christmas one might talk about: pagan, early Roman, medieval, or Anglo-American, there remains a discernible continuity running through all of them, namely, that of the season's organizational character. From early pagan rituals, through the Christian piety and royal court shenanigans of the Middle Ages, up to and including the (re) invented or reimagined urban Christmases of the Victorians, there exists a shared concern with the efficient and effective coordination of a range of practices and activities that gives Christmas a distinctive organizational quality.

At times, such practices and activities have operated in the interests of the common good (Connelly, 1999) while, at others, in those of a smaller political or economic elite (McKay, 2008). Nonetheless, they have all come to define what, in large part, Christmas is and how people feel it should be celebrated. Not that the importance of context can be overlooked when making such claims. Significant differences would no doubt have existed between, for example, the importance and role ascribed to Christmas by a Roman priest of the early Christian church and a nineteenth-century British or American industrialist. Nevertheless, as I argue throughout this chapter, they would both have likely realized, in a similar fashion, how the ideas and feelings that Christmas evokes might be wielded to particular ends and interests, both spiritual and secular.

In this chapter, I identify a history of these underlying organizational ideas and practices that were not only features of Christmases past but continue to characterize how we experience and celebrate Christmas today. In doing so, and as I stated in the introduction, I adopt and use the term organization in such a way that it can refer to both a bounded and relatively enduring social system or institution as well as an active process, one typically aimed at the ordering and rationalizing of people and their activities (Cooper and Burrell, 1988; Clegg, 1990). In doing so, I consider the history and features of organizations traditionally associated with the celebration of Christmas, such as the Roman Catholic Church, as well as explore how Christmas itself has contributed to both the development and growth of such organizations as well as those social relations that have helped promote and sustain their institutional position and often dominance.

I commence with the season's likely origins in our earliest attempts to weather the trials and tribulations of the winter months. I then explore how the festival subsequently developed as an attempt, in large part, to help consolidate a minority Roman religious sect and its role in becoming one of the most potent organizational forces in the known world. Next, I journey through the early expansionist days of the Christian church into the middle and early modern ages, considering the emergence of what became a distinctively Anglicized version of the festive season. Finally, I consider how Victorians, in both the old and new worlds, envisaged the role Christmas might play in mitigating some of the worst excesses of the industrial revolution and the threat it was believed to pose to the burgeoning middle-class order of the era. In doing so, it then becomes possible to identify how this helped popularize the celebration we know today and many of the values and practices underpinning its subsequent rise as a global and largely secular festival.

In the Bleak Mid-Winter

It is widely agreed amongst scholars that the contemporary celebration of Christmas owes as much, if not more, to a pre-Christian pagan culture than it does to the birth of the Christian saviour. Indeed, Christian Puritans of the 1600s not only refused to celebrate what they considered to be the blasphemy of Christmas but made it a matter of punitive ecclesiastical and legal intervention. Today, Christian sects such as the Jehovah's Witnesses still refuse to observe the season due to its pagan associations and lack of biblical evidence. As such, many historians, both religious and secular, agree that to understand why we celebrate Christmas the way we do we must first journey back to a time prior not only to the nativity but to organized religion itself (cf. Miles, 1912; Harrison, 1951; Sansom, 1968; Pimlott, 1978; Forbes, 2007; Storey, 2008).

As Bruce Forbes (2007) stresses, to honestly understand the pagan origins of Christmas as it first emerged in the northern hemisphere, it is incumbent on us that we first know winter and its consequences for human life, both physical and cultural. The northern hemisphere is, of course, a large place. Depending on one's degree of latitude, the shock of winter is experienced differently. Nonetheless, wherever one resides, it shares some common features to which Forbes (2007) directs our attention. The most significant of these is the ebbing of the daylight and the life that it brings. It is the time when, as William Sansom (1968: 9) poetically observes, the seasonal colour of mid-winter is not that of red, green, or gold as we might find in contemporary Christmas imagery, but in fact black:

> Black of winter, black of night, black of frost and of the east wind, black of dangerous shadows beyond the firelight.

When put like this, it is perhaps no surprise that our European ancestors found ways, particularly in the form of feasts and festivals, of coping with the sense of abandonment and isolation that must have come with the descent of the dark and relative cold of those brumal days and nights.

Having said this, as Hutton (1996) notes, we have relatively scant information about what any such ancient mid-winter celebrations might have looked like, save from those tales handed down in folklore to predominantly Christian scholars, many of whom would have had reason to portray them in a less than generous manner. Nonetheless, from what is known, a few observations can be made with at least some confidence. First and foremost, it is likely that they did actually take place at around the same time each year (Hutton, 1996), which is a good start. Secondly, they would have been what Clement Miles (1912: 15) describes as 'life-affirming' events, an idea summed up by Llewelyn Powys when he observes:

> Ever since our Saxon ancestry in Germany set fire to their enormous Yule logs, and ever since our Druid ancestors cut down the mistletoe with sickles of gold, this time of the year has been a period of plenary indulgence.
>
> *(Powys, 2010: 7)*

Certainly, with one eye on the return of the mid-winter sun as it gradually began to climb back into the sky, and the other on those supplies of food and drink that needed to be consumed while at their best, these early celebrations were unlikely to have been for the faint-hearted being indicative, as Miles (1912: 15) suggests, of a 'lusty attitude towards the world, a seeking for earthly joy and well-being'.

In contrast to such a portrayal of hedonistic sensuality, however, these festivities were also most likely attuned to the need to maintain some semblance of social order and what we now term a civic sensibility during such difficult months. Such festivals not only celebrated life in the face of the 'tedium and melancholy' (Hutton, 1996: 34) of winter, but they would also have celebrated the community and those social relations that enabled it to endure the privations of the season. At a time when, in the north at least, winter could be like 'walking into death' (Forbes, 2007: 4), shared acts of feasting, storytelling, and ritual worship provided a space and time in which individuals could re-identify with each other, recognizing their mutual interdependence and reinforcing tribal and communal loyalties (Sansom, 1968). Furthermore, these rituals and practices also played an essential role in offering communities what could be considered to be magical protection from both natural and supernatural threats, not only during the dark months of winter but throughout the year, reinforcing further, as magic so often does, community solidarity (Mauss, 2001; Malinowski, 2011).

Moreover, many of the rituals and practices associated with pagan celebrations became, as Hutton (1996) notes, integral to the rural and eventually urban Christmases that emerged in later centuries. Alongside some more mundane examples, such as communal feasting and drinking or the telling of supernatural stories, take, for example, the ancient Anglo-Saxon practice of wassailing. Involving the ceremonial drinking of cider or ale and the singing of traditional songs through settlements and villages, it was a magical ritual said to banish malevolent spirits and bring good luck to the community for the forthcoming year. Subsequently, this became an essential part of Christmas celebrations up to around the early twentieth century and can still be found in some rural communities in the UK and US, and often elsewhere, in the form of door-to-door carol singing.

Such seasonal practices and rituals echo what anthropologists and early sociologists such as Emile Durkheim (1965) identified as an expression of the distinction between the *sacred* and *profane* dimensions of human experience. For Durkheim, the sacred is bestowed with otherworldly significance, representing the identity and unity of the group or collective manifested through sacred group symbols or totems. Mid-winter celebrations acted, in part, as just such symbolic events that established a sacred or enchanted relationship between the individual, the group, and their environment. Instead of a specific object gaining symbolic importance, however, it was the actual ceremony and practices associated with it, like wassailing, that represented a united effort to resist the bleakness of winter and to flourish rather than merely survive.

The Festivals and Politics of the Sun

Nor should our interest in those pagan celebrations associated with mid-winter end with the birth of the Christin saviour. For if we are to understand the Christian connection to Christmas, the place to start is not the Bible[1] but rather the political and social tinderbox that was Rome in the fourth century

AD. Having suffered invasion, civil war, and finally the rise of its first Christian Emperor, Constantine, Rome and its Empire was, albeit not for the first time, a fragile place. Moreover, when it came to religion, while Christianity was not the official creed of the Empire, with Rome at that time remaining a largely polytheistic culture (Beard, 2015), influential Roman Christians were increasingly working behind the scenes to cement the power of both the Church and its leaders within Roman society.

With pagan Gods drawn from many sources and mid-winter festivals forming a vital part of the Empire's religious and cultural calendar, such efforts had to be pursued with some care, however. The most important of these festivals were the *Saturnalia*, *Dies Natalis Solis Invicti*, meaning 'the birth of the Unconquered Sun', and the *Kalendae*. The first of them, the festival of *Saturnalia*, traditionally began on the equivalent of December 17 with a formal sacrifice to the god Saturn and then continued for up to seven days more. At its heart was not only indulgence but also the reaffirmation of social and familial ties. It was a time, already reminiscent of our modern Christmas, when work was suspended, homes and streets were decorated in greenery, people feasted, and small gifts were exchanged amongst family members and friends (Forbes, 2007).

Next came *Dies Natalis Solis Invicti*. Falling on December 25, this celebration of the winter solstice held particular importance for another powerful religion in the Empire, Mithraism. With its origins in Persian culture (Sansom, 1968), and while not reducible to sun worship, it appears in several accounts to have promoted the 25th as a day of celebration and worship (cf. Miles, 1912; Storey, 2008). What is significant about Mithraism and its accompanying festival is that it was not only popular amongst the lower orders of the Empire, but it was, as Michael Harrison (1951) observes, also the recognized religion of the Roman military and the political elite. As such, to consolidate its spiritual and political legitimacy, Roman Christians understood that there was a clear case for ensuring that established celebrations such as *Solis Invicti* were allowed alongside Christianity and needed to be viewed as fundamentally compatible with it.

Before exploring this point further, it is also worth considering, however, the third and final festival in our pagan triumvirate, namely the *Kalendae*. As the name suggests, the Kalendae was the Roman recognition of the first day of each new month, which took on additional significance on the first day of the New Year. The extended January celebration occurred between January 1 and 3 and was a time of further collective feasting, partying, and exchanging gifts and money (Miles, 1912; Hutton, 1996). For many, it was the most economically active of the three festivals, encouraging consumption and extravagance closely akin to what today many identify as the worst characteristic of our current festive season. Indeed, the observations on the January Kalendae made by the fourth-century philosopher Libanius might sound very familiar to any contemporary ear concerned with seasonal excess:

> Everywhere may be seen carousels and well-laden tables; luxurious abundance is found in the houses of the rich, but also in the houses of the poor better food than usual is put upon the table. The impulse to spend seizes everyone. He who the whole year through has taken pleasure in saving and piling up his pence, becomes suddenly extravagant.
>
> *(cited Miles, 1912: 109)*

Furthermore, as Libanius also observed, such activities took place not just in Rome. As the seat of the world's greatest Empire to date, it exported its values and practices across the globe, including its religious and cultural festivals, laying the foundations for their later Christian uptake in Europe and beyond (Miles, 1912).

However, to fully understand the pagan origins of Christmas, one must also look beyond the Empire and to those lands where similar festivals were just as important and indigenous cultures, especially in northern Europe, fashioned similar observances of the mid-winter season. Perhaps the most well-known of these was, and indeed still is, the Nordic festival of Jul or Yule. While there is some dispute as to whether such a festival was related to knowledge of the solar cycle and turning of the year (Miles, 1912), there is general agreement that it existed prior to the arrival of Christianity and served a similar role in providing respite from the travails of the season, and an opportunity to reassert existing social solidarities. Steeped in folklore and magic, the importance it placed on communal feasting and drinking, alongside its practices of ancestor worship (Figure 1.1) once again suggests the significance of this time of year to the renewal of existing relations and hierarchies and the reaffirmation of established forms of social organization and authority.

There is reason, therefore, to speculate that many of the early winter festivals that predated and influenced Christmas can be understood as serving a valuable organizational as well as a spiritual function. That is, they often acted as a pressure valve for social tensions and anxieties and a means by which sacred social relations and solidarities could be sustained or reasserted at a time when they were tested most (Etzioni, 2004). Furthermore, because they were often likely to have been relatively large social events, these festivals would also require the organization of scarce economic resources such as food, fuel, and labour. As Libanius observed, commercial transactions undoubtedly underpinned access to these resources for many involved, ensuring, in turn, that they were busy times for many traders and merchants of the day.

FIGURE 1.1   Illustration of an Ancient Nordic Yule Festival, *Die Gartenlaube*, 1880.

Christianity and the Selling of Christmas

Even if the origins of many of the practices we associate with Christmas can be traced back to the pagan mid-winter festivals celebrated in Ancient Rome and beyond, the question remains nevertheless, why, in turn, did these festivals largely become Christianized and converted to the celebration of the nativity? It is generally accepted that prior to around the fourth century, Christians had not shown much interest in celebrating the birth of their saviour. As Kelly (2004: 53) observes, 'in the Bible only pagans like Pharaoh, or sinful Jews like the Roman puppet king Herod Antipas, celebrated their birthdays'. As such and compounded by a lack of biblical evidence to suggest that the nativity was all that significant or even when it took place, celebrating the birthday of Jesus was not really of concern to many early converts.

However, with the conversion of Roman Emperor Constantine around 336 AD, Christians, after being both vilified and intermittently persecuted for generations, started to gradually move into the ascendency. Looking to cement both their religious and political power, it was in this context that this emerging Christian establishment started to see how the nativity could, in fact, contribute to their spiritual and secular ambitions. For while the mid-winter festivals of the Empire remained so popular, it was evident that it would be difficult to supplant pagan belief systems when what was on offer was a faith whose primary and austere festival of Easter did not take place until the spring.

This conundrum is encapsulated, if somewhat light-heartedly, by Forbes (2007: 30):

> I try to imagine Constantine, as a devotee of Sol Invictus, announcing to his soldiers and his government officials that he planned to accept Christianity and that he wanted them to become Christians too. If his next comment was 'The bad news is that you will have to give up all of your three winter parties', how many people do you think will have followed him into his new religion?

While there is no evidence that Constantine himself was responsible for setting the date of Christmas, with its first recorded appearance on December 25 not appearing until 354 AD, 17 years after Constantine's death, nevertheless there is still much to be said for Forbes's interpretation of events. In particular, it recognizes the genuine likelihood that the date set for the Christmas we know today was essentially an act of, at best, cultural appropriation and, at worst, one of political expediency. An act designed to help integrate swathes of the Roman political and military hierarchy into an increasingly organized Christian church.

It was not only non-believers who needed to be won over, however. Such pagan celebrations had become a significant part of everyone's calendar, including Christians, who were often enthusiastic participants during the mid-winter months. As the Christian scholar Scriptor Syrus observed sometime in the late fourth century:

> It was a custom of the pagans to celebrate December 25th as the birthday of the Sun, at which they kindled lights in token of festivity. In these solemnities and revelries, the Christians also took part. Accordingly, when the doctors of the Church perceived that the Christians had a leaning to this festival, they took counsel and resolved that the true nativity should be solemnized on that day.
>
> *(cited Hutton, 1996: 1)*

This is not to claim, of course, that the decision, most likely taken by Julius I, the first Bishop of Rome, to set December 25 as the official birthday of Christ was solely a consequence of such considerations. Such matters are always far more complicated. Nevertheless, it seems highly plausible that it did play a significant role which supports the idea that, in part, Christmas was initially established as a mid-winter festival to ease the reorganization of Roman culture and politics under a newly emerging Christian leadership.

Also worth mentioning here, and something we shall see reappearing throughout the festive seasons of years to come was the role various social and political inversions played as part of established pagan celebrations and their impact on the infant Christian festival. Once again, Miles (1912) is an essential source of insight into the nature of such practices, especially during the Roman transition from pagan to Christian celebrations. Discussing the reversal of roles and positions that often took place during the festival of Saturnalia, for example, he points to the popularity of a figure called the 'mock king' (Miles, 1912: 108). Drawn from the ranks of ordinary revellers, the mock king was chosen as the lawmaker of parties and feasts, upturning established hierarchies and with all ranks subject to his decrees and whims. Miller (1993: 9) makes a similar observation regarding most mid-winter festivals of this era whereby 'we find the master feasting the slave', once again in an inversion of social hierarchies. Such practices played a prominent role in how the season playfully mediated class tensions and inequalities while helping to sustain the traditional organizational character of Roman society and, as we shall see, were to retain a similar function at Christmas festivities over the forthcoming centuries.

Spreading the Word

The heartlands of the Empire were not the only places where Christmas played a role in securing the devotion of non-Christian believers and contributing to the maintenance of social order, however. The increasingly organized Christian church also brought Christmas to western and northern Europe as it expanded in search of converts and new opportunities to evangelize. Moreover, just as the early Christian establishment in Rome had to deal with the power and attraction of established pagan celebrations and their popular and often magical rites, so did its missionaries as they ventured along and increasingly beyond the Empires' borders. Many of these celebrations remained, of course, Roman in origin, for as Sansom (1968: 33) observes, while we might talk of festivals such as the Saturnalia and Kalends in relation to Rome and its immediate territories, they were also equally prominent in 'Bath or Colchester or any other parts of occupied Europe'. Nonetheless, at the same time, the northern regions of Europe enjoyed their own mid-winter celebrations, most notably that of the aforementioned Yule that, like its Roman counterparts, was associated with feasting, drinking, and mystic fireside tales of gods and ancestorial spirits.

Furthermore, the fact that so many of these traditions continue to feature as part of contemporary Christmas observances is due in no small part to how Christian missionaries and church leaders were encouraged to address them. For rather than seeking to eradicate such practices, under what became known as the doctrine of *Interpretatio Christiana* (MacMullen, 1986) they took a more inclusive approach. Seeking to assimilate or Christianize them in such a way as to render them amenable to a Christian interpretation, they endeavoured, in Pimlott's (1978: 6) words, 'to acquiesce in the lesser evil for the sake of the greater good'. Such acquiescence was not purely indicative of a pragmatic disposition on behalf of the Church, however. In the language of contemporary marketing, it also positioned Christmas as something of a loss leader. So, while a certain price would have to be paid in terms of tolerating some practices that might not be considered wholly devout, the greater profit in saved souls and the extended authority of the Church appeared to make this an acceptable trade-off, a position exemplified in Pope Gregory's instruction to Augustine's mission to England in 597 AD:

> Nor let them [the Anglo-Saxons] sacrifice animals to the Devil, but to the praise of God kill animals for their own eating, and render thanks to the Giver of all things for their abundance; *so that while some outward joys are retained to them, they may the more easily respond to inward joys.*
> *(cited Pimlott, 1978: 6, emphasis added)*

As it was back in the heart of the Empire then, conversion to Christianity continued to provide opportunities for native populations to indulge in their established mid-winter rites and rituals, many of which were believed to possess magical qualities that would entice good fortune while repelling dark and malevolent forces. Again these included the adornment of homes and halls with greenery, feasting, and, as it came to be known, making merry, but all while now ostensibly directing such activities towards the glory of the Christian saviour, consolidating and, in turn, furthering the influence, spiritual, political, and organizational, of the Church across Europe.

Charity, Misrule, and Court

The relationship between Christmas and the organizational structures of political and religious order did not end with the early days of what was to become the Roman Catholic Church, however. Instead, it remained influential throughout the move into what is referred to commonly as the middle-ages and beyond. In England, much of what became of Christmas during the early centuries of this period is often unclear. Nonetheless, it is generally agreed that the Anglo-Saxon celebrations of this time were widespread and characterized by activities, such as drinking and gaming, that owed more to their pagan origins than Christian piety (Sansom, 1968; Pimlott, 1978; Hutton, 1996).

As Pimlott (1978: 9) observes, by the time of the Norman Conquest in 1066, Christmas was established as the country's 'main annual holiday and the season of religion, rest from labour, and traditional merriment which they were to remain until the age of Puritanism'. Indeed, William the Conqueror elected to be crowned on December 25 of that year, perhaps in order to add a little more divine legitimacy to his coronation. At this time those who were able would observe the 'twelve days of Christmas' which the Church in 567 AD had declared to be the proper duration of the season. With feasting and festivities commencing on December 25 they continued on through to 'Twelve Night' on January 5 or 6, depending on local customs, when a last huge feast would take place.

Now as one might suspect, such feasting, at least for those who could afford it, required a high level of economic and organizational activity to happen. This was particularly true of royal banquets, where extravagance was very much the name of the seasonal game. Pimlott (1978: 21) catalogues many of the items provided for King John's Christmas of 1213, which included over 400 heads of pork, 3,000 hens, and over 10,000 salt eels, while by the reign of Henry VII, a single courtly Christmas dinner could consist of somewhere in the region of 'a hundred and twenty dishes' (Sansom, 1968: 47–48). Moreover, although the primary objective of such extravaganzas was largely pleasure, with the economic and organizational symbolism and consequences being secondary, other forms of seasonal activity were perhaps more instrumental. For instance, as Pimlott (1978) further observes, this was also the time when Christmas gift-giving, especially amongst the wealthy, became increasingly important as a way of cementing social solidarities and currying favour with patrons and the powerful. While the English court and its officers, including the monarch, expected cash gifts, there was also an increasing trend for personal gifts and presents, especially by the time of the reign of Elizabeth I· who was known to have favoured receiving gifts of clothes and jewellery.

In addition to feasting, merriment, and gift-giving, another notable feature of these medieval English Christmas was the importance ascribed to practices of hospitality and charity (Hutton, 1996; Nissenbaum, 1997; Powys, 2010). Expectations surrounding hospitality by the wealthy, an established form of *noblesse oblige*, represented a continuation of the ancient pre-Christian practices that celebrated the inversion of established regimes of order and hierarchy (Nissenbaum, 1997). Simply put, the powerful were expected to feed and amuse those obligated to serve during the rest of the year. Such charitable practices also often combined traditional and dutiful giving with more ritual and often riotous activities. The poor usually initiated the exchanges through house-to-house visits while masked and dressed in outrageous clothes or costumes. Popularly termed 'mummers, maskers or guizers' (Hutton, 1996: 12), these revellers saw it as their right during the festive season to make demands of the wealthy for charitable provision, as well as for celebratory food and drink.

Also featuring during the season, and derived from the aforementioned mock kings of Rome, were the Lords of Misrule. Often playing a prominent role in Christmas festivities at this time, they upturned established social hierarchies and contributed to the general 'topsy-turvidom' (Harrison, 1951: 68) of the season. Indeed, across most major English houses of the time, seasonal revelries were usually overseen by such a figure who was elected or chosen from servants or, in the case of the royal household, lower officers of the court. They appear to have exercised significant authority not only to organize activities over the course of the 12 days of Christmas, but to speak their mind even to the highest of ranks. As Alison Weir and Siobhan Clarke (2018: 75) observe:

> Will Wynesbury was Lord of Misrule in the first year of Henry VIII's reign and impudently asked his sovereign for £5 towards his expenses. 'If it shall like Your Grace to give me too much', he added mischievously, 'I will give you none again, and if Your Grace give me too little, I will ask more!' Henry was greatly amused.

Similar inversions also took place in religious institutions such as cathedrals and monasteries with the election of Abbots of Misrule and Boy Bishops. They were said to possess authority comparable to their secular counterparts over their institution's festive and often everyday practices during the 12 days of observance and celebration.

While such activities might suggest a breakdown in social order and organization and, one could argue, established principles of economic distribution, there is much to favour an alternative interpretation, however. As Susan Davis (1982) has noted, such 'misrule' continued to serve the critical role established in Roman times of reaffirming established social relations and hierarchies. For by allowing them to be inverted in a relatively harmless and short-lived manner, they served to cement the political legitimacy and longevity of the existing political order. Indeed, when it came to Christmas charity in particular, a similar argument is taken up in Stephen Nissenbaum's (1997: 11) discussion of Christmas in America who, citing E.P Thompson, suggests that the utility to be found in Christmas altruism and hospitality was that by showing generosity and goodwill at Christmas the powerful could make up 'for a year's accumulation of small injustices, regaining in the process their tenants' good will'.

This is suggested most clearly by the actions of Elizabeth I. Elizabeth possessed her father's enthusiasm for Christmas festivities, and her seasonal revelries featured the organization of lavish banquets, plays, and other often rowdy activities. Unfortunately, the quality of her hospitality purportedly drew many of her landed nobles to the court for Christmas, leaving local communities and tenants with little or no source of festive food or entertainment. In response, Elizabeth took to insisting that her nobles returned to their country seats at Christmas in order to 'keep hospitality amongst their neighbours' (Pimlott, 1978: 32). Yet this was no arbitrary exercise of royal power. Rather it was a measured action designed to sustain both loyalty and order amongst her subjects who benefitted annually from the largesse of the nobility during the season, as well as to maintain the continuity and legitimacy of the local government of the day.

A Midlife Crisis at Christmas

Up until the mid-seventeenth century, Christmas remained largely unchanged, following the same traditions it had for centuries, and remaining the foremost religious celebration in the English calendar. However, with the civil war between the forces of the Crown and Parliament, and the rise of the Commonwealth of England with its largely puritanical value system, Christmas was soon to find itself officially persona non grata across most of the British Isles. While much has been made of the idea that it was Oliver Cromwell who personally outlawed Christmas during his time as Lord Protector of the Commonwealth, evidence suggests that this is not quite the case, given that most legislation opposing the festival was driven by pressure from hardliner groups within the parliament (Pimlott, 1978).

Having said this, Cromwell was undoubtedly not well disposed towards the season. As was the case for most of those sharing his puritanical predilections, he viewed Christmas as a pseudo-Christian celebration for which there was, as I have noted, scant biblical evidence. He was also somewhat repulsed by the distinctively un-Godly revelry that tended to accompany it, including gambling, drunkardness, debauchery, and the pursuit of pagan practices that, in his mind, verged on witchcraft and magic (Golby and Purdue, 2000). Nonetheless, as a man with more significant political issues facing him at the time, outlawing the season was not necessarily uppermost in his mind.

For his supporters in the powerful Scottish Presbyterian Church, however, the season was symptomatic of what they believed to be the decline of a more pious Christianity across the British Isles as a whole. The required Scottish military support for the Parliamentary cause in England came at a cost, therefore, including greater Presbyterian influence over the theological and political policies of the emerging state (Armstrong, 2010). This, in turn, led to a series of parliamentary interventions into the celebration of the season, culminating with Acts of Parliament in both 1647 and 1652 that sought to ban the personal, public, and religious observance of Christmas, with soldiers actively deployed to ensure that churches remained shut and shops remained open on December 25 (Storey, 2008).

Not that this resulted in the complete eradication of Christmas and its observance. Instead, its role as a medium of political organization and a battle of ideas once again came to the fore. For while in the minds of those pursuing a Presbyterian agenda, it represented a means by which legal and ecclesiastical reform might be undertaken, for those who opposed their rule, it also became a mobilizing cause for anti-Puritan sentiment. In 1647, for example, and in stark defiance of Parliament's recent decrees, heady festive celebrations were reportedly held in Suffolk and Norfolk towns, as well as ecclesiastical centres such as Oxford and Canterbury that became, as Hutton (1996: 30) observes, rallying points for the 'condemnation of the government'.

In addition, this season offered a wealth of material for a wider array of anti-government stances, as well as those that were specifically targeted at the move to eradicate Christmas (Golby and Purdue, 2000). Perhaps the most famous example is Taylor's 1652/3 pamphlet, *The Vindication of Christmas.* Here the Puritan's attack on Christmas was not only rejected as an act of religious repression but it was also condemned as part of a far broader set of governmental policies and actions. This was especially true concerning taxation and what was considered the government's tendency to 'plunder' the means of ordinary folk to pursue wars such as that being waged in Ireland (Pimlott, 1978).

Beyond the Restoration

With the restoration of Charles II in 1660 and the repeal of all Commonwealth laws, while never fully resolved, such disquiet essentially ended in England and Wales, if not Scotland, as Christmas once again became something that could be observed publicly. Nonetheless, the struggle over Christmas retained its significance elsewhere, most notably in colonized North America. For while many of those who went to the new world took their festive traditions and customs with them, others carried their religious opposition and intolerant practices as well. As Golby and Purdue (2000) observe, in the Colony of Virginia, for example, from around 1607 Christmas was celebrated very much in the English style with country gentleman feasting and dispensing hospitality. Nevertheless, in the New England colonies that came to be settled predominantly by Presbyterians and Calvinists, things were much more reminiscent of ongoing developments across the Atlantic under Cromwell. As a result, Christmas was shunned as a largely pagan or Roman Catholic mystification and, in certain areas, entirely outlawed. In Massachusetts in 1659, for instance, a fine of five shillings was threatened should anybody be caught observing the season in any way whatsoever (Forbes, 2007).

However, such legislation was not, as Stephen Nissenbaum (1997) notes, simply an isolated attack on the popular celebration of Christmas in one American colony. Instead, for those aligned to a Puritan worldview, Christmas again represented just one aspect, albeit a highly significant one, of what they considered to be the corrupted and Godless old world they were escaping. So, while Christmas was ostensively the immediate target of Puritan legislation, such legislation was part of a more significant attempt to pursue widespread social and cultural reform. Its adherents sought to at least modify, if not eradicate, ideas, behaviours, and attitudes that were deemed antithetical to the idealized social order envisaged by a significant swathe of American colonists. Indeed, as late as 1870, it is reported that the public schools of Boston continued to hold classes on December 25 despite the day being declared a public holiday by the US Congress that same year (Marling, 2001). And while, as in Britain, the direct influence of Puritan laws and structures would ultimately wain, they went on to shape many aspects of the country's post-colonial culture, not least of all what Max Weber (1976) referred to as the 'spirit of capitalism' with its emphasis on hard work and, just as importantly, an ascetic lifestyle.

Gradually, however, a new spirit of Christmas did emerge across the US and Britain. One that combined the iconography, tales, and traditions of Europe with the dynamism and commercial sensibilities of the new world into what would ultimately become a globally annual event. Exactly why and how this came to be at this juncture in history is itself, however, a further and fascinating tale of attempted social and economic engineering that reflected the concerns and organizational interests of the modern and increasingly industrial age in which it arose.

The Coming of Anglo-American Christmas

A broad consensus exists that, in Britain at least, the late eighteenth and early nineteenth centuries were not a particularly healthy time for Christmas (Pimlott, 1978; Golby and Purdue, 2000; Miller, 1993). Despite its restoration in 1660, the season had lost much of its lustre following the years of Puritan repression. For Harrison (1951: 146), this can largely be blamed on the lack of enthusiasm the restored Charles II held for it, resulting in an end to 'tournaments', 'disguisings', 'masques' and 'Christmas and Twelfth Night revels at the Inns of Court'. As such, and having for so long been associated with royal patronage and power, once such patronage slipped away, Christmas and its supporters found it hard to reassert its previous popularity or cultural importance, particularly in the minds of the wealthy and influential.

To say this is not to side with those who suggest that the celebration of Christmas in Britain entirely died out during this period, however. On the contrary, rural communities, especially those in English areas where the influence of the Commonwealth had been less marked, continued to observe many of the feasts and revelries of the season, albeit in a slightly more subdued manner. Nonetheless, as the locus of power, taste, and influence gradually began to shift to the emerging urban centres of the country, the festive season increasingly took on the mantel of something of a superstitious anachronism appropriate neither for the increasingly worldly passions of the ascendant middle classes nor the time and resource-poor working orders.

Despite this, some mid-winter celebrations continued to be enthusiastically observed even in the towns and cities. For example, New Year's Day was still a day of festivities and relaxation, especially amongst the working population. At the same time, most British Government departments continued to have December 25 as a holiday throughout the eighteenth and early nineteenth centuries. What had undoubtedly dissipated, however, was any recognition of the 12 days of Christmas as an annual interval of merriment. Furthermore, as the demands of industrial production extended their hold on society, the notion that Christmas was a unique event that could unify the population in worship and celebration was increasingly outweighed by its perceived cost to productivity (Pimlott, 1978). This lack of urban festive activity is aptly illustrated by Golby and Purdue (2000: 40), for example, who observe how between '1790 and 1835 *The Times* did not mention Christmas at all, and for the remaining years its reports were extremely brief and uninformative'.

Matters were slightly different in the US, however. Especially on the east coast, where Christmas had gradually released itself from the grip of Puritan repression, seasonal celebrations started to take on a form that, while originating in Europe, were often very distinct from those we tend to associate with the Victorian era today. Most notably, from England and Germany in particular, the old pagan practices of mumming and wassailing, so despised by the Puritans, had found new homes in cities such as Philadelphia, Boston, and New York. By the 1800s, much as their predecessors had in earlier times, the predominantly working-class participants in such activities saw them as an opportunity to rile the established social orders and raise a little Christmas hell into the bargain.

Such misrule quickly came to be viewed, however, less as just seasonal hijinks and more as actively criminal, especially by the aspiring and law-abiding middle classes of the US east coast. Davis (1982), for example, tells of the disquiet and increasing despair at the roaming Christmas gangs of 'callithumpians' and 'fantasticals' who purportedly caused panic in early nineteenth-century Philadelphia. Taking to the streets over the Christmas period, they were frequently masked, drunk, and often violently inclined towards demanding monies and drink with menaces, with the editor of one Philadelphia paper reporting how on Christmas Eve, 1833:

> riot, noise and uproar prevailed, uncontrolled and uninterrupted in many of our central and most orderly streets. Gangs of boys howled as if possessed by the demon of disorder.
>
> *(Davis, 1982: 190)*

Similar problems were also emerging in other major cities such as New York, where bands of predominately young men reportedly terrorized not only their neighbourhoods but also the commercial centres and those of the wealthy elites, often tarnishing Christmas itself into the bargain (Nissenbaum, 1997).

Christmas to the Rescue

While on the face of it, these two ways of engaging with Christmas, the first by largely ignoring it and the second by turning it into an increasingly riotous affair, could not appear more different, both helped trigger the season's urban resurrection and, in many ways, contributed to what would eventually become its global popularity. In England, for those concerned by such matters, it was felt that the demise of Christmas was symptomatic of a broader decline in society's moral and spiritual order, a decline driven by rapid industrialization and urbanization (Golby and Purdue, 2000). In the US, as Nissenbaum (1997) states, the increasing impact of roaming bands of festive revellers was viewed similarly if expressed in more disruptive and challenging terms. Either way, they were both considered symptomatic of a genuine and present threat to the authority of these emerging liberal democracies and the class system that, albeit unofficially, underpinned them. In both instances, therefore, and particularly amongst what today we might call the liberal intelligentsia, there was a widespread feeling that something had to be done to head off such challenges and that if Christmas was part of the problem, it could also be part of the solution.

In America, writer Washington Irving was one of the leading cultural figures at the forefront of such efforts. First, in 1809, and under the pseudonym of Diedrich Knickerbocker, Irving published his largely satirical account of the Dutch settlement of what became New York. As Forbes (2007) observes, this story partly focused on the possibly imagined significance to the city's early Dutch inhabitants of Christmas in general and the figure of St. Nicholas as a mysterious gift giver, in particular. Then, in his *work, The Sketch Book of Geoffrey Crayon, Gent*, published between 1819 and 1820, Irving (2009) went on to present his readers with a highly romanticized but still influential account of Christmas in an English country house; one bathed in the romance of medieval enchantment and imagined aristocratic practices of hospitality. More than this, however, Irving presented Christmas as a celebration that was best experienced not as a riotous and bawdy outdoors affair but in the secure domestic setting of hearth and home:

> [Everyone] were variously occupied; some at a round game of cards; others conversing around the fireplace; at one end of the hall was a group of young folks, some nearly grown up, others of a more tender and budding age, fully engrossed by a merry game; and a profusion of wooden horses, penny trumpets, and tattered dolls, about the floor, showed traces of a troop of little fairy beings, who having frolicked through a happy day, had been carried off to slumber through a *peaceful night*.
>
> *(Irving, 1886: 55, emphasis added)*

And it was Irving's publications that went on to have a significant impact on how New Yorkers and east coast residents thought about the season, eventually establishing a template for its observance as an increasingly home-based celebration with the figure of what was to evolve into Santa Claus as the provider of gifts for well-behaved children. Furthermore, as Marling (2001) observes, his work also influenced a second great literary figure lauded for the refashioning of Christmas on both sides of the Atlantic during the nineteenth century, the English author Charles Dickens.

The Power of a Carol

While the often-heard claim that this Victorian author can be credited with inventing the contemporary Christmas (cf. Standiford, 2008) is an exaggeration, there can be no doubt that Dickens's influence on how we view and celebrate Christmas today is significant. While during the 1800s, the perceived threat of an unruly culture of festive revelry was not as pronounced in the UK as it was in the US, nonetheless, as the seat of the industrial revolution and the immense social and economic changes that accompanied it, the UK was facing its own problems in respect of an increasing lack of social integration and economic stability. As Golby and Purdue (2000: 51) observe, this was a time when the ascendant British middle class had particular and somewhat pressing 'preoccupations' with the destructive impact industrialization was having on the lower orders and the threat of social conflict it was engendering.

For those with a more liberal social conscience, including Dickens, the solution to such preoccupations was not to build more prisons and recruit more policemen, solutions prevalent in the press of the time, but rather to tackle what they saw as the roots of such 'ugliness', both at the economic and socio-cultural level. Furthermore, like so many romantic critics of modernity, for Dickens it was partly to the past he looked to for solutions. In doing so, however, he provided much impetus for what was to become the defining celebration of the modern age, mainly through the pages of a short, if albeit now timeless, novella.

Like Irving and others, such as the Scottish author Walter Scott, what Dickens offered the world was what he considered to be a redemptive vision of Christmas that harked back to a rural and romantically coloured pre-industrial English landscape. In *The Pickwick Papers* (1992) of 1836, and under his then pseudonym of Boz, Dickens had first regaled his readers with such imagery during his tale of a festive visit to Dingley Dell Farm. Here, Christmas was a warm-hearted time of feasting and merriment when everything was in abundance, especially goodwill. It was not, however, until his 1843 novella, *A Christmas Carol* (2006), that Dickens established himself as perhaps the preeminent voice of the Victorian Christmas, as well as a man who believed that industrial society could be improved through the power of social sentiment and a touch of Christmas magic.[2] And to illustrate the final stages of this chapter's argument, it is on this story I now focus.

Misery at Christmas

While today a global bestseller, Dickens's most famous piece of writing, *A Christmas Carol*, was initially a financial disappointment due mainly to the high cost of production that he bore himself. Nonetheless, it eventually helped sustain him for the rest of his life, mainly through reprints and an increasingly lucrative market for his public readings of the story across the UK and the US. Since its publication, it has become what Paul Davis (1990: 4) describes as a *culture-text*, having undergone an untold number of performances and adaptations across theatre, radio, television, and cinema, giving it a life that is well beyond any intentions the author may have had for it. Its importance, however, cannot be reduced simply to its popularity and longevity. In a similar vein to Irving's work, this tale of the fall and redemption of Ebenezer Scrooge also represented a deliberate intervention into Victorian Britain's political and cultural organization in general and, in particular, the relationship between social classes.

At the time of its writing, London offered little more comfort to working people than what the likes of, say, Friedrich Engels (2009) had observed in the industrial north of England. The newly found wealth and influence of the professional and industrial middle classes were matched only by the increasing poverty and despair of those working men, women, and children for whom the new order often meant inhuman labouring conditions and barely subsistence-level payments. And while Dickens supported social reform, it was the importance of charity and the altruistic responsibilities of the wealthy to the poor that he sought to highlight in his festive tale. One of the earliest scenes in the story used to illustrate Scrooge's character, for example, is his refusal to contribute to a collection for the poor at Christmas, declaring that the premature death of such people would help 'decrease the surplus population' (Dickens, 2006: 14). Equally, one of his first acts of redemption is to revisit the same collectors on Christmas Day, offering them an undisclosed but significant sum designed not only to meet that year's obligations but, equally, his 'many back-payments (Dickens, 2006: 80).

Not that charity is all Dickens champions in response to the destitution and squalor around him. His emphasis on the importance of the family at Christmas also aims to spur all quarters of society to focus on what resources they have in pursuing domestic festive activities and concerns rather than those that might lead to ever greater poverty and ruin. As Sheila Whiteley (2008: 99) observes, 'salvation, it seemed, lay in the family, an axiom central to the Victorian belief that a good home life would produce a stable and worthy population'. From the wealthiest to the poorest characters, family in *A Christmas Carol* is presented as an axial institution through which the good life might be realized despite, it must be said, Dickens's own failing and adulterous marriage.

Nevertheless, it is a spirit of generosity that Dickens returns to repeatedly throughout the story, emphasizing it as the true calling of those observing the season. A prominent example of this, and one particularly pertinent to the organization of work, is his nostalgic telling of the young Scrooge's exuberances at the lavish annual Christmas party held by his first employer, 'Mr Fezziwig'. Here Dickens presents a tale of what he considers to be an employer's paternalistic responsibility for his workforce and the comfort this can bring. For as Scrooge reports when questioned by the first of the Christmas spirits as to why he seems to display such affection for his old boss, he notes how Fezziwig 'has the power to render us happy or unhappy; to make our service light or burdensome; a pleasure or a toil ... The happiness he gives is quite as great as if it cost a fortune' (Dickens, 2006: 56).

Such a statement was not only expressive of Dickens's sentiment towards the well-being of others, however. It also reflects an awareness that if the casualties of industrial progress, both the employed and unemployed, are to be reconciled to the new moral order, they would need to feel as if they shared in its benefits, as well as its ills. Nowhere is this made more evident than in Scrooge's encounter with *Ignorance* and *Want* (Figure 1.2).

Described as the 'children of man', while they hide beneath the robes of the Ghost of Christmas Present the warning the Ghost gives is unambivalent:

'... This boy is Ignorance. This girl is Want. Beware them both, and all of their degree, but most of all beware this boy, for on his brow I see that written which is *Doom*, unless the writing be erased. Deny it!' cried the Spirit, *stretching out its hand towards the city*.

(Dickens, 2006: 62, emphasis added)

Dickens, therefore, presents Christmas to Victorian society as both an opportunity for individual redemption and a chance to protect itself from the threat of an impoverished and increasingly disenfranchised urban proletariat. In a similar vein to his American cousins, it reflected this increasingly prominent Victorian unease about the state of this new industrial, urbanized society, alongside a commitment to an albeit limited social and cultural reorganization through, in this instance, philanthropy and voluntary associations such as the family. In doing so, therefore, Dickens drew upon and reproduced older ideas about the role Christmas could play as a stabilizing force in society, with Scrooge embodying the message that 'by learning to share a little, a great deal more will remain secure' (Storey, 2008: 27).

IGNORANCE AND WANT

FIGURE 1.2 Scrooge encounters Ignorance and Want.

Shopping for Redemption?

While such an interpretation of Dickens's work is not entirely new, what is commented on less frequently, however, is the importance he places on market economics and the pursuit of sound business regarding his festive prescription for the ills of nineteenth-century society (Hancock, 2016). While the likes of Irving, for example, appealed predominantly to medieval ideals and family tropes, Dickens was also quite prepared to celebrate what he considered to be the capacity of capitalism to improve the condition of all men and women, whatever their relative class position. With the financial crash of 1825 (Haupert, 1997), the first real cracks in the new economic system were starting to show while debates surrounding the problems of under-consumption (de Sismondi, 1990), and subsequently over-production (Marx, 1992), were beginning to haunt economic thinkers. And it was in this context that men like Dickens started to realize that industrial-scale production would also require a comparable increase in consumption if it were not to collapse under the weight of its own expectations. Not that the mass of the British population could meaningfully afford to buy that much more, not at first anyway. Instead, it was the increasingly affluent middle classes who, still restricted by a predominantly ascetic worldview, needed to be coaxed out into the pleasures of the marketplace. In doing so, or so Dickens believed, they would channel wealth down to the masses through employment and altruism so that all might eventually benefit from this new world of plenty.

This, however, would require an ethos of consumption, preferably one that was both self and other-orientated, and it is as such that *A Christmas Carol* can also be understood as a direct intervention into the economic life and values of Victorian society. So while Dickens's credentials as a social reformer appear genuine, and his despair at the attitudes and values of a character such as Scrooge sincere, it is also clear that he had no problem with the principle of accumulating wealth through commerce. Instead, what concerned him was that such wealth should be allowed to return into economic circulation for the betterment of all. A clear believer, therefore, in what contemporary liberal economists would describe as the virtues of the trickle-down effect, Dickens felt that wealth acquired by the rich should re-enter the economy via wages, consumption, and, indeed, philanthropy and, in doing so, improve the security of rich and poor alike.

As such, the virtuousness of consumption in *A Christmas Carol* is a theme Dickens frequently returns to, portrayed through the general notion that Christmas should be a time for plenty and that Christmas goodwill is best communicated through spending. This is picked up on by James Carrier (1993), who observes how the purchase of food and its consumption are central to the image of a hearty English Christmas for Dickens. In the novella, this is perhaps best illustrated by the arrival of the second of the Christmas spirits, the Ghost of Christmas Present, who is described as sitting on a 'throne' comprising of a veritable cornucopia of every festive foodstuff that could be imagined (Dickens, 2006). A hearty and joyful Christmas is not only defined by the possession and consumption of abundant foodstuffs, however. Just as important is the image Dickens presents of how successful commerce can ensure that such delicacies become accessible to the masses at Christmas. As the same spirit leads Scrooge through the streets of London, his first observation is of the shops and stalls bustling with the goods and trades of the season. Images of shops heaving with delights of all sorts pervade the text, from meats to fruits, from vegetables to sweets, leaving Dickens (2006: 46) to declare 'The Grocers'! oh the Grocers'!' while describing the event in effusive terms.

While Dickens was writing at a time just before the appearance of industrially produced Christmas goods, his message is clear, therefore. To produce, sell, and consume on such a scale and with such positive enjoyment in its undertaking should be integral to the season's generosity, happiness, and spirit. Moreover, this motif reappears at various points throughout the text. For example, it is seen in the pleasure of a goose dinner for the Cratchits and the evident joy when the redeemed Scrooge can demonstrate his care for his clerk by purchasing the big 'prize' Turkey for him and his family. Scrooge's spiritual redemption was achieved not only through charity, therefore, but through a willingness to fully commit to the ideal of the market as a means by which he, and all others, may (re)enter the social sphere in a manner that is, for Dickens at least, positively virtuous.

A Christmas Carol is not only a remarkable story, therefore. It also brings to the fore a series of continuities that reflect an organizational interpretation of the festive season, a 'hidden history' (Benjamin, 1970) that exists at the margins of Christmas and organizational scholarship. Along with its more widely recognized concern with Christmas as a medium of redemption through charity and altruism, the story tells a tale of the organized pursuit of social stability through the virtues of Christmas trade and consumption. It champions the role the season will come to play in nurturing and sustaining a mass production and consumer economy, as well as those organizations that have come to be so closely identified with such activities and that, in many cases, have become objects of celebration themselves.

Moreover, not only does Christmas mobilize economic, cultural, and social resources to realize its own ambitions and objectives, a process personified by Dickens in the form of the various Christmas spirits. It also witnesses the preliminary structuring of a new form of modern seasonal subjectivity whereby Scrooge is transformed through his contact with the lights, sounds, smells, and values of Christmas into an ideal festive subject. One that keeps Christmas in his heart all year and revels in all it has to offer, from purchasing a couple of bowls of smoking bishop and a new coal scuttle, to the promise of money spent on charities, parties, and festive events galore. The reader is left with a tale of transformation whereby a subject of misery becomes one that lives for Christmas, and indeed by living this way brings into being its seasonal hopes and joys. One who internalizes a childlike belief in dreams, with or without ghosts, and who understands that at Christmas such dreams are more likely if one embraces business in such a way as to ensure that its benefits are not hoarded but, like manure, spread around.[3]

Notes

1   As I noted in the introduction, the Bible has very little to say about the nativity being limited as it is to extracts from the gospels of Matthew (1:18–25, 2:1–12) and Luke (1:26–38, 2:1–20).
2   What is often termed his carol philosophy (Callow, 2012).
3   An idea that is widely cited but rarely attributed.

References

Armstrong, N. (2010) *Christmas in Nineteenth Century England*. Manchester: Manchester University Press.

Beard, M. (2015) *SPQR: A History of Ancient Rome*. London: Profile Books.

Benjamin, W. (1970) [1955] 'Theses on the Philosophy of History' (trans H. Zohn). In, H. Arendt (ed.) *Illuminations*. London: Fontana/Collins. Pp. 255–266.

Callow, S. (2012) *Charles Dickens*. London: Harper Press.

Carrier, J. (1993) 'The Rituals of Christmas Giving'. In, D. Miller (ed.) *Unwrapping Christmas*. Oxford: Oxford University Press. Pp. 55–74.

Clegg, S. (1990) *Modern Organizations: Organization Studies in the Postmodern World*. London: Sage.

Connelly, M. (1999) *Christmas: A Social History*. London: I.B. Tauris.

Cooper, R. and Burrell, G. (1988) 'Modernism, Postmodernism and Organizational Analysis: An Introduction'. *Organization Studies* 9(1): 91–112.

Davis, P. (1990) *The Lives and Times of Ebenezer Scrooge*. New Haven, MA: Yale University Press.

Davis, S.G. (1982) '"Making Night Hideous": Christmas Revelry and Public Order in Nineteenth-Century Philadelphia'. *American Quarterly* 34(2): 185–199.

De Sismondi, J. (1990) *New Principles of Political Economy*. Piscataway, NJ: Transaction Publishers.

Dickens, C. (1992) *The Pickwick Papers*. London: Wordsworth Classics.

Dickens, C. (2006) 'A Christmas Carol in Prose: Being a Ghost Story of Christmas'. In, *A Christmas Carol and Other Christmas Stories*. Oxford: Oxford University Press. Pp. 5–83.

Durkheim, E. (1965) *The Elementary Forms of the Religious Life* (trans. J. Swain: 1915). New York, NY: The Free Press.

Engels, F. (2009) *The Condition of the Working Class in England* (ed. D. Mclellan). Oxford: Oxford University Press.

Etzioni, A. (2004) 'Holidays and Rituals: Neglected Seedbeds of Virtue'. In, A. Etzioni and J. Bloom (eds) *We Are What We Celebrate: Understanding Holidays and Rituals*. New York, NY: New York University Press. Pp. 3–40.

Forbes, B.D. (2007) *Christmas: A Candid History*. Los Angeles, CA: University of California Press.

Golby, J.M. and Purdue A.W. (2000) *The Making of the Modern Christmas*. Stroud: Sutton Publishing.

Hancock, P. (2016) 'A Christmas Carol: A Reflection on Organization, Society, and the Socioeconomics of the Festive Season'. *Academy of Management Review*, 41(4): 755–765.

Harrison, M. (1951) *The Story of Christmas: Its Growth and Development from the Earliest Times*. Watford: Odhams Press.

Haupert, M. (1997). 'Panic of 1825'. In, D. Glasner and T.F. Cooley (eds) *Business Cycles and Depressions: An Encyclopedia*. New York, NY: Garland Publishing. Pp. 511–513.

Hobsbawm, E. (2012) 'Introduction: Inventing Traditions'. In, E. Hobsbawm and T. Ranger (eds) *The Invention of Tradition*. Cambridge: Cambridge University Press. Pp. 1–14.

Hutton, R. (1996) *The Stations of the Sun: A History of the Ritual Year in Britain*. Oxford: Oxford University Press.

Irving, W. (1886) *Old Christmas* (5th edition). London: Macmillan & Co.

Irving, W. (2009) *The Sketch Book of Geoffrey Crayon, Gent.* Oxford: Oxford World Classics.

Kelly, J.F. (2004) *The Origins of Christmas*. Collegeville, MN: Liturgical Press.

MacMullen, R. (1986) *Christianizing the Roman Empire, AD 100–400*. New Haven, CT: Yale University Press.

Malinowski, B. (2011) *Magic, Science, Religion and Other Essays*. London: Souvenir Press.

Marling, K.A. (2001) *Merry Christmas: Celebrating America's Greatest Holiday*. Cambridge, MA: Harvard University Press.

Marx, K. (1992) *Capital: A Critique of Political Economy Vol. III* (ed. F. Engels). Harmondsworth: Penguin.

Mauss, M. (2001) *A General Theory of Magic* (trans. R. Brain). London: Routledge.

McKay, G. (2008) 'Consumption, Coca-colonisataion, Cultural Resistance and Santa Claus'. In, S. Whiteley (ed.) *Christmas, Ideology and Popular Culture*. Edinburgh: Edinburgh University Press. Pp. 50–67.

Miles, C.A. (1912) *Christmas in Ritual and Tradition, Christian and Pagan*. London: T. Fisher Unwin.

Miller, D. (1993) 'A Theory of Christmas'. In D. Miller (ed.) *Unwrapping Christmas*. Oxford: Oxford University Press. Pp. 3–37.

Nissenbaum, S. (1997) *The Battle for Christmas: A Cultural History of America's Most Cherished Holiday*. New York, NY: Vintage Books.

Pimlott, J.A.R. (1978) *The Englishman's Christmas: A Social History*. Hassocks: The Harvester Press.

Powys, L. (2010) *Christmas Lore and Legend: Yuletide Essays*. Sherborne: The Sundial Press.

Sansom, W. (1968) *Christmas*. London: Weidenfeld and Nicolson.

Standiford, L. (2008) *The Man Who Invented Christmas: How Charles Dickens's "A Christmas Carol" Rescued his Career and Revived Our Holiday Spirits*. New York, NY: Broadway Books.

Storey, J. (2008) 'The Invention of the English Christmas'. In, S. Whiteley (ed.) *Christmas, Ideology and Popular Culture*. Edinburgh: Edinburgh University Press. Pp. 17–31.

Weber, M. (1976) *The Protestant Ethic and the Spirit of Capitalism*. London: Allen & Unwin.

Weir, A. and Clarke, S. (2018) *A Tudor Christmas*. London: Jonathan Cape.

Whiteley, S. (2008) 'Christmas Songs – Sentiments and Subjectivities'. In, S. Whiteley (ed.) *Christmas, Ideology and Popular Culture*. Edinburgh: Edinburgh University Press. Pp. 98–112.

2

THE BUYING AND SELLING OF A SEASON

Introduction

If there is one criticism commonly voiced when it comes to Christmas, it is that it has become 'too commercial'. This usually rests on the idea that by prioritizing shopping for increasingly expensive gifts and other seasonal accoutrements, people have forgotten the season's true meaning, either the celebration of the Christian nativity or, from a more secular perspective, spending bounded time with family and friends. Now Christmas is, without doubt, a time of excess, and for those who can afford it – and just as often for those who cannot – it is a celebration that embraces eating more, drinking more, and generally spending more than one would at any other time of the year. Nevertheless, is this necessarily the same as Christmas having *become* too commercial?

The relationship between Christmas and commerce is complex (Bartunek and Do, 2011). As I observed in Chapter 1, those winter festivities in which Christmas originates were always concerned with celebrating life in the face of winter's darkness and what better way to do so than by indulging in earthly pleasures such as eating, drinking, and sharing gifts and gratitude? As such, the amount of current commercial activity associated with Christmas should not be all that much of a worry, should it? After all, somebody has to provide all the food, drink, toys, gifts, cards, and the like, and if they can also make a bit of a profit, then why not?

Such a counterargument only really tells half the story, however, predicated as it is on the idea of a festive marketplace in which the seasonal reveller not only recognizes their needs but that the market then passively obliges to supply them. For to accept such a demand-led version of events misses the frequently

DOI: 10.4324/9781315637969-3

active role that commerce plays in shaping the season and creating many of the demands and desires we have come to consider essential to an enjoyable Christmas (McKechnie and Tynan, 2006). Indeed, not only has Christmas long been a period of intense commercial activity, a 'costly purveyor of excess' as Pimlott (1978: 126) puts it, but it has itself also been shaped in equal part by a series of cultural interventions, innovations, and invocations that, as I shall argue, have starkly commercial origins and motivations.

Take, as an opening example, something as straightforward as when we celebrate the season. While December 25 has remained the date identified with the birth of Christ and, as such, the season's 'big day', what once constituted the 12-day extended holiday has shifted in line mainly with commercial priorities and a drive for profit maximization. So, while the medieval Christmas ran from December 25 to January 6, with its re-popularization during the 1900s the Christmas holidays were shortened to perhaps no more than two or three days largely to prevent them from interfering with industrial production. At the same time, Christmas activities increasingly started to commence around the beginning of November to maximize opportunities for pre-festive consumption. Equally telling is that those who tend to decry the commercial character of the season do so most vocally with one eye on an albeit more recent past, namely an idealized image of a Victorian Christmas. Extolling the virtues of a season characterized by falling snow, carols being sung around an open fire, and charity and goodwill to all in abundance, they are either unaware of or ignore the fact that it was such Victorians who were the first to fully recognize Christmas to be the business opportunity it is.

Yet whatever one's view of the origins, or indeed the rights and wrongs of the commercial aspects of the season, what is hard to deny is that not only is it now the preeminent global festival, but it is also probably *the* economic event of the year. Over the course of just six weeks, from late November to the end of December, retail spending average reaches around £70 and £80 billion across major European economies such as France, Germany, and the UK.[1] Employment levels rise, hospitality booms and even third-sector organizations such as charities see their financial health improve as the spirit of Christmas leads people to put their hands in their pockets not just more deeply but more frequently as well. As writer and journalist Katherine Whitehorn (1962: 183) observed, 'from a commercial point of view, if Christmas didn't exist it would be necessary to invent it'.

Not that it is all necessarily good news, even for commerce and the economy. For example, a report based on work by *The Centre for Economics and Business Research*, published in 2015 by *KPMG*, claimed that Christmas costs the UK economy over £2.3 billion a year due to time off work and reduced employee performance.[2] Striking a similarly cautious note is the widely publicized work of the American economist and management professor Joel Waldfogel.

Waldfogel's original *American Economic Review* Paper (1993) and later book (2009) entitled *Scroogenomics: Why You Shouldn't Buy Presents for the Holidays* makes the argument that rather than creating value, the giving of Christmas presents actually destroys it by generating what, in economic terms, he considers a 'deadweight loss'. This is because, by his reckoning, more often than not the recipients of such gifts neither need nor want them. As such, they constitute nothing more than economic waste.

Despite, or perhaps because of such tensions and contradictions, in this chapter I focus on several aspects of the relationship between Christmas and various forms of commercial activity. Commencing with the explosion of Christmas goods and services during the 1800s, it tells of the rapid development of the festive season as the most important economic event of the year, especially in respect of growing levels of consumption and the role of the big department stores of the early twentieth century in perpetuating the glamour and popularity of the season. The organization of Christmas trade and commerce is then further explored as an increasingly globalized and globalizing force; one that has helped carry the values and practices of the Anglo-American Christmas across national and cultural borders alongside, it must be said, other national and political interests. Finally, the chapter brings these issues up to date, exploring the scope and impact of seasonal commerce today, including the growth of an increasingly significant Christmas industry in its own right.

Back to the Victorians

For cultural sociologist John Storey, the contemporary Christmas was invented by the Victorians 'first and foremost as a commercial event' (Storey, 2008: 20). Born of the entrepreneurial spirit of the age and resonating with the industrial and urbanizing priorities of nineteenth-century modernization, the Christmas we know today was in many ways a creation of the Victorian manufacturer, the shopkeeper and, increasingly, the advertiser. Moreover, if one stops to consider it, even today, so much of what we enjoy at Christmas, such as presents, trees, decorations, food, films, and the like, all have at least one notable thing in common; they can all make someone, somewhere, a profit.

Indeed, by the second half of the nineteenth century, especially across the UK and US, Christmas had already become the annual highpoint of the commercial year, affording the production and retailing of a host of novel consumer goods and services all designed for the newly burgeoning festive marketplace. Take as an illustration of this the humble Christmas card. While greetings cards had been popular for some time, with New Year and Valentine's Cards having been around for hundreds of years (Forbes, 2007), the first official Christmas card did not appear until 1843, the same year as the publication of Dickens's *A Christmas Carol* (Buday, 1964).

FIGURE 2.1 Henry Cole's Christmas card of 1843.

A relatively minor matter, this inaugural card was personally commissioned by Sir Henry Cole, the founder of the Victoria and Albert Museum in London and an instigator of the UK's 'penny post'. Designed by an artist friend, J.C. Horsley, it was initially to be sent to some of Cole's friends instead of a written letter, something which had remained a seasonal custom amongst the British upper classes. While it was commissioned as a private seasonal token, from what was an initial print run of around a thousand, those that remained were then sold commercially from an office in London (Harrison, 1951),[3] instigating one of the first of many new seasonal markets (Figure 2.1).

While Christmas cards may not have been an immediate hit, within 25 years they had become the accepted medium through which seasonal good wishes would be spread. In the UK, their popularity was increased further by the introduction, in 1870, of the 1/2d stamp for postcards (Golby and Purdue, 2000). They had also become increasingly cheaper to produce due to advances in design and printing and an ability to employ, more than a little ironically, child labour in their manufacture (Buday, 1964). By 1880, this had led to over 11 million Christmas cards being sold in the UK, often featuring what to today's eye might appear to be wholly un-Christmas-like images, including everything from dying animals to barely dressed young nymphs.[4] By the latter years of the century, however, more familiar imagery had established itself with the staples of a snowy landscape, a Christmas pudding, and even the occasional traditional British Father Christmas, ushering in what today we might consider the traditional style and form of card.

In the US, a similar pattern of commercial activity also developed. While it is broadly accepted that cards were being bought and sent in the US by the late 1850s, the wider popularity of the American Christmas card is credited primarily to the work of Prussian immigrant Louis Prang (1824–1909), who was a lithographer and publisher (Forbes, 2007). Having published his first cards in 1875, by 1881, he was purportedly selling five million a year until cheaper imports from the European continent began to undercut his margins (Kavanagh, 2012). Either way, by the latter years of the nineteenth century, the Christmas card had become big business on both sides of the Atlantic, with their popularity quickly spreading across continental Europe and beyond.

Returning to the UK, despite what might appear to be their somewhat trivial character, as Llew Smith and Pam Smith (2012) have observed, Christmas cards also quickly came to play a part in social and eventually organized political struggles. Cole's original card, for example, while depicting at its centre a somewhat idealized middle-class Victorian family enjoying a Christmas feast was flanked by images of the destitute receiving acts and gifts of charity at its periphery. This not only emphasized the responsibilities that came with personal wealth and security but also, as Dickens was concerned to do, the message that to continue enjoying plenty, some of it might also have to be shared with those less fortunate. By the latter decades of the century, however, cards that were overtly political and designed and published often for Britain's burgeoning trade union movement were also emerging. As well as offering season's greetings, they often acted as reminders of the political struggles both behind and in front of workers, depicting events such as the 1887 Trafalgar Square demonstration known as 'Bloody Sunday' given the violent response of the police and military to the demands of its participants (Smith and Smith, 2012: 15).

Today, Christmas cards come in all sizes and varieties and depict every shade of the political and cultural spectrum while their commercial importance is as great as ever. Even despite the increasing inroads made by the internet and the use of e-cards, or indeed just emails, there remains a continued enthusiasm for sending physical cards during the season.[5] For example, the British Greeting Cards Association estimated that in 2020 around 80 million single Christmas cards were sent in the UK, with consumers spending around £1.4 billion on them in the process,[6] while in the US, approximately 1.6 billion cards are purchased each year,[7] proportionally less than in the UK, but which is worth around $2 billion to the US economy.

Another product of Victorian entrepreneurship worth mentioning, and which would also shape the celebration across several continents, is the humble Christmas cracker. Once again invented in the UK and remaining a largely, although not exclusively, British and Commonwealth cultural tradition, the cracker was the brainchild of confectioner Tom Smith.[8] While little is known about the man himself (Kimpton, 2004), what is known is that somewhere around 1840, Smith had travelled to Paris and had seen the French 'bonbon' sweets, which were almonds wrapped in tissue paper and twisted at both ends. On his return to London, he imitated and sold these, gradually adding an insert of a piece of paper with a rhyme or riddle, and later on the now famous snapping inserts, all of which proved highly popular. By the end of the nineteenth century, Christmas crackers had become a staple of the British and imperial Christmas. Increasingly featuring elaborate designs on the crackers themselves and the boxes they were shipped in, as well as mottos, they also started to contain small gifts and novelties, making them a further part of the gift-giving tradition. Today, it is estimated that over 300 million crackers are pulled every Christmas in the UK (Rainey and Zhang, 2013), and while the custom might appear bizarre to celebrants in some countries,[9] it remains another enduring legacy of festive Victorian entrepreneurialism.

Cards and crackers are not the only festive products that emerged during the Victorian era as the Christmas we know today began to crystalize, however. As Storey (2008) acknowledges, this was also the age when items such as decorations, printed collections of carols and, perhaps above all else, a host of goods that could be given as seasonal presents not only appeared in stores but became increasingly accessible to the wider population. This all added to the sense that Christmas had become a time of the year defined as much by what one could purchase as by anything else. For instance, Gavin Weightman and Steve Humphries (1987) observe how an 1895 article in *The English Illustrated Magazine* reports on the growth in the seasonal Christmas Tree trade in London. It would seem that even at that relatively early point in the Christmas tree's national popularity, one of the city's most prominent retailers had, for several decades, been selling nearly 30,000 trees a year, with buyers ranging from major department stores to local households.

To further understand such developments and the expansion of Christmas as a season of commerce, we need to move beyond the nineteenth century, however, and further into the realms of consumption and the burgeoning retail sector, especially the growth and cultural importance of another uniquely modern commercial phenomenon, the department store.

From Cathedrals of Christmas Consumption to Festive Superhighways

The first dedicated Christmas retailers reportedly appeared in the US sometime during the early nineteenth century when, according to Marling (2001: 44), what today we might refer to as 'pop-up shops' appeared providing 'greenery for the decoration of churches, stores, civic buildings, and private homes'. Then as Christmas increasingly became synonymous with the buying and selling of Christmas-related goods, a range of shops and markets started to annually stock Christmas related products. Nowhere was this trend embraced more enthusiastically than in the increasingly popular department stores appearing in major towns and cities across Europe and North America (Connelly, 1999). While these embryonic 'cathedrals of consumption' (Ritzer, 2005) first emerged during the eighteenth century, with *Bennets* of Derby[10] and *Harding Howell and Company's Grand Fashionable Magazine* of London,[11] both in the UK, vying for recognition as the first of their kind, it was not until the nineteenth century that the contemporary department store started to stake its claim on the high street.

As stores such as *Marshall Field's* (1852) in Chicago, *Macy's* (1858) in New York and, more latterly, *Selfridges* (1909) in London, adopted an increasingly customer-orientated approach, it became quickly apparent that Christmas was not only an opportunity for 'working off the end of year surplus' (Twitchell, 1996: 178) but also for encouraging people to shop not only as an economic activity but as a social and cultural pastime as well. Critical to promoting such seasonal consumption was a drive to shift consumers away from the perception that Christmas decorations and gifts should be small and often handmade and towards a normalization of the idea that the kinds of mass-manufactured commodities that predominantly featured in such stores, and that would generate significant profits due to economies of scale in both production and distribution, could also be considered legitimate tokens of seasonal love, respect ,and celebration (Carrier, 1993; Waits, 1994).

While it was Marshall Field's general manager and soon-to-be London department store magnate Harry Selfridge, that coined the now infamous phrase, 'x number of shopping days to Christmas' (Woodhead, 2012), it was Macy's in New York that led the way in making Christmas the festival of mass consumption that we know today. By 1867 it had, for the first time, opened its doors until midnight on Christmas Eve, leading the store to set a $6,000 sales record for the day (Twitchell, 1996). Then, in 1874, the store started what was to become an annual Christmas attraction in many large cities and beyond, the themed Christmas window display. While relatively simple by today's standards, displaying a collection of around $10,000 worth of imported dolls, it attracted throngs of existing and new shoppers to its store both to buy and to look and dream (Snyder, 1985). From then on, department stores across the US and UK (and eventually beyond) became not only the place to purchase gifts and Christmas products but, for many families, an important Christmas destination in their own right.

Furthermore, as George McKay (2008) observes, it was through their open access and by acting as safe spaces that such stores also became social and cultural hubs in which women, in particular, could act out public lives based not on work but leisure. Moreover, given that women at this time were, and arguably still are, considered the primary homemakers and, therefore, responsible for

Christmas preparations and shopping (Bella, 1992), such stores were perforce increasingly considered to be not only the first stop for Christmas gifts and decorations but one of the few places in which women could partake in a communal celebration of Christmas outside of the home and church.

Stores Come into Their Own

As the twentieth century progressed, department stores played an increasingly integral role in defining both commercially and culturally many of the qualities and expectations surrounding Christmas. Their window displays, in particular, became increasingly lavish and technologically sophisticated, reinforcing their status as stand-alone Christmas attractions. Today, stores such as *Harrods* and *Selfridges* in London invest thousands in their festive displays,[12] with preparations and designs in place not only for the windows themselves but for the entire Christmas theme of the store 18 months or more in advance. Indeed, the unveiling of such designs has also become big news in itself. In 2016, for example, *Selfridges* hit the headlines for seeking to steal a march on its competitors by revealing its Christmas window displays in October – something generally reserved for the following month. Featuring, for the first time in nearly a decade, the central character of Santa Claus, they comprised 12 Santa mannequins, each wearing a suit of around 6,000 sequins which took 193 hours to make. In addition, 114,000 baubles were featured in a series of displays that took over 168 working hours to assemble (Cliff, 2016).

And while individual window displays remain popular, increasingly sophisticated marketing and merchandising strategies have now developed such that a store's Christmas appearance is often conceived and designed following a holistic Christmas style guide. These include not only windows but interior store design and decorations, as well as many of the actual products on sale, all curated and merchandised to maximize their impact on consumers. As one member of the design team based in a central London department store recounted to me, when dressing the store for Christmas:

> There're two elements to it really. One is that there's the core product at Christmas that we do, and it doesn't necessarily fit with the theme; it's just the stuff people need to buy at Christmas, so it's like your jumpers, your socks, your gifts, all of that kind of stuff. And then, we develop another range *that sits specifically with the concept*. So, we kind of do two different directions for products.
>
> *(Emphasis added)*

This degree of commitment to creating a 'total Christmas experience' reflects aptly the continued importance of the season for the retail sector, especially department stores and shopping malls. Despite an ongoing decline in customer footfall and in-store expenditure, Christmas remains known as the golden quarter with stores still often expecting a 25% uplift in annual sales during the season, with one manager of a major outlet I spoke to explaining that they can anticipate doing anything up to 60% of their business between October and December. Not that the Christmas retail period necessarily waits until as 'late' as October to commence. Department stores have increasingly started to open their dedicated Christmas shops in late summer, selling decorations and other branded Christmas items that have previously been sourced at events such as *Christmasworld*, a vast Christmas decorations exhibition held in the southwestern German city of Frankfurt each January.[13] In 2019, for example, *Selfridges* announced its Christmas store was open for business from July 30, with *Harrods*, amongst others, following suit a few weeks later, something that, like the revealing of the windows, caused annual media excitement and outrage, in equal measure.[14]

Nonetheless, for store managers themselves, this is considered an increasingly necessary approach, attracting as it does overseas summer tourists eager to take a piece of the traditional 'English' Christmas home with them.[15] Indeed, during one visit to a London department store, a manager recalled the story of a Chinese retailer who annually purchased several thousand pounds worth of decorations from the store early in the season. The reason for this being that they would fetch a premium price in China due to what customers would perceive to be their country of origin, namely the UK. Needless to say, the irony was not lost on the manager in question, reflecting as he did on the fact that they had been purchased from a Chinese manufacturer and wholesaler in the first instance.

Despite the continued importance of Christmas to such stores, some of their festive glamour has been usurped, however, by the ever-ubiquitous shopping malls. As it is for department stores, many of which are today housed in such malls, Christmas remains the most important retail event of the year for such outlets. As one mall manager told me quite bluntly, 'If we get Christmas wrong, we've had it. Plain and simple'. Planning for Christmas was once again, therefore, a year-long process with in-depth analyses of trading patterns and the success of the previous year's Christmas decorations, events, and activities starting from the moment the New Year sales are over. One illustration of this urgency is how trade publications such as the UK's *Shopping Centre Magazine* publish their Christmas specials early in the new year. The February 2017 edition, for example, is at pains to stress that it is never too early to start planning for Christmas noting that as customers increasingly demand more excitement from their visits to physical retail outlets, malls must be ready and able to rise to the challenge of creating 'magical environments' that are more interactive and that will 'further enhance the visitor experience and encourage people to stay longer' (*Shopping Centre Magazine*, 2017: 23).

Not that Christmas is necessarily a recipe for retail success. While festive trading figures are often used as a barometer for the health of an economy, relying so heavily on a three-month window for trading survival is dangerous for any business. Each January, the season's winners and losers are reported in the press, with some of those losers facing everything from falling share prices and layoffs to complete collapse. So, while major UK high street stores such as *John Lewis* and *Marks and Spencer* found themselves in a precarious position because of poor trading over the 2019 Christmas period,[16] previously well-known if albeit smaller retailers such as the camera store *Jessops* and video chain *Blockbusters* have in the past lost it all, with both folding directly after a poor performance during the season. Nonetheless, despite the risks, the overall rewards for the retail economy can be significant, with consumer expenditure figures for the season quite astounding. In the UK, the average consumer reportedly spends around an extra £800 at Christmas each year,[17] with the total Christmas retail spend for the period, that being sales between mid-November to the end of December, equalling nearly £80 billion in 2018, while in the US, the figure is closer to £516 billion.[18]

Consuming the Experience

A similar story of seasonal plenitude can also be told of the leisure and hospitality sectors. As people head out to attend parties and indulge in increased luxury consumption, Christmas is equally as important for restaurateurs, hotels, and bar owners, as it is for the retailers of goods and commodities. For venues such as bars and pubs, average turnover can increase by around 50% during the season,[19] while between 2012 and 2017, UK restaurants reported a 240% increase in Christmas lunch bookings.[20] Tourism equally benefits from this Christmas bounce. Often this is directly related to the consumption of Christmas destinations, such as, for example, the increasing popularity of European-style Christmas Markets both aboard and at home. In the UK, the biggest such markets are to be found not only in London but in provincial cities such as Lincoln and Birmingham, with the latter attracting around 5.5 million visitors a year and improving the local economy by something in the region of £400 million (Bentley, 2018).

At what is perhaps the extreme end of the Christmas tourist spectrum, there are also those select international venues that often trade on their northern locations and the association of Christmas with winter snow. The most notable example of this is the city of Rovaniemi in Finnish Lapland (Pretes, 1995). Situated on the Arctic Circle, it was designated in 2010 as the official home of Santa Claus[21] and claims a host of Santa-themed attractions, including his home 'village' that attracts over 500,000 visitors a year,[22] his official post office, and an underground theme park aptly named *Santa Park*[23] which is built in the

FIGURE 2.2   A publicity image for Rovaniemi, the Arctic home of Santa Claus. © Visit Rovaniemi.

city's vast nuclear shelter. Not only are themed attractions such as the Santa Claus Village permanently open to welcome visitors all year round, however, but elements of the Christmas story are integrated into everyday aspects of the city's life, from football tournaments (one of the two local clubs is called FC Santa Claus) to a city tourist board that requires local businesses, if they are to receive official support, to publicly commit to believing in Santa Claus and refraining from acting in a manner contrary to the ethics of Christmas.[24] Combining these links to 'Santa Claus and the magic of Christmas',[25] with a host of snow-based attractions and activities, elements of indigenous Lappish culture, and arctic flora and fauna, Rovaniemi has sought to become, therefore, what one might consider the world's first Christmas city, an 'experience' destination (Pine and Gilmore, 1999) that embraces the magic of Christmas all year round (Figure 2.2).

Despite the obvious festive appeal of such a place, if you live in the UK and cannot make it to northern Finland, there are, however, options closer to home. Throughout Christmas, numerous attractions and events appear across the country, each offering a unique festive experience. While some have become somewhat notorious for poor standards and customer disappointment,[26] a number stand out as credible substitutes. Alongside destinations such as London's annual Hyde Park *Winter Wonderland*, which is effectively a large but popular fairground, *Lapland UK*, situated each year in the county of Berkshire has become a successful alternative attraction to the real thing. Founded in 2007 by a retired City of London finance trader, this Christmas theme park attempts to offer a UK-based experience that rivals the authentic Lappish one, describing itself as:

> a secret immersive adventure based on an original reimagination of the Father Christmas myth. We introduce you to an ancient elven civilization through a magical world of storytelling that fuses the spectacle of a filmset with the performance of theatre, all experienced within the intimacy of your own family.[27]

Here a combination of character performance, set design, visual effects, and some particularly slick marketing are brought together to bring the spirit and magic of Christmas to its family audience. Mobilizing the mythos, expectations, and symbolism of the season to create a popular destination, Lapland UK has become a commercially profitable venture that also increasingly attracts visitors from outside the UK, establishing itself as an international Christmas destination in its own right.

Retail Makes Christmas

Returning to the realm of the department store and retail, it is also worth considering the extent to which such retail organizations have not only responded to but also directly contributed to creating of some of the season's most enduring cultural motifs, mythologies, and practices. While I discuss the seasonal gift giver Santa Claus in more depth in a forthcoming chapter, it is difficult to entirely bypass either the importance of the character to department store trade itself or the role that stores have played in refining and propagating his contemporary image and identity. For while Santa has both mythological and, as we shall see shortly, commercial origins, the first and often very real encounter most children have with him, one that could make or break a belief in Christmas, is usually within such retail settings (Blanchet, 2020).

The first appearance of Santa Claus in a department store, or at least a Santa Claus within what is now considered a 'traditional' grotto environment, is like so many other Christmas 'facts', somewhat disputed. According to Connelly (1999), for example, the first recognized sighting of Santa in a store grotto occurred in the run-up to Christmas 1888 at the East London store of J.P. Robert (Connelly, 2019). In contrast, alternative sources (cf. Pimlott, 1978) claim it was at the 'Christmas Fairyland' opened at Lewis's Bon Marche Department Store nearly ten years earlier in 1879.[28] In the US, the first appearance of Santa Claus is credited widely as taking place slightly later when James Edgar started dressing up as Santa in his Massachusetts department store in 1890 (Snyder, 1985), albeit not in a grotto. Whatever the truth about any of these dates and places, what is certain, however, is that the presence of Santa Claus has become a seasonal necessity for most major department stores and shopping malls. Indeed, he has become so integral to the season that attempts to downgrade his role or even remove him from the seasonal store calendar altogether have often met both employee and public opposition.[29]

Another essential Christmas character that this time has its immediate origins within the world of retail is Santa's perhaps most famous magical helper, *Rudolph the Red Nose Reindeer*. The idea that Santa flies through the air on a sled pulled by eight magical reindeer is traditionally traced back to Clement Moore's[30] 1823 poem, 'A Visit from Saint Nicholas' or, as it is more popularly known, 'The Night Before Christmas' (Snyder,1985). It is likely, however, that Moore himself was influenced by North European pagan culture and tales of Teutonic god Wodan's white eight-legged flying horse, Sleipnir (Struthers, 2012), as well as by an earlier Christmas poem in 1821, entitled 'The Children's Friend' (Bowler, 2005), that I discuss in further detail in a later chapter. Whatever the case, however, it was his tale of 'eight tiny reindeer' named Dasher, Dancer, Prancer, Vixen, Comet, Cupid, Dunder, and Blixem[31] that went on to become Christmas canon.

That was until 1939, when a manager at the *Montgomery Ward* department store in Chicago decided that the store should produce, in-house, a storybook to give to children over Christmas. The task of designing this was given to advertising copywriter Robert May who went on to create the character and story of *Rudolph the Red Nose Reindeer* (Hawkins, 2013). Despite some initial opposition from store management – the character's red nose seemingly speaking of alcohol abuse – the story of Rudolph was eventually adopted for the book, with some 2.5 million copies produced for stores across America. Within a decade, further releases ensured that Santa's ninth reindeer became a staple of the Christmas story in the US. In 1949, his global popularity was also assured when May's brother-in-law, Johnny Marks, turned the story into a song, making it a hit for the 'singing cowboy' Gene Autry (Forbes, 2007). Today, following numerous films, 'further adventures of' stories, and more cuddly toys than could fit even in Santa's sack, this product of marketing genius has become perhaps the second most recognized of Christmas icons.

Christmas Online?

Despite their continued importance, the commercial and cultural dominance of physical department stores and shopping malls today faces a significant threat as consumers turn to the internet and online shopping to fulfil their own and others' Christmas dreams. This has meant that even well-established stores have to rely more and more on their online presence to catch up with those virtual retailers, such as *Amazon*, that emerged in the mid-1990s. Indeed, many large stores are now finding that online transactions represent the bulk of their seasonal turnover, with one senior retail manager admitting that 'while the physical stores provide us with a vital high street presence, the online business is increasingly where Christmas happens'.

Certainly, the online figures bear out this perspective. According to the *Centre for Retail Research*, while total Christmas retail sales rose in 2021 in the UK by 7.3%, actual in-store sales lost a total retail market share to online retailers of 6.9%. The aggregate total of online sales during Christmas 2021 was £17.618 billion, up 36.1% on 2019, while online retailers achieved an overall share of UK retailing of 28.4% during 2021.[32] Consumers also appear to increasingly use mobile devices to order retail goods and services and to check and compare store prices while in-store. While some of this can be accounted for by the increasing use of devices such as tablets as desktop replacements, the fact that in the US and UK, as well as parts of continental Europe, such devices currently account for around 50% of all online Christmas shopping is significant suggesting a further shift in consumer behaviour.[33]

Another challenge that bricks and mortar retailers face has been the growth in pre-Christmas discount events, such as Black Friday and, more recently, Cyber Monday. While there is some dispute about the origins of the name Black Friday, ranging from its associations with traffic jams to retailers heading out of the red (loss) and into the black (profit), from the 1950s onwards, it has referred to the Friday directly proceeding Thanksgiving, the day in the US when the Christmas shopping season traditionally starts. Since then, retailers, not only in the US but increasingly in the UK and beyond, began to apply significant discounts on the day, enticing shoppers to spend early and spend big. In 2005, Cyber-Monday also emerged as a term designed to promote predominantly online Christmas shopping on the following Monday (although most Black Friday offers can now also be purchased online).[34]

The problem for retailers is, however, that while such discounting might increase turnover and, for physical outlets, footfall, volume is one thing but profit is another as retailers face a race to the bottom when it comes to pricing. Nor do such events only undermine commercial sustainability. They can also create a more cutthroat environment in which other concerns, such as environmental sustainability, are all too easily jettisoned, resulting in an even more inequitable and potentially destructive retail economy over Christmas (Schiffling and Kanellos, 2021).

Global Christmas Commerce

While drawing above on examples and illustrations from the UK and, to a lesser extent, the US, the commercial importance of Christmas is a global one that appears unlikely to wane anytime soon. Moreover, as Christmas has become an increasingly international celebration, it is even harder not to be struck by how central economic interests and demands are to how it is experienced and celebrated worldwide. Outside of Europe and the US, the global presence of Christmas can be traced back mainly to the British Empire of the nineteenth and early twentieth centuries. On the one hand, this can be attributed to the relatively simple desire of British colonists and imperial officials to continue practising their national festive traditions in other lands and, in doing so, often influencing the indigenous populations. On the other hand, however, the British Empire also played a more organized role in globalizing the festival through deliberate political and economic interventions.

By the end of the nineteenth century, the celebration of Christmas and a sense of British imperial nationalism had become comfortable bedfellows. As Weightman and Humphries (1987) point out, it was not uncommon for Christmas trees to be bedecked with Union flags and for the season to be self-consciously understood as a reflection of a particular notion of Christian Britishness.[35] Furthermore, as subjects of the Empire appeared to be maturing and, in doing so, threatening to loosen some of their bonds with the mother country, promoting the celebration of Christmas was increasingly viewed as something that might help reintegrate the Empire's population much as it had previously been seen to do at home. Wherever one was, therefore, to know how to keep Christmas was presented as a sign that one was a subject of the British Empire such that 'Christmas was like a homing signal, drawing people together, reminding them of their roots, whatever local conditions may be' (Connelly, 1999: 104).

By the 1930s, nothing embodied this idea more than the voice of the reigning British monarch, broadcasting across the Empire by radio each Christmas Day. Suggested by the then General Manager of the *British Broadcasting Corporation* (BBC) John Reith, the inaugural speech in 1932 by George V placed a particular emphasis on the status of the Empire as a family, reflecting one of the dominant themes of the Anglo-American celebration (Weightman and Humphries, 1987). It was not just for the benefit of those who populated the lands of the Empire that the BBC helped establish a very particular idea of Christmas, however. Throughout the century, both at home and beyond, BBC radio, and more latterly, television, has helped establish a series of crucial punctuation points for the Christmas season. These included nativity plays, carol services, and even an annual performance of Dickens's favourite festive novella, all of which became defining features of a vision of a British Christmas (Connelly, 1999) and which, in turn, left their mark on its global celebration.

As well as an opportunity for citizens of the Empire to support and celebrate their shared identity as subjects of the Crown, as the twentieth century developed Christmas also provided, however, an important opportunity to promote trade specifically amongst countries within the Empire while avoiding the excesses of protectionism and enabling the importation of rare and luxury foodstuffs for the seasonal home market. One of the most widely known attempts to encourage British consumers to purchase their Christmas fayre in this way was the film produced by the *Empire Marketing Board* in 1930 entitled 'One Family'.[36] This short documentary featured the daydream of a schoolboy who travels the dominions of the Empire to collect the ingredients for the King's Christmas pudding, demonstrating that 'patriotism, support for the Empire and Christmas could therefore all be celebrated and expressed by buying the right articles' (Connelly, 1999: 125).

Interestingly, the 'Empire pudding' has become something of a vintage style icon and an educational resource for history students, mainly because of the widely reproduced 1927 poster by F.C Harrison that shows the necessary ingredients and their countries of origin. Just as importantly, however, it provides a concise illustration of how Christmas was used to promote trade and demonstrate the emergence of an increasingly interdependent, if albeit at this point in time, geo-politically limited, seasonal global economy.

Beyond Empire

While the British Empire provides an essential context for the global expansion of Christmas, one cannot overlook the even more enduring impact of increasing American economic reach during the twentieth century. While beset with setbacks, not least those of a world war and a global recession, by the 1930s, the US had emerged as the world's dominant economic power. Nonetheless, much remained to do to increase domestic consumer confidence. One notable contributor to such an effort was the burgeoning advertising industry and the influence of Madison Avenue in New York. With its new and distinct approach to focusing on potential consumers' emotional concerns and fascinations, it would also significantly impact Christmas as we know it today.

While the importance of Christmas advertising in the US can be traced back to the mid-nineteenth century (McKay, 2008), it was during the 1930s that it came into its own due to an increasingly ubiquitous mass media and the rapid growth of the US economy and the demands this created. Nowhere was this more evident than in the impact of Haddon Sundblom's Christmas advertising illustrations of Santa Claus for the *Coca-Cola* company that went on to define a global image of Santa that endures today. For while Sundblom's illustrations did not, as is often claimed, invent the modern Santa Claus, something that even *Coca-Cola* admits is a popular misconception, what he did achieve was the creation of a globally ubiquitous image and associated him with a particularly American notion of how to celebrate the season.

Throughout his 33, official illustrations, one a year between 1931 and 1964 (Charles and Taylor, 1992), Sundblom not only fulfilled the company's original objective of convincing consumers to drink a cold, carbonated soda in the winter as well as the summer, but he also popularized the image of a benevolent, child-centred gift-giver; one who is lavishly attired, rotund, and unfailingly jolly. An image that, as Paul Hawkins (2013: 213), author of *Bad Santas*, observes, eventually became 'defined and inescapable'.[37]

By the 1950s, US-style advertising campaigns and an ethic of mass consumption dominated Christmas at home and increasingly worldwide. Santa Claus, in particular, remained a staple of such work, not only due to increasing national and global recognition but also, as Gerry Bowler (2005) observes, his image was in the public domain, and advertisers could use it without paying royalties. Santa or no Santa, however, both advertising at Christmas and Christmas advertising had become big business in the US and, increasingly, across Europe, bringing with it American seasonal practices and values. This expansion of the influence of the Anglo-American celebration is illustrated by French anthropologist Claude Lévi-Strauss (1993: 40), who, in a 1952 essay, described what he considered to be the novel but also, in his view, malign influence on his home country of American commercial practices that included, for example:

> decorated wrapping paper for Christmas presents; illustrated Christmas cards and the custom of displaying them on the mantlepiece for the fateful week ... and finally people dressed up as Father Christmas listening to the requests of children in department stores.

Nevertheless, despite the reservations of the likes of Lévi-Strauss, there are few countries today where Christmas is not experienced as a period of acute economic and commercial activity, and the most prominent illustration of this can be found in the world's second-largest economy, China. While only around 2% of the country's population is Christian, China's increasing integration into the global economy has meant that Christmas has become the focus of not only retail activity but also a means of expressing a less traditional sense of national identity, especially amongst the country's younger population. While the season is not encouraged by the ruling Communist Party, across Chinese cities and urban areas Christmas has become an important event with city streets, malls, and department stores all decked out with the same Christmas trees, lights, and decorations one might find in any western town or city.

Similarly, seasonal events take place across the country, such as an annual parade of Harley Davidson riders dressed as Santa Claus,[38] while Christmas carols can be heard piped out through PA systems throughout December. And even though it is unlikely that many shoppers will either know or be particularly concerned about the spiritual message often attached to such music, it encourages similar levels of spending as those seen in Europe and the US, with Christmas Eve purportedly now the largest shopping day of the calendar year in many major Chinese cities.[39] Purchases usually range from Western style decorations to high-end luxury products and brands, as well as what has become an established Chinese seasonal gift, the Christmas Apple (Fisher, 2012). Even 'traditional' European Christmas markets have started to appear in more cosmopolitan centres such as Shanghai, featuring many Western staples such as German pretzels, bratwurst sausages, and mulled wine and mince pies (Song, 2022). Such consumer activity is particularly significant for those with young families or younger people who embrace the season as one of frivolity and romantic gift-giving in a similar vein to Valentine's Day in Western cultures.

Another notable example of Christmas's impact on Chinese sensibilities was the planned building of a Christmas theme park in the city of Chengdu, the capital of southwestern China's Sichuan province.[40] Encouraged by the increasing numbers of Chinese visitors to its aforementioned Santa Park in Rovaniemi, Finland, the company which owns Santa Park was approached to replicate its attraction in China. The proposed Chinese version would have been a 13-square-kilometre open-air park – becoming one of the largest theme parks in China – and was based on the original design featuring, for example, Santa Claus's office and his Elvin workshops. Alas, due to the impact of the COVID-19 pandemic, amongst other possible factors, the plans were never realized, but nonetheless, the very fact that the project came so far attests to the popularity of Christmas in the country.

Similarly, in another predominately non-Christian culture, that of Japan, Christmas has also been embraced by the urban young, who again approach it as a season for shopping and giving gifts as tokens of young love (Moeran and Skov, 1993). While not entirely new to the Japanese, given America's close post-war ties to the country (cf. Plath, 1963), as in China, Christmas in Japan is not an official holiday. Nonetheless, it is increasingly celebrated, mainly through luxury consumption and partying, while as Junko Kimura and Russell Belk (2005: 326) have observed, it is incessantly promoted as a special time 'by a number of multinational companies, media, and brands, including Universal Studios-Japan, Disney, the Muppets, Coca-Cola, Visa, Hyatt Regency, KFC, McDonald's, Vogue, Martha Stewart, and many others', all of whom see the profit to be made in nurturing the season's popularity in the country.

Following on from this, perhaps the most well-known, if somewhat perplexing to Western eyes, aspect of Christmas celebrations in many Japanese cities is the now almost traditional Christmas dinner of *Kentucky Fried Chicken*. Started by American ex-pats during the 1970s, today it is estimated that around 3.6 million Japanese families enjoy a festive bucket of fried chicken from the American fast-food giant each year, spending around $63 million in the process (Barton, 2016). In fact, due to widespread advertising and publicity by the company, it is so popular that to be sure of one's Christmas dinner, these buckets usually need to be ordered in early November simply in order to ensure supply matches demand.

The Global Making of Christmas

Such a globalization of Christmas consumption, albeit in what might often appear to be a 'glocalized' form (Robertson, 1995), with chicken instead of turkey and a Santa Claus that looks suspiciously like Colonel Sanders for starters, only tells half the story, however. For despite the importance of consumption, one must recognize the equally important realm of production if one is to seriously talk about the globalizing impetus of Christmas commerce. And, as such, we must now return to China and some of its near neighbours.

In 2012, Chinese journalist Phoenix Lee offered a stark if somewhat tongue-in-cheek illustration of the intimate relationship between Christmas, manufacturing, and China. Lee suggested that rather than criticizing Chinese-made goods, American consumers should welcome their arrival at Christmas, declaring that Santa Claus is really Chinese and that, on Christmas morning, Americans should readily 'accept their gifts with gratitude' (Lee, 2012). And while such a statement is perhaps more about rattling nationalist cages and playing out new economic rivalries, the claim that China is now the country where Christmas is actually made or created is not, it should be said, without foundation.

Since 1990, China has grown from undertaking around 3% of world manufacturing to just under 29% (Richter, 2021). In doing so, it has become a global economic power, especially when it comes to consumer goods, producing, for example, 60% and 70% of the world's shoes and mobile phones, respectively.[41] As such, if we are lucky enough to receive gifts and presents on Christmas Day, then it is likely that a significant proportion of these will have indeed been made in China, if not in one of its East Asian neighbours. This is especially true if young children are involved, given that the country produces around 49% of all the world's toys.[42] However, perhaps the most direct and visible correlation between Christmas and its global manufacturing capacity is to be found in the industrial production of those objects and artefacts that, for many, embody the magic of the season, namely Christmas ornaments and decorations.

As I noted earlier in this chapter, one could not escape the irony of a Chinese-based retailer purchasing authentic 'British' Christmas decorations from a London department store that were, in fact, manufactured originally in his home country. Nevertheless, unless one almost entirely favours the purchase and display of locally produced 'craft' items, then the likelihood that most of any Christmas decorations we might purchase in the UK are made in

China is inescapably high. While figures vary, the US census bureau produces some of the most accurate statistics in this respect, demonstrating how much a 'traditional' Christmas depends on Chinese exports.

For example, in 2019 the value of US imports of Christmas ornaments from China reached $2.1 billion, representing 92.4% of all imports of this type.[43] In the UK, while similar statistics are harder to come by, my own conversations with both importers and retailers of such decorations have suggested that we should expect up to 90% of those decorations that dominate shops and shelving from October onwards and which play such an integral part in how we celebrate the season, to have been made in China or a regional neighbour. Furthermore, it is not only possible to narrow down the national origin of the bulk of the world's Christmas decorations but also the city from which most of them originate, namely Yiwu, in the Chinese province of Zhejiang. For while Yiwu is known as an important centre for commodity production and trading more generally, including, for example, socks and jewellery, it is its status as China's Christmas city for which it is most well-known.[44] Popularly attributed with producing over 60% of the world's supply of Christmas decorations, Yiwu is estimated to contain around 600 factories dedicated to making festive ornaments and Christmas paraphernalia.

It is a place where one can buy anything from life-size saxophone-playing Santas, a favourite portrayal in contemporary Chinese festive culture, to 'authentic' Victorian-style tree baubles and nativity sets, all via a combination of the city's small decoration stores, its giant wholesale market, and even online providers such as Alibaba.com that, at the time of writing this, advertises more than 338,800 individual Christmas items. And while orders from the US and Europe have been reportedly falling over recent years,[45] much of the slack has been taken up by consumption from Russia and South American countries, including Brazil, meaning that it is unlikely that we will be 'running out of Christmas' anytime soon.

Business for Christmas

While China has become the preeminent global manufacturer and exporter of Christmas-related goods and ornaments, in this section I want to turn my attention to what I described earlier as an, if not altogether new, then burgeoning industrial sector that consists of businesses that often only exist to utilize such goods while servicing the demands of consumers during the festive season. The increasing pressure to ensure that each Christmas is somehow more spectacular, better prepared for, and more magical than the one before has led to a growth in companies, both small and large, that cater almost exclusively to the more experiential end of the Christmas market and taking responsibility for a relatively consistent and untroubling reproduction of the purportedly perfect Christmas experience.

For example, while not the most widely recognized of such businesses, those with the biggest and most visible impact are those that design, install, and manage Christmas lighting and decorations across shops, streets, and homes throughout November and December. In the UK, European companies such as *MK Illuminations* have a major presence in the market, having gained a significant number of UK malls with the collapse of its UK rival, *Fuzzwire*, in 2013. Similar companies in the US include, for example, *American Christmas*, which is responsible for lights across numerous cities, including New York. Back in Europe, however, *MK Illuminations* boasts an average €100 million turnover while operating across 120 countries and employing around 350 permanent staff.[46] At the same time, they continue to vie with indigenous operations such as those offered by the UK's *Springfield Decorations and Display*, which design, install, and project manage festive decorative displays for clients from *Harrods* to *Heathrow Airport*.

Perhaps somewhat counterintuitively, as trade has shifted towards online shopping, the importance of the Christmas designs and innovations provided by such companies for stores and shopping malls has increased as the experiential dimension of Christmas shopping is considered central to retaining seasonal footfall. As John Riordan, managing director at *MK Illuminations*, has noted, to keep shoppers coming to physical stores and shopping malls, the priority is enabling them to experience the traditional 'feelings of joy and happiness that the festive season brings' (Shopping Centre Monthly, 2017: 14). As such, attempts to decorate such locations in a way that rekindles what are often nostalgic cultural images and memories of an idealized magical Christmas, through the increased use of standardized if technologically advanced interactive and 3D decorative experiences, has become a core development in what is a critical seasonal market.

Not that all the interactive features and decorations in the world would count for much without the presence of the previously alluded to number one Christmas icon, Santa Claus. Yet whatever the perennial popularity of the character himself, visitors tend to expect much more these days than a quick chat and perhaps a present from their visit. Instead, they are increasingly seeking a complete seasonal experience when visiting Santa in his grotto, with the design, production, and ongoing management of Christmas grottos themselves having become big business. For example, UK companies such as *Magenta Star* or *Great Grottos* offer managed grotto services that provide a setting to meet Santa and festive landscapes that can feature everything from magical train rides to 3D cinemas to fully immersive animatronic winter wonderlands.

As it is with the broader provision of Christmas decorations and lighting, however, the needs of consumers are often tricky to reconcile, demanding as they do, to quote one such supplier, 'traditional with a modern twist' that will keep the festive experience intact throughout the entire visit. This has led to the introduction of what another grotto manager described as 'pacifier grottos' that are designed to manage children's expectations in particular and quell their behaviours before they reach the main feature so that:

> nowadays there's more of an attraction at a grotto, while Santa's just a *part* of the experience. You know, there's lots going on. So, with the sort of introduction of the 3D cinemas and writing letters to Santa before they go in and those kinds of stuff, I think, especially from the customer's perspective, a good grotto is if something else is going on to keep the kids happy.

For every grotto, there must, of course, also be such a Santa. And while I return to this subject in greater depth in Chapter 5, there is no doubt that the provision of suitably experienced, trained, and garbed performers also represent an increasingly important component of this Christmas industry. Grotto suppliers not only provide and manage the design and operation of the grotto environment but also often recruit and train the Santa Claus performers themselves, ensuring clients receive a closely integrated and regulated package. At the same time, other companies provide them as an exclusive activity or as part of a more extensive portfolio of character offerings.

One example of the latter is *The Ministry of Fun*, a London-based events and PR company that provides Santa Claus performers to an often-exclusive market of major department stores and corporate parties and events. Known nationally for its activities, the company also runs an annual Santa School as a training and publicity event. In the US, similar training schools for such performers are also spread across the country. Santa performer and entrepreneur Tim Connaghan runs one prominent example in the form of his *International Santa Claus University*, or *School4Santa*. Holding events across the US and beyond, they cover everything from personal grooming and attire to crowd management and child protection,[47] seeking to ensure that children receive the same magical experience each time they encounter one of his trained performers.

Not all such businesses operate at such a scale, however. Returning to the realm of lights and decorations, for example, UK company *The Christmas Decorators*, while having increasingly branched out into large-scale civic and corporate decorations, continues to provide a decorating service for domestic clients. For those who are either time-poor or simply who enjoy Christmas without too much effort, companies such as this can help alleviate the strain. Boasting offices around the UK, *The Christmas Decorators* will supply, fit, and dismantle either purchased or hired domestic decorations and lights that:

> includes the lighting of roofline contours, bushes, shrubs and trees as well as highlighting driveways and entrances with garlands, wreaths and potted

trees. Inside, an array of beautiful Christmas decorations can be provided to add a large sprinkle of Christmas spirit including Christmas trees, doorway, banister and fireplace garlands, and festive floral arrangements.[48]

Moreover, for those who require even more help, premier personal shopping services, such as those provided by companies such as *The Organizers*,[49] can service your festive shopping needs, while *Theme Traders* can ensure your Christmas party will go with a (well-managed) swing,[50] meaning that Christmas can be handled professionally from almost start to finish.

Today, then, business appears to be everywhere at Christmas. As such, it is no great surprise that many people continue to lament the idea that the season has become 'too' commercial and lost something in the process. Nonetheless, while this might indeed be an accelerating trend, perhaps the greatest irony is that when mourning the loss of a more innocent and even 'pure' notion of Christmases past, the usual point of reference, as noted previously, is that of a late Victorian celebration. But, on the contrary, this is the very point at which Christmas emerged as the most commercial of times. It was when our festive season came to celebrate not only the birth of a Christian saviour but also another birth, that of industrial mass consumption and production and the entrepreneurial energies of the ascendant middle classes.

And from this point on, there was little that could stop it. Today, the season is the focus for various industries and organizations dedicated to making Christmas more extravagant and profitable year on year, if not always for consumers, then at least for their owners and shareholders. At the same time, its global recognition and popularity can largely be attributed to many of the seasonal activities of such organizations, purveying everything from fast food and fizzy drinks to decorations and Christmas experiences, amongst so much more.

Notes

1 www.retailresearch.org/shopping-for-christmas.html
2 https://home.kpmg.com/uk/en/home/insights/2015/12/economics-roun dup-the-true-cost-of-christmas.html
3 In 2001, a surviving card, signed by Sir Henry Cole himself, was sold at auction for a record £22,500. http://news.bbc.co.uk/1/hi/england/1679110.stm
4 For examples of the former, amongst others see Bell (2015).
5 www.royalmailgroup.com/sending-traditional-christmas-cards-still-more-popu lar-e-cards-reveals-royal-mail-research-0
6 www.gca.cards/who-sent-the-first-christmas-card/
7 www.greetingcard.org/abouttheindustry/tabid/58/default.aspx
8 As is often the case, there have been others for whom this claim has been made, but the broad historical consensus appears to be that it was Smith's ideas and work that brought them into the popular consciousness.

9 www.nytimes.com/1987/12/25/world/britain-s-rather-silly-christmas-tradition. html

10 http://news.bbc.co.uk/local/derby/hi/people_and_places/newsid_9250000/9250 059.stm

11 www.bbc.co.uk/culture/bespoke/story/20150326-a-history-of-the-department-store/index.html

12 www.harrods.com/christmas/christmas-events-in-store

13 https://christmasworld.messefrankfurt.com/frankfurt/en.html

14 www.independent.co.uk/life-style/christmas/selfridges-christmas-shop-2019-open-day-world-record-department-store-london-a9025151.html

15 One should remember, of course, that dedicated Christmas shops frequently open all year round, often relying on tourists to get them through the non-festive months. For example, see www.nutcrackerchristmasshop.co.uk/default.asp, while perhaps the most famous was London's The Christmas Shop until it closed in 2015. It now has an online presence at www.thechristmasshop.co.uk

16 www.bbc.co.uk/news/business-51049894

17 www.bankofengland.co.uk/knowledgebank/how-much-do-we-spend-at-christmas

18 www.retailresearch.org/shoppingforxmas.php

19 www.bighospitality.co.uk/Events-Awards/Planning-for-Christmas-2012-Why-prep aration-is-key-to-success

20 www.verdictfoodservice.com/news/christmas-day-restaurant-dining-rises/

21 www.visitrovaniemi.fi/love/santa-claus-magic-of-christmas/

22 www.visitrovaniemi.fi/media/facts-figures-highlights/

23 https://santaparkarcticworld.com/santapark

24 www.visitrovaniemi.fi/about/brand/

25 www.visitrovaniemi.fi/love/santa-claus-magic-of-christmas/

26 www.bbc.co.uk/news/av/uk-12507480

27 https://portal.laplanduk.co.uk/visit

28 www.liverpoolpicturebook.com/2012/12/department-store-santas-grotto.html

29 www.edinburghnews.scotsman.com/news/christmas-cancelled-at-jenners-as-fest ive-grotto-axed-1-2583882

30 Although Moore is credited with writing the poem, there is also evidence to suggest that the original author was a man called Henry Livingstone (Struthers, 2012) and that Moore had obtained a copy through his governess.

31 The latter were eventually changed to Donner and Blitzen.

32 www.retailresearch.org/shopping-for-christmas.html. Such figures have been somewhat distorted due to the COVID-19 pandemic and periods of lockdown.

33 www.retailresearch.org/shopping-for-christmas.html

34 www.independent.co.uk/life-style/cyber-monday-black-friday-when-is-it-online-shopping-retail-thanksgiving-a8648106.html

35 As previously noted, this was not an exclusively British practice, with Perry (2010) observing a similarly close relationship between German nationalism and expressions of the season.

36 www.colonialfilm.org.uk/node/40

37 Somewhat ironically, given the fact that Sundblom's illustrations had played such a prominent role in making Santa such a family-friendly character, his last illustration produced in 1972 was a return to his days as a pin-up artist and was of a naked young woman in an open-fronted Santa costume for the cover of *Playboy* magazine.

38 www.chinadaily.com.cn/regional/2016-12/26/content_27777686.htm

39 http://europe.chinadaily.com.cn/china/2012-12/25/content_16049147.htm

40 This was discussed with me during a visit to the Finnish resort. Although, as I understand it, plans are still in place, the actual building project has yet to commence.
41 www.economist.com/news/leaders/21646204-asias-dominance-manufactur ing-will-endure-will-make-development-harder-others-made
42 www.statisticbrain.com/china-manufacturing-statistics/
43 www.census.gov/newsroom/facts-for-features/2020/holiday-season.html
44 www.chinadaily.com.cn/business/2014-12/08/content_19043207.htm
45 www.reuters.com/news/picture/2012/09/15/chinas-christmas-factories?articl eId=USRTR37ZGS
46 www.mk-illumination.co.uk/Media/Pages/About-us
47 www.school4santas.com
48 www.thechristmasdecorators.co.uk/residential-christmas-decorating.html
49 http://theorganisers.com/personal-shopping/
50 www.themetraders.com/christmas-party-organisers

References

Barton, E. (2016) 'Why Japan Celebrates Christmas with KFC'. *BBC Culture*, December 19. Available at: www.bbc.com/worklife/article/20161216-why-japan-celebrates-christmas-with-kfc

Bartunek, J. and Do, B. (2011) 'The Sacralization of Christmas Commerce'. *Organization* 18(6): 795–806.

Bell, B. (2015) 'Frog Murder and Boiled Children: "Merry Christmas" Victorian Style'. BBC News, December 21. Available at: www.bbc.co.uk/news/uk-england-34988154

Bella, L. (1992) *The Christmas Imperative: Leisure, Family, and Women's Work*. Halifax: Fernwood Publishing.

Bentley, D. (2018) 'Birmingham German Christmas Market Dates for 2018'. Birmingham Live, November 28. Available at: www.birminghammail.co.uk/whats-on/whats-on-news/birmingham-german-market-2018-dates-14801504

Blanchet, V. (2020) 'Happy Christmases Are All Alike; Each Unhappy Christmas Is Unhappy in Its Own Way'. *Marketing Theory* 20(2): 175–184.

Bowler, G. (2005) *Santa Claus: A Biography*. Toronto: McClelland and Stewart Ltd.

Buday, G. (1964) *The Story of the Christmas Card*. London: Odhams Press.

Carrier, J. (1993) 'The Rituals of Christmas Giving'. In, D. Miller (ed.) *Unwrapping Christmas*. Oxford: Oxford University Press. Pp. 55–74.

Charles, B.F. and Taylor, J.R. (1992) *Dream of Santa: Haddon Sundblom's Vision*. Washington, DC: Staples & Charles.

Cliff, M. (2016) 'A Partying Santa, 72,000 Sequins and 114,000 Baubles: Selfridges Becomes the First London Department Store to Unveil its Festive Window (65 days before Christmas)'. *Mail Online*, October 20. Available at: www.dailymail.co.uk/femail/article-3854834/A-partying-Santa-72-000-sequins-114-000-baubles-Selfrid ges-London-department-store-unveil-festive-window-65-days-Christmas.html

Connelly, M. (1999) *Christmas: A Social History*. London: I.B. Tauris.

Connelly, M. (2019) 'Shop 'till You Drop: A Brief History of Christmas Shopping'. *History Extra*, November 14. Available at: www.historyextra.com/period/victorian/christmas-shopping-history-commercial-victorian/

Fisher, M. (2012) 'Eight Fascinating Facts About Christmas in China'. *The Washington Post*, December 24. Available at: www.washingtonpost.com/news/worldviews/wp/2012/12/24/seven-fascinating-facts-about-christmas-in-china/

Forbes, B.D. (2007) *Christmas: A Candid History*. Los Angeles, CA: University of California Press.

Golby, J.M. and Purdue A.W. (2000) *The Making of the Modern Christmas*. Stroud: Sutton Publishing.

Harrison, M. (1951) *The Story of Christmas: Its Growth and Development from the Earliest Times*. Watford: Odhams Press.

Hawkins, P. (2013) *Bad Santas and Other Creepy Christmas Characters*. London: Simon & Schuster.

Kavanagh, M. (2012) 'Louis Prang, Father of the American Christmas Card'. *New York Historical Society Museum and Library*, December 19. Available at www.nyhistory.org/blogs/prang

Kimpton, P. (2004) *Tom Smith's Christmas Crackers: An Illustrated History*. Stroud: Tempus.

Kimura, J. and Belk, R.W. (2005) 'Christmas in Japan: Globalization Versus Localization'. *Consumption Markets & Culture* 8(3): 325–338.

Lee, P. (2012) '"Made in China": A Christmas Gift'. *People's Daily Online*, December 24. Available at: http://en.people.cn/90778/8068957.html

Lévi-Strauss, C. (1993) 'Father Christmas Executed'. In, D. Miller (ed.) *Unwrapping Christmas*. Oxford: Oxford University Press. Pp. 38–51.

Marling, K.A. (2001) *Merry Christmas: Celebrating America's Greatest Holiday*. Cambridge, MA: Harvard University Press.

McKay, G. (2008) 'Consumption, Coca-colonisataion, Cultural Resistance and Santa Claus'. In, S. Whiteley (ed.) *Christmas, Ideology and Popular Culture*. Edinburgh: Edinburgh University Press. Pp. 50–67.

McKechnie, S. and Tynan C. (2006) 'Social Meanings in Christmas Consumption: An Exploratory Study of UK Celebrants' Consumption Rituals'. *Journal of Consumer Behaviour* 5(2): 130–144.

Moeran, B. and Skov, L. (1993) 'Cinderella Christmas: Kitsch, Consumerism and Youth in Japan'. In, D. Miller (ed.) *Unwrapping Christmas*. Oxford: Oxford University Press. Pp. 105–133.

Perry, J. (2010) *Christmas in Germany: A Cultural History*. Chapel Hill, NC: University of North Carolina Press.

Pimlott, J.A.R. (1978) *The Englishman's Christmas: A Social History*. Hassocks: The Harvester Press.

Pine, J. and Gilmore, J. (1999) *The Experience Economy*. Boston, MA: Harvard Business School Press.

Plath, D. (1963) 'The Japanese Popular Christmas: Coping with Modernity'. *The Journal of American Folklore* 76(302): 309–317.

Pretes, M. (1995) 'Postmodern Tourism: The Santa Claus Industry. *Annals of Tourism Research* 22(1):1–15.

Rainey, S. and Zhang, J. (2013) 'It Just Wouldn't be Christmas Without Crackers'. *The Telegraph*, December 17. Available at: www.telegraph.co.uk/topics/christmas/10522935/It-just-wouldnt-be-Christmas-without-crackers.html

Richter, F. (2021) 'China Is the World's Manufacturing Superpower'. *Statista*, May 4. Available at: www.statista.com/chart/20858/top-10-countries-by-share-of-global-manufacturing-output/

Ritzer, G. (2005) *Enchanting a Disenchanted World: Revolutionizing the Means of Consumption*. Thousand Oaks, CA: Pine Forge Press.

Robertson, R. (1995) Glocalization: Time-Space and Homogeneity-Heterogeneity. *Global Modernities* 2: 25–45.

Schiffling, S. and Kanellos, N.V. (2021) 'Dark Side of Black Friday: The Major Drawbacks with this Shopping Bonanza'. *The Conversation*, November 25. Available at: https://theconversation.com/dark-side-of-black-friday-the-major-drawbacks-with-this-shopping-bonanza-171713

Shopping Centre Magazine (2017) 'Making the Most of Christmas', *Shopping Centre Magazine*, February: 11–23.

Smith, L. and Smith, P. (2012) *Glad Tidings of Struggle and Strife*. London: Fonthill.

Snyder, P. (1985) *December 25th: The Joys of Christmas Past*. New York, NY: Dodd, Mead & Company.

Song, C. (2022) 'Christmas Shopping in Shanghai 2023 (Best Christmas Markets)'. *China Highlights*, December 23. Available at: www.chinahighlights.com/shanghai/article-christmas-markets.htm

Storey, J. (2008) 'The Invention of the English Christmas'. In, S. Whiteley (ed.) *Christmas, Ideology and Popular Culture*. Edinburgh: Edinburgh University Press. Pp. 17–31.

Struthers, J. (2012) *The Book of Christmas: Everything We Once Knew and Loved About Christmastime*. London: Ebury Press.

Twitchell, J.B. (1996) *Adcult USA: The Triumph of Advertising in American Culture*. New York, NY: Columbia University Press.

Waits, W. (1994) *The Modern Christmas in America: A Cultural History of Gift Giving*. New York, NY: NYU Press.

Waldfogel, J. (1993) 'The Deadweight Loss of Christmas'. *The American Economic Review* 83(5): 1328–1336.

Waldfogel, J. (2009) *Scroogenomics: Why You Shouldn't Buy Presents for the Holidays*. Princeton, NJ: Princeton University Press.

Weightman, G. and Humphries, S. (1987) *Christmas Past*. London: Sidgwick & Jackson.

Whitehorn, K. (1962) *Roundabout*. London: Methuen & Co.

Woodhead, L. (2012) *Shopping, Seduction & Mr. Selfridge*. London: Profile Books.

3

THE MAGICAL ATMOSPHERICS OF CHRISTMASTIDE

Introduction

It is often said that come December, as the high-street decorations go up, the temperatures fall, and a sense of panic is evident as the number of shopping days starts to count down, that Christmas 'isn't a season' but 'a feeling' (Ferber, 2001: 206). And if there is one aspect of it and how it is organized that continues to fascinate me, it is why Christmas feels like it does, who is behind it all, and, quite frankly, how do they pull it off year after year? Academically speaking, these are questions of what one might term Christmas's sensuality, affect, and atmospherics. For all these terms speak of things we experience and almost intuitively know but are not always able to put into words. They refer to the sense of a place or a situation we all have from time to time, those things we know by just being there and immersed in the sounds, sights, smells, and sensations around us. My questions can perhaps only be answered, therefore, with reference to other somewhat esoteric ideas, such as those of symbolism and aesthetics, of ideas that try to take us beyond the intellectual and require us to engage with what are often deeply engrained cultural, and indeed visceral, responses to the season as we experience it.

As I observed in the opening chapter, the importance of sensuality and symbolism at Christmas has a long history. From the firelit gatherings of the earliest mid-winter festivals to the sight of twinkling Christmas lights and decorations, the touch of cold air on the skin, the smells of winter spices, and the sounds of Christmas songs characteristic of celebrations today, Christmas has always been a feast not only for the palate but all senses. And while individual stimuli are more than capable of making us feel seasonal, they have the greatest

DOI: 10.4324/9781315637969-4

impact when combined, particularly when they evoke half-forgotten memories and recollections of Christmases past. For example, they might take the form of a tightly integrated combination of stories, pictures, and songs to be found in a favourite Christmas film that is being watched in an appropriately decorated room. Alternatively, they can be found in the more mundane sights, sounds, and smells we experience during the annual unveiling of a small town's Christmas lights, a school's nativity play, or when shopping in one of the department stores or malls I have previously considered.

One way of thinking about all of this, and the approach I take in the forthcoming chapter, is to understand such a combined impact as productive of what I term the atmospherics of Christmas. While somewhat challenging to define, for German philosopher Gernot Böhme (1993, 2003, 2016, 2020), to talk of atmospherics or atmospheres is to recognize the impact the external environment has on how we feel and act and how, in turn, our experience and response to that environment contributes to this. So in the case of Christmas, it could encapsulate, for instance, the joyous or celebratory feelings one might experience and, in turn, be part of reproducing in, say, a communal space such as a church or town square during a carol service or Christmas singalong. On the other hand, it could equally describe the somewhat less pleasant but no less acute sense of loss or unhappiness in a home at Christmas due to the absence of a loved one or family member, or perhaps when just anticipating the arrival of some particularly truculent relatives.

Böhme's approach also acknowledges, however, that atmospheres are not some purely spontaneous manifestation of an environment and how it is responded to. Instead, it also points to the need to think about how such atmospheric conditions can, in part, be manufactured, manipulated, and organized to promote or encourage particular ways of feeling and acting. In doing so, it brings to the fore concerns surrounding what one might term the production and impact of aesthetic commodities. These can include forms of mass or popular culture such as film, television, or music, as well as how everyday aesthetic experiences, such as shopping in a decorated department store, can encourage feelings that can be harnessed to encourage particular ways of behaving at Christmas, particularly when it pertains to consumption.

The chapter opens with a brief but useful consideration of the idea that there exists, drawing on the critical work of Adorno and Horkheimer (1973), something that can broadly be described as a Christmas culture industry, one concerned with the organized production and distribution of mass-mediated forms of Christmas entertainment. Following this is a discussion of two of the most prominent products of this industry, Christmas films and [popular] music. The focus then shifts onto how we are increasingly encouraged to feel about Christmas in a given way through our encounters with themed and festively enriched spaces that, while predominantly commercial such as department stores are landscaped and managed to generate, in the words of those responsible, *'magical atmospheres'*.

Facing the Christmas Culture Industry

Public entertainment at Christmas existed well before the introduction of contemporary technologies such as cinema, recorded music and, of course, television. We can trace back tales of seasonal games and public entertainment as far back as the Saturnalian festivities of Ancient Rome (Hutton, 1996). More latterly, there was the popular carol singing and mumming of the middle ages that continued to compete with more lavish and aristocratic events such as the seasonal plays performed before the royal courts, such as William Shakespeare's *Twelfth Night* first performed before Queen Elisabeth I on January 6, 1601 (Ackroyd, 2006). Nonetheless, perhaps the first real example of modern mass public entertainment at Christmas, excluding, for example, fairs which could happen at any time of the year, was the emergence in England during the 1800s of pantomimes (Connelly, 1999).

While the origins of the pantomime stretch back to the sixteenth century and the Italian 'Commedia dell'Arte', during the 1800s, it developed into a peculiarly British type of Christmas entertainment. Often anarchic in form and anywhere between radical and nationalistic in content, pantomimes quickly became associated with the festive season combining drama, humour, song, and dance into an albeit decidedly low-brow but increasingly child-friendly spectacle (Weightman and Humphries, 1987). Today, a visit to the pantomime remains a staple of the Christmas season for many British families, with figures released in 2019 suggesting that theatres sold over £60 million worth of pantomime tickets across the UK during the season (Carpani, 2019). The popularity of such events and activities notwithstanding, however, there can be little doubt that during the twentieth and into the twenty-first centuries, film became the preeminent industrial medium for spreading Christmas's cultural values, ushering in a far more extensive and technically sophisticated form of Christmas culture industry that, for many, continues to define the season.

The term culture industry was first coined in the 1940s by Adorno and Horkheimer (1973) and refers to the mass production of popular entertainment that emerged during the early and mid-twentieth century. While multi-faceted, it is characterized by the mass production and distribution of cultural products, including film, music, literature, art, and so on, that, on inspection, are largely standardized in both form and content. While regrettable, Adorno and Horkheimer considered such standardization an inevitable outcome in a world in which culture had become simply another commodity in a market for entertainment. This meant that consumers demanded assurance of consistency in what they were buying and, as such, to placate this market, the culture industry offered standardized entertainment that provided consumers with the expected over the innovative and the predictable over the challenging. For example, from this perspective, popular music requires recordings that, while superficially distinct from each other, possess an underlying structure that is essentially the same so that consumers will know what they are buying and feel good about it when they do. Similarly, films must follow specific anticipated plots and patterns to be commercially successful, repeating ad nauseam expected tropes, characterizations and outcomes with victorious heroes, vanquished foes, and happy families.

For Adorno and Horkheimer, such standardization results in cultural products becoming the ideal media of ideological forms of communication in a society in which dominant interests – particularly those of capital – prevail. As such, their criticism of these cultural forms focused not so much on their quality but rather on their structure and the messages they promoted. For while the mass production of cultural products and events was presented as an expansion of choice to people, this was an illusion due to the limited number of authentic differences between products. Instead, people today are exposed to fewer and less challenging ideas or cultural experiences, reducing their capacity to enjoy or value anything beyond what is offered in the marketplace and ultimately attenuating cultural discrimination and blunting individual critical faculties. Furthermore, they considered products of the culture industry as integral to stabilizing and retaining forms of established social organization and control as they not only encourage cultural and intellectual passivity but also promote particular values and ways of being necessary for reproducing a market economy that benefits only a small minority in society. These include, for example, the idea that in order to be happy, one must constantly consume and that support for established principles of social organization, such as family life, patriotism, and romantic love, is essential if one is to live a good life.

As history has shown, however, while such standardized cultural products abound, and messages to consume as a personal and social good continue to dominate, there is also more diversity available in art and entertainment than Adorno and Horkheimer appeared able to countenance. Furthermore, there are examples of what they might have considered to be 'cultural products' that have inspired and enacted social critique and inspired solidarities (Benjamin, 1970) at the same time as being entertaining. Some forms of rock music are the obvious example here, with the likes of Greil Marcus (2011) arguing that while aesthetically unreconcilable, punk rock of the 1970s, for instance, actually captured Adorno's spirit of social criticism.

Nonetheless, the film industry, described as 'the greatest of the industrialized art forms' (Nowell-Smith, 1997: xix), remains a significant global carrier of our particularly Anglo-American version of Christmas and how it should be celebrated (Connelly, 2000); one that perhaps reflects far more closely Adorno and Horkheimer's (1973) vision of mass culture than say the lyrics of John Lydon. And it is such films, as both examples of this Christmas culture industry and as particularly stylized atmospheric media, that I now consider.

Christmas Tinsel Meets Tinsel Town

While for the larger film studios, Christmas remains the favoured season to release big-budget blockbusters, whatever the genre, it is also the time of year for the release of appropriately festive outputs. And while dedicated Christmas films are less popular than they once were, they have still fared well over the decades. To date, the most financially successful Christmas movie at the box office, Chris Columbus's 1990 hit *Home Alone*, has grossed somewhere in the region of $285 million, followed closely by the 2000 adaption of Dr Seuss's *How the Grinch Stole Christmas* at around $260 million.[1] At the same time, whatever their financial success, festive titles such as *White Christmas*, *It's A Wonderful Life*, and *The Santa Clause*, to name but a few, have become seared into the seasonal consciousness across generations. In fact, films have, ever since their inception, played a hugely significant role in the organization of popular attitudes towards and feelings about Christmas.

The first known Christmas film, George Albert Smith's 1898 seventy-six-second British silent production, *Santa Claus*, is an interesting example of this. A pioneering piece of film-making by virtue of its use of cinematic techniques not previously seen,[2] this short piece depicts Santa's visit to two young children on Christmas Eve, bringing together a host of images and themes that remain integral to the 'spirit' and 'magic' of Christmas today.[3] The film commences with two excited but well-behaved children being put to bed by a domestic servant on Christmas Eve, with stockings for both tied to the end of the bedstead. Once the bedroom light is extinguished, the background scene shifts to a bearded and berobed Santa Claus appearing on the roof (albeit minus his reindeer), carrying what looks to be a Christmas Tree covered in presents. He then disappears down the chimney stack and magically appears in the children's bedroom, where he takes toys from the tree and places them in the children's stockings. He then appears to bless them before vanishing and leaving the children to wake, much enthused by their gifts.

Leaving to one side the film's aforementioned technical innovations, which themselves bring a certain magical quality to the film, it provides a fascinating insight into Christmas at the end of the 1800s and what would become the increasingly standard Anglo-American narrative. Despite this being a British film, the titular character is not the Father Christmas of British tradition but the American Santa Claus, which suggests that even by this time, the idea of a universal Santa Claus who visits at night and comes down the chimney had become widely accepted. Perhaps more telling, however, is the film's portrayal of a warm domestic setting with happy but well-disciplined children. Tucked up safely in a respectable and comfortable middle-class home, they are presented as the natural recipients of the good grace of the season embodied in the visit by Santa. Hence, while a relatively simple exercise in storytelling, the underlying content of this film is one that not only propagates a Dickensian vision of idealized domesticity and the magic of Christmas but, as we shall see, helps establish a template that film-makers will continue to draw upon for decades to come.

Hollywood Beckons

As the twentieth century unfolded, the value to be found in presenting the warm bosom of the family as the ideal condition in which one might truly experience the joys of Christmas became central to the Hollywood vision of Christmas. As John Mundy (2008) observes, even when Christmas films have been prepared to portray the darker aspects of the season, including loneliness, guilt, and even family breakups, the underlying message is always that things will inevitably turn out for the best; usually in the form of familial reconciliation and a rediscovery of the stability and happiness within which the 'miracle' or 'magic' of Christmas is ultimately embedded.

One of the most critical and influential cinematic examples of this is George Seaton's *Miracle on 34th Street*. Originally released in 1947 and subsequently readapted and remade in 1994 (dir. Les Mayfield), the film ostensibly tells the story of a department store Santa Claus performer – calling himself Kris Kringle – who appears to believe that he is the real thing (Figure 3.1).

More importantly, however, it is also the tale of a divorced mother whose six-year-old daughter desperately wants a father and sibling. While such notions are far from entertained by her career-focused and somewhat Scrooge-like parent, working through the medium of the elderly Kris Kringle, the film concludes with the miracle the daughter seeks as both love and procreation come to pass in a relationship between the mother and a dashing lawyer who is not only kind but, most importantly, a believer in the spirit of Christmas. Despite the presence of divorce, cynicism, and, at one stage, persecution in the form of the prosecution of Kringle on trumped-up charges, the family unit not only endures, therefore, but thrives. At the same time, Kringle is effectively revealed to be the authentic Santa Claus after all. As such, the magical combination of Christmas, consumption, and the nuclear family unit remains untarnished.

Furthermore, if, as Miller (1993: 35) suggests, Christmas helps mediate the relationship between the local and the global, the domestic and the 'cosmological', then Christmas films such as *Miracle on 34th Street* also represent an important and, as I have noted above, culturally ubiquitous intervention into that mediation. Through a range of aesthetic and narrative

FIGURE 3.1   A publicity poster for the 1947 version of *Miracle on 34th Street*.

practices, they provide a saccharine enactment of the family unit's continuing normative and organizational supremacy as a site of emotional and cultural solidarity and consumption. Nor is any family unredeemable at Christmas. From the classic tale of suicide, familial love, and redemption in Capra's *It's A Wonderful Life* (1946) to the hapless and socially dysfunctional Griswalds of *National Lampoon's A Christmas Vacation* (1989), the Christmas film recurrently demonstrates that even if we cannot always choose our families, they will always be central to achieving peace and goodwill to all and, as such, deserve our enduring allegiance.

One can also understand how the appearance of such films in the cinema, or, more importantly today on TV, might contribute to a season defined by feelings of familiarity, continuity, and solidarity. For however estranged from family life one might feel, as a disgruntled teenager or an alienated adult, Christmas is a time when home – or the idea of home at least – pervades our aesthetic, even if not our lived sensibilities. Moreover, the fact that, especially since multi-channel television has appeared, the same films tend to appear at the same time every year reinforces this sense of punctuation and predictability, a symbolic and indeed material continuity with both a familial past and future.

Not that this is a wholly uncontested ideal. As Thom Swiss (2008) recalls, families at Christmas are no less complex arrangements than at any other time of the year. Indeed, it is likely that the kinds of expectations generated by these very same movies place impossible demands and expectations on family members and friends alike. Nonetheless, the romanticization of the family and home at Christmas remains hard to resist, as I shall discuss further in Chapter 6. For however negative one's experience of them might be, the aesthetic stylization, underlying content, and seasonal punctuality of Christmas films make them significant players in reinforcing the idea that at Christmas, at least, there truly is no place like home.

Christmas and War in Cinema

While significant, the importance of portraying familial solidarity at Christmas through popular media such as film is not confined, however, to the nurturing and redemptive functioning of the nuclear or extended family as we know them. It can also play an essential role in mediating broader social tensions, especially between the particular demands of the family and the more universal needs of the wider society. Moreover, by representing or embedding the importance of family life within a broader ethical framework, Christmas can promote a sense of identity between society and the family unit in that the latter's survival is recognized as dependent on, if not subservient to, the latter. And, nowhere is this fact more evident than when Christmas is invoked in times of crisis or conflict, such as war, when not only is the family potentially under threat, but so are those social institutions and practices that purportedly support and enrich it.

While the use of Christmas as a medium of wartime propaganda can be traced back to the American Civil War (Nissenbaum, 1997), the Second World War witnessed the season become an overtly cinematic tool of national and military intervention, with the defence of Christmas becoming a rallying cry for populations on all sides of the conflict. An example of this is the 1941 British GPO Film Unit production *Christmas Under Fire*, a short but perhaps unsurprisingly atmospheric documentary about the life and struggles of the English[4] experiencing the season during the Blitz. As Sarah Street (2000) notes, the film was aimed at a predominantly American audience that was still largely reluctant to enter the conflict attempting, as it did, to win over the average citizen through a shared vernacular, namely that of Christmas. While, due to its wartime setting, it lacks some of the traditional festive symbolism, the film nonetheless utilizes rich seasonal imagery such as carol singers, paper decorations, and Christmas trees to highlight the hardships faced by the population of England alongside their determination to celebrate the season in the face of adversity.

As the film unfolds, images of a limited Christmas on the home front also form a cypher for the enduring bond between family and society and its institutions. Children remain a focal point throughout, signalling not only their position at the heart of what is so unique and so important about Christmas but also the family's vital role in their upbringing and, more widely, in what is considered to be the healthy organization of social reproduction. However, this role is also portrayed as intimately embedded in the continuation of social institutions such as the church, school, and the state's armed forces that also feature prominently. Ultimately, what they all have in common, however, is they are carriers of an idealized and highly aestheticized Anglo-American vision of Christmas and the shared values that underpin it, values that America is being invited to help defend in the face of the Nazi onslaught.

Songs and Music for Christmas

Leaving film to one side for the moment, another form of mass-mediated entertainment that has left a significant mark on the aesthetic organization of Christmas and how we are encouraged to relate to it is popular music. While films, by virtue of their content and timeliness, play a central role in reproducing many of the standardized tenets of our contemporary Christmas, they are a largely static cultural medium. By this, I mean that generally speaking, one must go to them, be they in the cinema on the television screen or even accepting their increased portability, the laptop or tablet. They also tend to demand, if not always receive, one's sole attention to the exclusion of all other stimuli. On the other hand, music can be experienced wherever one is, especially at Christmas. It frequently provides both focus and background and often accompanies other activities and displays, complementing and reinforcing seasonal atmospherics rather than distracting from them (Jarman-Ivens, 2008). Indeed, hearing Christmas music is perhaps not only the first sign that the season has arrived but the most powerful and evocative of all of them.

For obvious reasons, Christmas and music also have a much longer mutual history than film can offer. As Barry Cooper (2008) notes, the existence of

Christmas hymns can be traced back to the fourth century AD, and by the Middle Ages what we know today as the Christmas carol, a popular religious song characterized by a regular rhythm designed for singing and dancing, was well-established. Particularly popular in rural areas where communal activities such as wassailing were common, villagers would memorize and sing such carols from house to house to gain favour and gifts from the homes they visited, contributing to an idealized image of the countryside Christmas that inspired the Victorians so much, and which continues to inspire to this day.

Yet, despite such ancient origins, as Golby and Purdue (2000) have suggested, by the end of the eighteenth century, carol singing, like many other Christmas customs had, as a consequence of the general decline in the observance of Christmas by the urban middle classes, receded in popularity. Once again, though, it was the revitalization of the Christmas spirit that took place during the mid-1800s, combined with the industrial production of sheet music and songbooks, that served to rescue both ancient songs and give birth to new ones, with contemporary favourites such as *O Little Town of Bethlehem* and *Good King Wenceslas* appearing during this period. Christmas carol services also started to reappear in British churches while, at the same time, as Whitely (2008) notes, collections of seasonal songs, such as the 1847 publication of *Songs of Christmas for Family Choirs*, became commercially available, heralding their mass production and leading to a resurgence in both their accessibility and popularity.

Certainly, by the mid-twentieth century, the singing and playing of live and recorded Christmas carols had become a central feature of the season's sonic landscape. Today they regularly compete with more contemporary festive music in commercial and civic spaces, with the distinction between religious and popular music becoming blurred beyond much meaningful recognition. Nonetheless, Christmas is rarely complete for many people without at least one visit to a traditional carol service. At the same time, the commencement of Christmas itself is often considered to be signalled by the sound, broadcast around the world, of the opening verse of the 1848 carol *Once in Royal David's City*, atmospherically delivered by a lone choir boy at the start of the 'Festival of Nine Lessons and Carols' from King's College Chapel at the *University of Cambridge*.

In addition to the mass circulation and consumption of carols, Christmas also represents a commercially important time for the popular music industry. Even in an age of multiple music formats where the significance of record sales has declined, a certain kudos is still attached to being on or near the top of the popular music charts during late December. Interestingly, in the UK, at least, only a minority of the songs that have achieved the coveted Christmas number-one spot in the music charts have ever involved a specific Christmas theme. While the most successful Christmas number-one is such a song, namely the

1984 charity track *Do They Know It's Christmas*, which was re-rerecorded in 1989 and 2004, and sold a total of 3.7 million copies in the UK and over 50 million worldwide,[5] the second and third biggest seasonal sellers are Queen's *Bohemian Rhapsody* (1975, 1991) and Paul McCartney's *Mull of Kintyre* (1977), neither of which are particularly festive.

Returning to the specifics of Christmas music, however, as I have acknowledged, it is now ubiquitous throughout the season due to its constant, if not incessant, broadcasting over radio and television as well as in stores and shopping malls. Indeed, the arrival of mechanical technologies of musical reproduction and broadcasting, including the gramophone and radio during the 1920s, was as much a factor in the global popularization of Christmas as anything else. Functioning mainly as a medium of Anglo-Americanized commercial and cultural imagery, these new recordings of Christmas songs ensured that celebrants knew, for example, that there were 'toys in every store' while encouraging them to 'hang a shining star upon the highest bough' while Irving Berlin's *White Christmas*, purportedly the biggest selling Christmas single of all time coming in at over 50 million copies sold,[6] helped establish the ideal of a snow-covered celebration while spawning its own festive movie in which Christmas is not indeed Christmas until the snow begins to fall.

Pop and Rock for Christmas

By the late 1950s' pop and rock-styled Christmas hits started to emerge, taking the festive importance of recorded music to a new level both artistically and, perhaps more importantly, commercially. Building on the successes of seasonal swing favourites such as Benny Goodman, Art Lunt, and Peggy Lee's 1942 hit *Winter Weather*, and Louis Armstrong's 1953 rendition of *Cool Yule*, amongst others, in 1957, the release of Elvis Presley's *Christmas Album* brought the mass consumption of rock'n'roll into the Christmas mainstream. With its combination of traditionally delivered carols and edgy renditions of secular numbers, such as Coot's and Gillespie's 1934 song, *Santa Claus is Coming to Town*, it opened the floodgates for a host of artists to contribute to what was to become a new Christmas canon. From Chuck Berry in 1958 with *Run Rudolph Run*, through the 1960s and Phil Spector's wall of sound renditions of tracks such as *Frosty the Snowman* and *Sleigh Ride*, by the 1970s, Christmas and popular music had become inexorably entwined.

As products of the Christmas culture industry, it is perhaps no surprise, however, that what such songs have in common, whatever their genre, be it reggae, rock'n'roll, or even electronic dance music, is they continue to rely on many of the structural features and musical themes of more traditional Christmas songs and carols while reproducing a standardized set of lyrical motifs appropriate to the season. Most evident are their accessible singalong qualities reminiscent of early carols and the widespread incorporation of bells or other metallic instruments 'located in the table range' (Jarmen-Ivens, 2008: 113) that give a sense of sleigh travel across snow-covered landscapes. Another perennial feature of such recordings is the frequent use of children's choirs to evoke both religious and family-orientated feelings of seasonal solidarity, alongside the enduring belief that Christmas is experienced best through the medium of childhood innocence.

Take, for example, the success of such repeating musical devices in Jona Lewie's 1980 UK song, *Stop the Cavalry*. While released in December of that year, Lewie has always insisted that he did not write it as a Christmas song. Instead, in his mind, it was an anti-war song produced during rising Cold War tensions. Nevertheless, while the song only tangentially refers to Christmas in the line 'wish I was at home for Christmas', its singalong structure, replete with themes of peace, love, and the desire to be at home with family, ensures that it adheres to several standard seasonal tropes. Similarly, while lacking the choir, the instrumentation and arrangement of the song features the requisite tubular and sleigh bells and a Salvation Army brass band reminiscent of those once seen on street corners at Christmas. All of which gives this ant-war anthem those expected qualities of a Christmas 'hit', as it indeed went on to be.

While rare, actual anti-war sentiments and celebrating Christmas values and ideals are not entirely inimical to each other either. Another prominent example is John Lennon's and Yoko Ono's 1969 recording of *Happy Christmas (War is Over)*. Whiteley (2008), however, places such songs within a more comprehensive and relatively contemporary approach to seasonal music that attempts to organize ideas around themes of altruism and care at Christmas within, much as Dickens did, a broadly political, if albeit charitable agenda. Another candidate Whiteley identifies is *The Pogues'* 1988 seasonal hit, *Fairytale of New York*, which she situates within, amongst other things, the context of a concern for the impact of alcoholism on families and the disadvantaged and poor. For despite the dark romance of its male and female protagonists, the song is a painful warning that without the stability of the family as the cornerstone of social life, the future of Christmas is not so much a magical one of peace and joy but more likely an evening in the 'drunk tank', despised even by those we love.

Whatever the prevalence of such moral components, pop music at Christmas has never entirely abandoned the more pagan and arguably hedonistic legacies of the season's origins, however. As Etzioni (2004) argues, while Christmas can, on the one hand, function as an assertion of tradition and a reaffirmation of order, as we have seen, it can also represent a cathartic opportunity to invert social norms and hierarchies in a relatively safe and bounded time and space. In this context, pop music has also served the cause of Christmas as something of a safety valve, legitimizing not only rampant consumption as in Eartha Kitt's original 1953 recording of *Santa Baby* and letting one's hair down through tracks such as Brenda Lee's 1958 hit *Rockin' Around the Christmas Tree*, but also the encouragement of romantic liaisons exemplified in say *All I Want for Christmas Is You*, a 1994 hit for Mariah Carey. Indeed, tracks such as *Back Door Santa*, released in 1968 by soul singer Clarence Carter, suggest an even more sexually active season, one very much in the spirit of celebrating the sensuality of life during the dark and cold of winter.

It is not only the often standardized aesthetic and lyrical qualities of such music that contribute to this musical landscape, however. As with the medium of the Christmas film, the appearance of carols and popular seasonal songs can also help organize a sense of temporal regularity and continuity with past seasons, experiences, and even generations. They help create an envelope in which idealized past, present, and possibly future memories and anticipations provide an affective context within which we can experience the season. As Martin Johnes (2016: 156) observes in this respect:

> Christmas pop music was nostalgic in evocation, if not actually in lyrics; it often conjured up simpler times. While this was often down to the whimsical or romantic feel of the songs, it was also because of the frequency with which they were played. They were heard so often that they represented Christmas itself.

Nonetheless, the festive sensibilities such music encourage are not confined, as I have suggested above, simply to the home or other more private spaces. Instead, they increasingly accompany us, especially as employees and consumers, across all kinds of public spaces and places throughout the season, reflecting the impact of this pervasive Christmas culture industry. And while it is uncertain if this is actually harmful to our emotional and mental health, according to Linda Blair (cited Petter, 2018), we can expend more energy trying to screen the music out rather than focus on other necessary activities. Nonetheless, there can be no doubt that for retailers, such music is integral to setting the aesthetic tone of Christmas and encouraging the upturn in the retail activity they rely on, something I will consider further in the next section.

Atmospheric Magic at Christmas

So far, I have discussed two kinds of often highly standardized artefacts, namely films and popular music, that can be regarded as produced by a Christmas-orientated culture industry. There are, of course, many others I could have considered, space permitting. Theatre and variety shows, television and radio broadcasts, books and magazines, and even advertisements are all immensely popular and often reproduce similar seasonal norms and expectations concerned with social solidarity, family, and tradition. In this section, however, I move beyond the idea of a culture industry that promotes such beliefs and values through the production and circulation of particular commodities and also consider how Christmas is also reproduced through the organization and direct spatial and aesthetic landscaping of common if largely commercial, seasonal environments.

While such environments can take many forms, particularly the home, this is a setting I consider in a later chapter. Here, my primary focus is on those prime organizing sites of Christmas consumption considered earlier, namely the shopping mall and the department store. This is for two reasons. Firstly, because it is in such spaces that the complex, in-situ interweaving of resources required to create a distinctly Christmas atmosphere are at their most self-conscious and visible. Secondly, these spaces promote more than simply consumption. Rather, they encourage and seek to mould the adoption of a more pervasive form of festive subjectivity amongst those that visit them; one that, while commercially valuable, exceeds the simple desire to shop *in situ*, and exists as an agent of everyday seasonal reproduction, realising the magic of Christmas not only in the public but also the most private of spheres.

Before I say any more about this, however, I want to briefly unpack the concept of atmosphere and explain a little more about how I am using it here. Although within organization studies, the idea that all organizations possess certain aesthetic qualities is nothing new (Gagliardi, 1992; Strati, 1999; Carr and Hancock, 2003), the idea that they can also generate particular atmospheric conditions is more recent (Borch, 2010; Biehl-Missal, 2013; Julmi, 2016; Hancock, 2019). Moreover, much of the current work tends to draw on the ideas, as mentioned earlier, of German philosopher Gernot Böhme (1993, 2003, 2016, 2020) and his stress on the importance of understanding how the creation of atmospheres is central to how consumer capitalism has continued to flourish despite inherent instabilities.

On one level, Böhme (1993) notes how atmosphere is a relatively simple concept, *describing* as it does the everyday ways in which a space or place feels to those who inhabit it, impacting, as it were, on their bodies and senses in a manner that usually invites little or no reflection. As he puts it:

> atmospheres are totalities: atmospheres imbue everything, they tinge the whole of the world or a view, they bathe everything in a certain light, unify a diversity of impressions in a single emotive state.
>
> *(Böhme, 2017: 29)*

However, while the importance of managing the atmospheres of organized spaces such as retail outlets has been recognized previously (cf. Kotler, 1974), for Böhme, the concept of atmosphere emerges from a deeper and more critical consideration of what he terms an *aesthetic economy* (Böhme, 2003).

For Böhme, this describes an aspect of the capitalist system of valuation and exchange whereby goods and the experience of services are exchanged based on what he terms their *staging value*; that is, value derived from their primary capacity to intensify pleasure. Integral to this form of valorisation is, he argues, the production of atmospheres that contribute to realizing such value and can be understood as the outcome of acts of deliberate spatial and aesthetic organization, combined with how those exposed to them react and respond. In considering how Christmas is experienced and reproduced atmospherically, what is of particular interest, therefore, is how the materiality of Christmas can be organized and managed to generate a way of feeling that favours specific ways of experiencing and valuing Christmas in what is hopefully an enduring and largely consumption-orientated manner.

It's Beginning to Look/Sound/Smell/ a Lot Like Christmas

By any standards, Christmas is a symbolically rich time of year. For those living in the cooler climes of the northern hemisphere, as the late autumn nights draw in and the temperatures fall, it is difficult not to be seduced by the lights, sounds, and fragrances associated with the season. From the sparkling lights on a Christmas tree in a neighbour's window to the first notes of a Christmas carol or song heard in a store or on the radio, such symbols can evoke a childlike anticipation that something big and exciting is about to happen. Furthermore, for those in need of greater levels of festive inducement, in many countries, one is not long into November before specialist Christmas programming starts to appear on multi-channel TV, enticing one to hunker down for the looming mid-winter and perhaps dream of a white Christmas.

However, while symbols might *tell* us that Christmas is on its way, it is more likely that it is their aesthetic qualities that make us feel a particular way about this fact appealing as they do to a more sensual, pre-reflective form of experiencing the world, one that, to cite Terry Eagleton (1990: 13), has its primary 'impact on the body' and our senses. Take, as a festive example, the case of the humble candy cane. While this Christmas staple reportedly derives its symbolic meaning from the crooked staff of the shepherds who, we are told, visited the infant Jesus in his manger somewhere in Bethlehem (Patel, 2008), for most people today this symbolism is a dim memory at best. Indeed, if it symbolizes anything, it is more likely to be the sweet treats expected throughout the season, especially by children. Nevertheless, either way, it is not so much such symbolism that makes it a Christmas favourite, but its aesthetic contribution to a more general festive atmosphere that makes it such an essential part of the seasonal landscape. Combining smell, colour, and design alongside past associations with childish innocence and the promise of Christmas, the very presence of such canes helps set the 'tone' and make it 'feel' like Christmas.

This is due to what one might term their sociomaterial qualities (Orlikowski, 2010) and their relationships to other symbols of the season through which artefacts such as candy canes can be said to contribute to making Christmas come into being. In this sense, we can understand Christmas artefacts and the atmospheres they help produce as what the anthropologist Alfred Gell (1992) describes as technologies of enchantment. Purposively manufactured to cultivate and normalize positive ways of feeling about and being at Christmas, they secure what, in Gell's (1992: 43) words, is 'the acquiescence of individuals' to those practices of the season deemed proper and profitable. Take, as a further illustration of this, the already extensively discussed content of *A Christmas Carol*. As I have previously observed, it is here that Dickens made his case for a Christmas grounded in celebrating the family unit, social solidarity, and the value of conspicuous consumption. However, what is significant about the story in the context of this chapter is that he does not make this case through rational argument. Instead, it is through the creation of a highly atmospheric entwining of sights, smells, and sounds, and indeed the highly sensual portrayal of his Christmas spirits, that the elderly miser Scrooge is eventually won over in the story.

Of course, as an artist, Dickens was naturally well aware of the capacity of aesthetic craftsmanship to win over hearts and minds. Nevertheless, in pursuing this path, he also recalled the priorities of a far older and pre-Christian template for Christmas, namely as a celebration of those sensual pleasures that seek to defy the privations of the mid-winter. In doing so, from the sights and sounds of bustling shoppers and excited children, through the smells and taste of food and drink, to the sentimentalized memories of festive seasons (not yet) past, Dickens was, despite the white on grey hue of the story's setting, able to re-establish the popularity of a sensually abundant Christmas. A skill that, as we shall see, still characterizes much of the labour that takes place in creating the magic of Christmas and a form of seasonal subject particularly attuned to it.

Making 'the Magic' of Christmas

In this section, I consider the views and experiences of those organizational employees who find themselves responsible for the everyday landscaping (Gagliardi, 1992) of public and commercial spaces to help further the atmospheric production of what they describe as the 'magic of Christmas'. While I have alluded to the idea that Christmas is considered, especially by those involved in marketing and selling it, a magical season, in this section, it is an idea that comes to the fore. For while a belief in magic in one form or another has characterized humanity since time immemorial, at Christmas it gains a far wider currency. This does not mean that it is easy always to be clear about what it means when someone talks of something being magical, however. As Randall Styers (2013: 258) observes, magic's 'amorphous and shape shifting' nature makes it a complex beast to pin down both semantically and ontologically', a problem that is no less the case at Christmas.

For anthropologists such as Marcell Mauss (2001) and Bronisław Malinowski (2011), while the supernatural qualities of magic itself were not something they were particularly interested in, what they did recognize was how a belief in magic was, across many cultures, both a detailed response to the negation of human desires by an external and hostile reality and a focus for social solidarity and cohesion. As such, and just like Christmas more widely, magic primarily draws together a host of actions and symbols to make human communities feel good about themselves (Lévi-Strauss, 1987). This is either by excusing their relative powerlessness in the face of overwhelming supernatural forces or offering them a form of power and redemption with which to assert their will. In a description that could just as easily apply to the men and women of advertising and marketing, then, for Mauss (2001: 175), the art of the magician, in particular, involves convincing other people that simply by utilizing their mystical skills, they can satisfy their desires and expectations. All it requires is a collective belief in the sacred powers they possess.

Not that when it comes to Christmas any uncertainties or ambivalences about the actual existence of magic appear to be allowed. Again, harking back to a time when it was believed the veil between the worlds of the living and the dead thinned, and supernatural symbolism and ancient beliefs in magic inhabited the mid-winter landscape, the origins of Christmas are to be found in the pagan world of magic and superstition (Hutton, 1996; Miles, 1912). However, even having supplanted its pagan origins, new magical narratives emerged and took hold as a cornerstone of the Christian celebration of the season. From the miraculous tale of the virgin birth and the visitations of an immortal flying gift giver and his army of elves and sentient reindeer to the possibility of capturing the love and affection of another just by buying the right gift, Christmas itself took on the mantle of the most magical time of the year.

Creating and Selling the Magic

Today, making Christmas magical has become an industrial-scale task. It relies on the intellectual and manual labour of a host of creatives, including designers, marketers, advertisers and craftspeople, as well as their managers and employers. Like Dickens, these people are well aware of the importance of the sensual and spectacular for getting the spirit of Christmas across to their target audience, be they seasonal readers, festive flaneurs or perhaps and most importantly, Christmas consumers. For few consider the atmospheric impact of Christmas to be more important than those who are charged with maximizing seasonal footfall, turnover, and ultimately profit through the landscaping and placement of seasonal features and events across stores, shopping malls, and other commercial centres.

This is not to ignore the fact that such festive landscaping, alongside the staging of Christmas events such as parades and fairs, is not always purely commercial in outlook. For example, the erection of Christmas trees financed by public bodies or charities in the US can be traced back to the 1900s with the first 'national' Christmas tree, replete with electric lights, displayed outside the White House in 1923.[7] In the UK, the nearest equivalent is perhaps the Trafalgar Square Christmas tree that dates to 1947 and is an annual gift from the Norwegian people in 'gratitude for Britain's support for Norway during World War II'.[8] Similarly, city and town councils across the globe each year sponsor and often erect public lights and decorations in honour of the season.

Nonetheless, such public activities are rarely without some commercial interest. The use of public money to decorate towns and cities in such a way is often defended, for example, by the claim that it promotes seasonal trade for local retailers and generates, as one town councillor in the UK I spoke to put it, 'the right atmosphere to bring shoppers into the town'. Furthermore, many ostensibly public decorations and events are privately or commercially sponsored for the same reason. In New York, *Macy's* Thanksgiving Day parade is one prominent example, while another is the annual placing of a giant Christmas tree at the Rockefeller Centre. Anchoring the surrounding shopping plaza, replete with an ice rink, despite its predominantly commercial function, this tree has been considered the public tree of New York City almost since its official inauguration in 1933 (O'Connor, 2007). Similarly, in London, the Regent and Oxford Street Christmas lights (Figure 3.2), while considered a public display, were originally paid for and organized by the local trader associations, while today, they only survive mainly through commercial sponsorship.

Nonetheless, while public Christmas displays and events are of commercial and indeed civic importance, the preparation of enclosed commercial venues such as department stores that rely heavily on the season for their annual financial performance remains the most significant site at which energy, financial resources, and time are put into crafting magical Christmas landscapes. Combining tradition, technology, and glamour, they set out to enchant children and adults, with their planning and design cycle ongoing throughout the year as the stakes get higher each season. Indeed, as one events manager at a major UK department store delighted in teling me, 'in this office, it's *always* Christmas'. Certainly, by early in the New Year in almost all major retail outlets, the past seasonal performance has already been quantified, and future seasonal trends have been analysed, with plans and visions for Christmas displays already well into the planning stage and ready for testing and submitting for costing and customer appeal. Furthermore, for those involved in merchandising activities,

FIGURE 3.2 Christmas lights on Regent Street, London. Photograph by the author.

the sourcing and stocking of Christmas goods usually commences just as early, especially if they are to follow a store's seasonal template that combines colour, texture, sound, and often even smell into a singular, seasonal identity across all designs, decorations, and select product ranges.

However, such a rolling, annual commitment to the season can throw up some unique challenges for those involved. For example, as one designer engaged in putting together a store's festive theme of a 'White Christmas' pointed out when discussing the 18-month cycle of their work, to achieve a magical atmosphere based on the theme of snowy whiteness that would reflect 'magic, beauty, ethereal wonder and playfulness' was more than a little challenging given that much of it took place during one of the hottest summers for years. Other employees I spoke to similarly reflected not only on the difficulty of keeping up with current trends when faced with such a long lead time, but also on the negative impact such year-round preparations could have on their ability to engage with the season when it finally arrived. As another interviewee in the same design department told me:

> One thing that's difficult is when you plan Christmas it's like in a period of the year when I suppose the last thoughts on your mind want to be Christmas, so getting into that spirit and creativity when it's finally here, you're almost so over it.

Despite such travails, most of the people I spoke to involved in designing and managing such commercial displays and spaces seemed to have a genuine enthusiasm for the season and the work they undertook in preparing for it. Below, I explore their activities as what Böhme (1993) might describe as aesthetic labourers whose responsibility is to promote consumption through (co)producing the requisite atmospheric conditions in which such activity might be maximized and more festive subjectivities realized. In doing so, I draw more extensively on my interview material than I have so far, focusing on how a magical Christmas atmosphere is brought into being, both technically and experientially, through work that takes place within such organizational settings.

Designing Christmas Magic

For those involved in designing and landscaping Christmas spaces and displays across such settings, it is crucial to get the festive feel 'just right' and ensure that it is conceived, created, and managed in line with existing commercial priorities. While it is recognized that such atmospheres always arise in the specific context of their production and reception, and that this inevitably causes problems when it comes to controlling them, those involved still tend to enter the process with an established idea about what the outcome of their efforts should be; namely, the 'magical atmosphere' of Christmas. As one leader of an events team at a large London department store emphasized:

> There's something rather intangible about getting Christmas right. Lots of time, money and hard work go into it, but at the end of the day it has to be magical … it's the atmosphere, isn't?

For those responsible for such activities, not only is magic *the* quality that defines Christmas, but it also chimes most closely with the kinds of anthropological accounts I referred to earlier. For this is a magic that, when appropriately enacted and with everyone believing in it, can result in magical and often miraculous outcomes for store owners and managers, namely shoppers spending more than they usually would or really should. As one store director observed in respect of their ambitions surrounding the design of their annual Christmas grotto:

> it's the most magical that you can make Christmas and I think that's what the customers enjoy and *that's when the customers buy* – because they get that feeling of Christmas magic and if they get that within the department that they're buying from, *they can take that magic home.*
>
> *(Emphasis added)*

The idea that magic, or a magical atmosphere, can be manufactured to entice customers to part with their money is not unique to Christmas, of course. *Disney*, for example, considers a magical experience to be a key component of attracting visitors to its theme parks employing as they do teams of *Imagineers* to design and build its rides and attractions (Bryman, 2004). What makes the magic of Christmas unique, however, is that it is not simply confined to a particular organizational setting. Instead, it infuses the cultural sensibility of the season through a festive network of locations such as the cinema, the pub and bar, and even the living room. Out and about, it can be wherever we hear Christmas music or see and hear Christmas advertising and, of particular interest here, whenever we enter markets, shopping malls and department stores, amongst other commercial and quasi-retail settings.

For this magic to do its work, however, it requires paying attention to the festive organization of an assemblage of resources and technologies, both human and non-human, across stores and shopping malls. The most important of these is the design and placement of primary decorative resources that help create a particular seasonal theme. The placement of, say, 'twinkling lights', 'snow' and 'decorations' of the right quality and 'feel', combined with the overall landscaping of the environment through the organization of material elements such as colour, texture, sound, and often smell, are viewed as foundational to creating an enchanting and magical atmosphere. This was emphasized by members of a team of designers and merchandisers who were in the process of planning a store's integrated Christmas 'identity' for the forthcoming two years:

> What's really important is that we get the feel right. We have to avoid anything that gives a sense of tackiness, or it at all being cheap. No cheap baubles or lights, everything has to fit with the image of the store. They [must] radiate magic, beauty, ethereal wonder, and playfulness.

For these designers, there is a direct link, therefore, between the design, quality, and arrangement of seasonal features and their capacity to enchant the consumer or visitor to the store, helping to produce an atmospheric outcome characterized as magical, ethereal, and playful; the very stuff of what they think and feel Christmas ought to be.

Santa's Grotto

Nowhere is this imperative more evident than in the design and operation of the primary Christmas attraction designed to enchant shoppers and other visitors each season, the Christmas or 'Santa's grotto'. Described by one manager as 'a parental apparatus to achieve the feeling of giving their children Christmas', such installations adorn stores and shopping malls throughout the season and, I was told at the time of writing this, can cost anywhere between £20,000 and £150,000 to build and install. While often featuring contemporary images and technologies, such as animatronic figures that include singing elves and dancing reindeer, as well as 3D projections and films, such grottos also continue to rely on more traditional imagery and artefacts associated with the home of Santa Claus. For instance, one elaborate grotto based at a mall in London was described by an employee in what is itself the most atmospheric of ways:

> When you approached [the grotto], it had old snowshoes outside and a reindeer harness hanging on the wall, and you could see through the little window inside. There was an electric log stove and ... oh, a beautiful log interior and Father Christmas sat on this bench with his big sacks of things and things all over the wall and a Christmas tree.

Furthermore, it is not just their material qualities that lend these grottos a unique position within the landscaping of the commercial Christmas experience. They also play a central role in incorporating the bodies and affective responses of visitors and consumers into the event itself, enhancing the atmospheric qualities of the space and helping create what the likes of (Orlikowski, 2007) might describe as an entanglement of both material and social, or non-human and human elements.

This 'sociomaterial' insight (Orlikowski, 2007, 2010; De Vaujany and Vaast, 2014) also recalls that atmospheres need to be understood as existing somewhere between the subject and the object, a property of both but, at the same time something more than simply either/or and where the whole is greater than the sum of its parts. To sustain the magic, therefore, grottos designers and managers must also be observant of how the spatial practices (Lefebvre, 1991) of shoppers and visitors contribute to or detract from the overall atmosphere while ensuring that anything that might prevent them from having an enjoyable visit is organized out of the experience.

Take, for instance, the notion that, as well as the bright lights and decorative designs in front of the house, manufacturing the perfect Christmas atmosphere also requires attention to the precise organization of the more mundane and ergonomic issues associated with crowd control and human movement through such spaces. For example, the necessary but often tiresome act of queuing to enter the grotto can be integral to the atmospheric context of the encounter as embodied activities and behaviours can be actively managed to sustain the desired mood or tone. This can be pursued by distracting and pacifying visitors, especially often restless children, through efficient design and a touch of technical trickery. As one manager of a Christmas grotto company explained:

> What's important is ensuring we keep the visitors feeling as Christmassy as possible. You can have the best grotto in the world, but if everybody is frustrated ... well. This is achieved using narratives based on traditional and Christmas tales that develop as the visitors proceed through the passages

and spaces leading to the grotto. Here, the sophisticated animatronics and installations discussed earlier often came into their own.

Similarly, as a grotto designer also observed:

> Sometimes people have been waiting half an hour to see Santa, but they've had all this fantastic show going on all around them, and lots of attention from the elves and helpers, so by the time they get to you *they're in the mood.*
> *(Emphasis added)*

The ability of the grotto to transform the humble queue into part of the experience is an integral outcome of its design and the sociomaterial organization of the available space. Artefacts, bodies, moods, and behaviours are all organized in order to sustain the feeling of something special, something magical, taking place. Not that all design and landscaping activities are equally as glamorous. Some are notably mundane but just as necessary in terms of their capacity, if not to enhance, then certainly minimize any possible distractions from the desired atmospherics of the experience. For example, as another grotto designer noted, 'you need a certain size operationally to have a distance between the queuing public and the Santa visit. You don't want to feel that everyone is looking at you while you are with Santa'.

At larger venues and events where multiple performers are often operating, there is also the need to ensure that the atmosphere is not shattered by, say, several Santas appearing at once. Something that again must be averted through the careful organization of space and the grotto design. Add to this the need to keep visitors in the proper 'Christmassy' spirit through appropriate ventilation, available and well-maintained toilets, emergency exits, and the quick and unobtrusive removal or rectification of non-seasonal litter and breakages, and it results in a complex process of sociomaterial production and activity all geared towards sustaining the magical experience of meeting Santa both for children and admission paying adults alike.

Furthermore, this entanglement of the human and the material continues beyond the physical encounter between the customers and the attraction. In an increasingly computer-dominated industry such as retail, information technology systems also play a significant role in directly enhancing the magical quality of the grotto visit. Alongside the programmed light shows and animatronics, as well as their role in the design process itself, the increasing use of computerized online booking systems associated with many Christmas attractions is crucial to commercial operators. This is due to their ability to facilitate the collection of targeted marketing data, a high-value commodity, as well as contribute to creating encounters that enhance the atmospheric qualities of the grotto experience. As one manager who was also a parent told me in respect of the impact such pre-collected customer data can have:

My daughter's ten, and doesn't believe anymore. She hadn't been anywhere where they do this [online booking] before. So, she goes in with her younger brother quite reluctantly and [Santa says] 'Oh William and Alice, how's your cat Tufty?' And she just turned to me and said, 'How does he know?' It was something really special and magical. It managed to re-spark that bit of belief.

Whether it be traditional Christmas decorations, hi-tech lighting shows and 3D visuals, or even remote data collection systems, manufacturing a magical Christmas atmosphere at these locations is, then, a profoundly socio-technical or sociomaterial undertaking that creatively combines the movements, rhythms, expectations, and attitudes of their human visitors with the operations and affordances of seasonal non-human technologies.

What is also notable about such attractions, however, is their additional capacity to produce what one might term an extended festive spatiality that seemingly extends beyond the physical context in which they are initially encountered. For Böhme (2017), the term that perhaps best encapsulates this atmospheric property is that of *ekstases*. Closely related to the term ecstasy and denoting individual experience of being outside or beyond oneself, here Böhme uses it to point to how it is less the internal properties of such attractions that are of central importance when understating their atmospheric qualities, but rather the way they can 'radiate outwards into space, to their output as generators of atmospheres' (Böhme, 2017: 32).

And as it is with Christmas films, music, and the like, what stands out about organizational phenomena such as the simple Christmas grotto is more than just their ability to generate a localized and immediate magical experience for the consumer. Rather, it is their ability to create a magical atmosphere that transcends time and space is what makes the holiday season so special. In doing so, they bring into being an atmospheric network that extends into the lived fabric of the season, one that both feeds on and, in turn, reproduces its magic, creating festive subjects that operate on the basis that if it now 'feels like Christmas' then acts of seasonal recognition, celebration and, most providentially, consumption are not only what is desirable, but necessary.

To summarize, then, having brought together two somewhat differing dimensions of the Christmas experience, mass-mediated Christmas films and music, and the design, landscaping, and operation of spaces of Christmas consumption, what they share in common is an underlying organizational blueprint that maps out the values and ways of feeling deemed conducive to the proper celebration of Christmas. In this sense, therefore, they can both be viewed as aspects of a larger Christmas culture industry dedicated to producing standardized but nonetheless seductive seasonal products and experiences. In the case of films and popular music, they are integral to the idea that Christmas, whatever the lived contradictions, speaks to an endurance of social institutions and family ties, particularly in times of personal or social adversity. By representing the sanctity of childhood and the magic of its innocence, or the nostalgic or cathartic musical qualities of seasonal hedonism, they attempt to organize how Christmas and, by extension, aspects of the social itself (Etzioni, 2004) are brought into being and experienced by what is an idealized seasonal subject.

When it comes to the design and landscaping of Christmas attractions, particularly within shopping malls and department stores, there is an equally powerful evocation of the feeling that Christmas is a somehow unique or enchanting time of year; and one that requires a similarly particular type of festive and, therefore, consuming subject to appreciate and sustain it. Conceived in such a way that they promote spatial practices (Lefebvre, 1991), whereby even 'happy queuing' is integral to the atmospheric experience (Julmi, 2016), these Christmas landscapes are central to the creation of an all-embracing Christmas atmosphere that structures both the tone and experience of the seasonal amongst swathes of the population. Through various sociomaterial technologies and practices, they structure individual feelings about and ways of relating to Christmas as a consumption event while reincorporating them as part and parcel of a closely managed, culturally and economically enchanting festive atmosphere.

Notes

1 www.statista.com/statistics/209295/domestic-box-office-revenue-of-the-most-successful-christmas-movies/
2 www.screenonline.org.uk/film/id/725468/
3 It is interesting to note that films about spirits and other supernatural entities – such as Santa Claus – were particularly important in the early years of cinema (Leeder, 2017).
4 While it was the UK and the Empire that was at war, most likely because the idea would be more familiar to its intended audience throughout the film, the terms 'England' and the 'English' are used.
5 www.officialcharts.com/chart-news/every-official-christmas-number-1-ever-__3618/
6 www.guinnessworldrecords.com/search?term=biggest+selling+christmas+single
7 www.nps.gov/whho/learn/historyculture/national-christmas-tree-history.htm
8 www.london.gov.uk/about-us/our-building-and-squares/christmas-trafalgar-square

References

Ackroyd, P. (2006) *Shakespeare: The Biography*. London: Vintage.
Adorno, T. and Horkheimer, M. (1973) *Dialectic of Enlightenment* (trans. J. Cumming). London: Verso.

Benjamin, W. (1970) [1955] 'The Work of Art in the Age of Mechanical Reproduction' (trans H. Zohn). In, H. Arendt (ed.) *Illuminations*. London: Fontana/Collins. Pp. 219–253.

Biehl-Missal, B. (2013) 'The Atmosphere of the Image: An Aesthetic Concept for Visual Analysis. *Consumption Markets & Culture* 16(4): 356–367.

Böhme, G. (1993) 'Atmosphere as the Fundamental Concept of a New Aesthetics'. *Thesis Eleven* 36(1): 113–126.

Böhme, G. (2003) 'Contribution to the Critique of the Aesthetic Economy'. *Thesis Eleven* 73(1): 71–82.

Böhme, G. (2016) *Critique of Aesthetic Capitalism* (trans. E. Jephcott). Berlin: Mimesis International.

Böhme, G. (2017) 'The Art of the Stage Set as a Paradigm for an Aesthetics of Atmospheres. In, G. Böhme, *The Aesthetics of Atmospheres* (ed. J-P. Thibaud). London: Routledge. Pp. 28–35.

Böhme, G. (2020) *Atmospheric Architectures: The Aesthetics of Felt Spaces* (ed. and trans. A.-Chr. Engels-Schwarzpaul). London: Bloomsbury Visual Arts.

Borch, C. (2010) 'Organizational Atmospheres: Foam, Affect and Architecture'. *Organization* 17(2): 223–241.

Bryman, A. (2004) *The Disneyization of Society*. London: Sage.

Carpani, J. (2019) Panto tickets sales gross over £60m for the first time, as millennials head to the theatre with parents. December 23. Available at: www.telegraph.co.uk/news/2019/12/23/panto-ticket-sales-gross-60m-first-time-millennials-head-theatre/

Carr, A. and Hancock, P. (eds) (2003) *Art and Aesthetics at Work*. Basingstoke: Palgrave.

Connelly, M. (1999) *Christmas: A Social History*. London: I.B. Tauris.

Connelly, M. (2000) 'Introduction'. In, M. Connelly (ed.) *Christmas at the Movies: Images of Christmas in American, British and European Cinema*. London: I.B. Tauris. Pp. 1–8.

Cooper, B. (2008) 'Christmas Carols'. In, S. Whiteley (ed.) *Christmas, Ideology and Popular Culture*. Edinburgh: Edinburgh University Press. Pp. 88–87.

De Vaujany, F-X. and E. Vaast (2014) 'If These Walls Could Talk: The Mutual Construction of Organizational Space and Legitimacy', *Organization Science* 25(3): 713–731.

Eagleton, T (1990) *The Ideology of the Aesthetic*. Oxford: Blackwell.

Etzioni, A. (2004) 'Holidays and Rituals: Neglected Seedbeds of Virtue'. In, A. Etzioni and J. Bloom (eds) *We Are What We Celebrate: Understanding Holidays and Rituals*. New York, NY: New York University Press. Pp. 3–40.

Ferber, E. (2001) *Roast Beef, Medium: The Business Adventures of Emma McChesney*. Champaign, IL: University of Illinois Press.

Gagliardi, P. (ed.) (1992) *Symbols and Artifacts: Views of the Corporate Landscape*. Berlin: de Gruyter.

Gell, A. (1992) 'The Enchantment of Technology and the Technology of Enchantment'. In, J. Coote and A. Shelton (eds) *Anthropology, Art and Aesthetics*. Oxford: Oxford University Press. Pp. 40–63.

Golby, J.M. and Purdue A.W. (2000) *The Making of the Modern Christmas*. Stroud: Sutton Publishing.

Hancock, P. (2019) 'Organisational Magic and the Making of Christmas: On Glamour, Grottos and Enchantment'. *Organization* 27(6): 797–816.

Hutton, R. (1996) *The Stations of the Sun: A History of the Ritual Year in Britain.* Oxford: Oxford University Press.

Jarman-Ivens, F. (2008) 'The Musical Underbelly of Christmas'. In, S. Whiteley (ed.) *Christmas, Ideology and Popular Culture.* Edinburgh: Edinburgh University Press. Pp. 113–134.

Johnes, M. (2016) *Christmas and the British: A Modern History.* London: Bloomsbury.

Julmi, C. (2016) 'The Concept of Atmosphere in Management and Organization Studies'. *Organizational Aesthetics* 6(1): 4–30.

Kotler, P. (1974) 'Atmospherics as a Marketing Tool'. *Journal of Retailing* 49(4): 48–64.

Leeder, M. (2017) 'The Haunting of Film Theory'. In, *The Modern Supernatural and the Beginnings of Cinema.* London: Palgrave Macmillan.

Lefebvre, H. (1991) *The Production of Space* (trans. D. Nicholson-Smith). Oxford: Blackwell.

Lévi-Strauss, C. (1987) *Introduction to the Work of Marcel Mauss* (trans. F. Baker). London: Routledge.

Malinowski, B. (2011) *Magic, Science, Religion and Other Essays.* London: Souvenir Press.

Marcus, G. (2011) *Lipstick Traces: A Secret History of the Twentieth Century.* London: Faber and Faber.

Mauss, M. (2001) *A General Theory of Magic* (trans. R. Brain). London: Routledge.

Miles, C.A. (1912) *Christmas in Ritual and Tradition, Christian and Pagan.* London: T. Fisher Unwin.

Miller, D. (1993) 'A Theory of Christmas'. In, D. Miller (ed.) *Unwrapping Christmas.* Oxford: Oxford University Press. Pp. 3–37.

Mundy, J. (2008) 'Christmas and the Movies: Frames of Mind'. In, S. Whiteley (ed.) *Christmas, Ideology and Popular Culture.* Edinburgh: Edinburgh University Press. Pp. 164–176.

Nissenbaum, S. (1997) *The Battle for Christmas: A Cultural History of America's Most Cherished Holiday.* New York, NY: Vintage Books.

Nowell-Smith, G. (1997) 'General Introduction'. In, G. Nowell-Smith (ed.) *The Oxford History of World Cinema: The Definitive History of Cinema Worldwide.* Oxford: Oxford University Press. Pp. xix–xxii.

O'Connor, M. (2007) *The Tree at Rockefeller Centre: A Holiday Tradition.* New York, NY: Melcher.

Orlikowski, W.J. (2007) 'Sociomaterial Practices: Exploring Technology at Work'. *Organization Studies* 28(9): 1435–1448.

Orlikowski, W.J. (2010) 'The Sociomateriality of Organizational Life: Considering Technology in Management Research'. *Cambridge Journal of Economic* 34(1): 125–141.

Patel, S. (2008) *The Christmas Companion: A Merry Little Book of Festive Fun and Trivia.* London: Think Books.

Petter, O. (2018) 'Listening to Too Much Christmas Music is Bad For Your Health', *The Independent.* Monday, December 17.

Strati, A. (1999) *Organization and Aesthetics.* London: Sage.

Street, S. (2000) 'Christmas Under Fire: The Wartime Christmas in Britain'. In, M. Connelly (ed.) *Christmas at the Movies: Images of Christmas in American, British and European Cinema.* London: I.B. Tauris. Pp. 77–95.

Styers, R. (2013) 'Magic and the Play of Power'. In, B. Otto and M. Stausberg (eds) *Defining Magic: A Reader*. London: Routledge. Pp. 255–262.

Swiss, T. (2008) 'Popular Culture and Christmas: A Nomad at Home'. In, S. Whiteley (ed.) *Christmas, Ideology and Popular Culture*. Edinburgh: Edinburgh University Press. Pp. 179–187.

Weightman, G. and Humphries, S. (1987) *Christmas Past*. London: Sidgwick & Jackson.

Whiteley, S. (2008) 'Christmas Songs – Sentiments and Subjectivities'. In, S. Whiteley (ed.) *Christmas, Ideology and Popular Culture*. Edinburgh: Edinburgh University Press. Pp. 98–112.

4

WORKING AT CHRISTMAS

Introduction

To be a success, every Christmas relies on the efforts of a vast seasonal as well as permanent workforce. Even Santa Claus himself, one of the hardest workers at Christmas, relies on a supporting cast of everything from professional set designers and engineers to temporary and part-time helpers to bring festive fun to the masses. At the same time, of course, many people work at Christmas even if their job appears to have little to do with the expectations of the season (Spicer and Cederström, 2014). In the UK, for example, and according to estimates by the *Trade Union Congress*,[1] in 2019, well over a million people were required to work on Christmas Day, with care workers and nurses perhaps unsurprisingly topping this festive chart, with hospitality staff close runners up.

Not that working over the holiday season is necessarily unwelcome. For some, it can provide an opportunity to earn extra income, often at enhanced rates, while for others, it can be a distraction from the loneliness or alienation they might feel at this time of year. For many, while perhaps not a happy obligation, it is just part of the job. It varies. Similarly, how people experience the possible trials and tribulations of working over Christmas can also vary depending on occupational and demographic factors. While it might mean nothing to many, for some younger people it is often a time when work can be combined with impromptu celebratory activities, especially if the job already involves a significant social dimension, such as in say retail or hospitality. Alternatively, and especially for those with family and other caring responsibilities, the intensification of work that often characterizes the months of November and

DOI: 10.4324/9781315637969-5

December can add to the myriad of personal and domestic pressures associated with the festivities.

Nor does Christmas solely involve paid labour. Given the values and ethos associated with it, voluntary and unpaid work is also an important feature of the festive period. There are many examples of charitable organizations that have, in one way or another, become synonymous with recruiting additional voluntary support over the season. Homeless support charities, hospitals, and those associated with children in need, in particular, are often responsible for providing opportunities for thousands of volunteers to contribute to the social good over Christmas.[2]

In this chapter, while I cannot offer an exhaustive account of all forms of labour that contribute to the organisation of Christmas, I consider some of the work that often contributes to making Christmas happen, often in very different ways. Moreover, I explore not only the contexts – spatial, economic and, of course, seasonal – that such work takes place within, but also the emotional and aesthetic demands that working at Christmas places on people. As such, as well as a historical overview, what I offer here is several snapshots of work in different sectors of the economy so as to generate a sense of both the specificities and commonalities of such work, as well as some of the background debates surrounding how work, Christmas, and organization, frequently intersect.

Seasonal Labours

First and foremost, it needs to be recognized that whether Christmas is considered a time of work or leisure is entwined closely with questions of class, gender, occupational status, and other forms of social stratification. From personal experience, I remember my days as a young man working as a relatively lowly technician in the British *National Health Service*. This role meant that the only leave I was typically entitled to over the festive period was the statutory holidays of December 25 and 26 and January 1. I was, of course, allowed to book additional days of annual leave to supplement these, but these were strictly rationed and, given my junior status, I usually missed out. Not that I would have complained. These few statutory days were often more than some of my colleagues in, for example, nursing, could be sure to receive.

Today, however, as a university professor, I usually expect at least eight working days away from my desk while I frequently encounter other professionals discussing how by December 20, they have 'finished for Christmas' and do not expect to return until at least the first Monday after New Year's Day. At the same time, I also know many people who work in the entertainment and hospitality industries for whom Christmas, including the day itself, is the most intensive working period of the year. Indeed, many of them rely on what they can earn throughout Christmas to provide an income capable of sustaining them throughout the year.

Social expectations surrounding the relationship between work and Christmas have also varied throughout history. As I discussed in Chapter 1, the pre-Christian origins of the season are to be found during a time when mid-winter offered a natural respite from the labours of the year. A lack of daylight, dormant crops, falling temperatures, and all being well, the attractions of a bountiful harvest and plentiful provisions combined to bring people together in collective expressions of reverence, solidarity, and occasional licentiousness (Forbes, 2007), allowing them to forgo their labours for at least a brief time. By the Middle Ages, the 'twelve days of Christmas' encompassed several holy days and ran from December 25 to Epiphany on January 6 becoming an almost continuous period of celebration when work took a back seat. In fact, many agricultural workers could expect additional time off until the day after what, in some parts, was called Plough Monday, the first Monday after Epiphany, when the farming year recommenced (Struthers, 2012).

Not that one should get too starry-eyed over the degree to which work halted during this period. The extent to which such predominantly religious holidays were actually observed remains uncertain (Pimlott, 1978), while women, servants, and the like would be expected to carry out their domestic duties as usual throughout the holiday. Furthermore, as formally organized Christmas entertainment became de rigueur, especially at the royal courts and aristocratic houses (Harrison, 1951), minstrels, actors, and other wandering entertainers would have started to find this a particularly profitable time of year. As such, they would hardly have been likely to reduce their labours, something that remains, as I have noted above, true to this day.

Nonetheless, it is probably fair to say that for many, the twelve days of Christmas were a period of some respite and one that remained so for several centuries. However, by the late sixteenth century, processes of social and economic differentiation started to take hold, and urban centres commenced their growth in influence and attraction, making the likelihood that most of the population could simultaneously down tools for around two weeks of the year a far less realistic possibility (Armstrong, 2010). And it was only in the mid-1800s, as Christmas started to reassert itself as a national festival, that questions surrounding just how much relief from work people should receive to celebrate it began to reopen. Having become a more pressing matter due to the demanding conditions brought about by the industrialization of many workplaces and the introduction of regimented regimes of clock-based discipline (Thompson, 1967), for the first time in around two hundred years, Christmas became a meaningful arena of social contestation, this time over the limits of work and the right to leisure.

With the Restoration, Christmas Day in England and Wales had regained its status as a religious holiday, while over 200 years later, in 1871, the 26, Boxing Day, also became a Bank Holiday.[3] By this time, however, actual practices in respect of paid holidays varied dramatically due to local customs and the power of often unscrupulous factory owners, which frequently resulted in little or no time off being given at all (Armstrong, 2010). Indeed, over the course of the century and beyond, several struggles and negotiations took place around how paid labour over Christmas should be organized and what holidays employees were entitled to. In the burgeoning manufacturing sector, for example, workers and their representatives increasingly lobbied to be allowed at least two consecutive days off at Christmas, something that did not become the norm until well into the late nineteenth century (Weightman and Humphries, 1987).

Even where such demands were successful, this second day was granted mainly to enable family members working in industrial towns and cities to visit familial homes, particularly as the improving rail networks continued to operate on Christmas Day. And while this opportunity was most likely welcomed by those workers who could take advantage of it, as Weightman and Humphries (1987: 88) acknowledge, it also represented a further expression of the kind of Victorian paternalism we have already seen in operation in that it was considered better to facilitate Christmas as a time for family celebrations that would unite 'sons and daughters living away from home with their parents', rather than allow them to fall foul of the increasingly ubiquitous 'temptations' to be found in the industrial towns and cities.

Such struggles were not just true of manufacturing, however, but were also taking place in sectors such as retail which, as we know, depends heavily on the season for profitability and often survival. As Johnes (2016) observes, issues such as whether employers should award a compensatory day's holiday to shop workers when say, Christmas Day fell on a Sunday or, indeed, even if such holidays should be paid at all, also continued to be disputed well into the nineteenth and even twentieth centuries. By 1913 the campaign to encourage people to 'shop early for Christmas' was also gaining momentum. Surprisingly, this was mainly promoted to reduce the burden on shopworkers and prevent them from being overwhelmed in those last weeks before the big day. Indeed, this was a matter of such concern that the campaign even gained royal support when, in 1923, the Queen and Princess Mary issued a statement attesting to its virtues and their own practice of early seasonal shopping so as not to overburden those employed in the retail sector.

Christmas at Work

Today, December 25 is a public holiday across the UK, Europe, and the US, while December 26 is recognized throughout most of Europe and many states in North America. This is not to say that there exists a concomitant right not to work on these dates, depending as it does on one's individual or collective contractual conditions. After all, as noted, many still have to work over Christmas even where such provisions are in place. Not that paid time off is the only benefit many employees expect during the season.

The Victorian emphasis on Christmas as a philanthropic time also spilt over into a hope, if not an expectation, that employees would exercise a broader ethos of generosity during the festivities. Early contemporary illustrations of such seasonal benevolence often took the form of Christmas gifts or 'boxes' being given to employees, with Neil Armstrong (2010) citing the example of food hampers being distributed to Coleman's mustard factory employees during the late 1800s. Similarly, for those working in domestic service, Christmas might have entailed being given not only a small and practical gift but also a Christmas party. This would have been held in the servant's quarters, with small amounts of Christmas food and drink provided by the family for the amusement of their staff. More recently, while the giving of Christmas gifts at work has declined, along with the payment of Christmas bonuses which are increasingly limited to specific sectors of the economy, most notably finance, the personal exchange of Christmas gifts does continue within some companies and industries (Lemmergaard and Muhr, 2011). These often take the form, if not explicitly, of a potlatch arrangement (Mauss, 1954) by which, in a not dissimilar manner to the royal courts of the sixteenth and seventeenth centuries, professional favours and alliances are formed, and debts both established and honoured through such gifting.

One common alternative to the Christmas gift that remains popular, if albeit increasingly maligned, is the office or workplace Christmas party. Customarily provided and paid for by the employer such events were immortalized in literary fiction by Dickens's (2006) description of the young Scrooge's attendance at Fezziwig's Georgian Christmas Eve party. While as with much of Dickens's take on Christmas, it was a somewhat idealized representation of actual practices at the time, by the late 1800s such events were becoming an annual occurrence across many industries in the UK (Johnes, 2016), bringing employees of all ranks together in celebration. Going from strength to strength throughout the twentieth century and arguably fully hitting their stride from the 1950s onwards (Mistry, 2017), such parties were frequently repositories of older Christmas traditions including the kinds of topsy-turvy inversions of authority discussed in Chapter 1. Indeed they developed a reputation for a degree of impropriety that might be considered verging on the Saturnalian (Gander, 2015) which still haunts them today.[4] And not only are they the subject of jokes, stories, and folklore, but they also have, from the perspective of organization studies at least, become one of the few aspects of Christmas that have generated any consistent research interest amongst those working in the field.

Academics such as Michael Rosen (1988), Ann Rippin (2011), and Anna Laura Hidegh (2015) have all, in particular, explored the role such events can play in both facilitating shared seasonal feelings of celebration and goodwill, as well as helping to ritually cement organizational cultures by temporarily suspending institutional hierarchies and allowing daily grievances to be forgotten. With their origins in the activities of medieval guilds that would celebrate the feast days of their patron saints (Rippin, 2011), contemporary workplace parties are particularly understood as organizational practices geared towards nurturing corporate loyalty and identification. They are what Rosen (1988: 478–479) describes as events 'where one is loved and may love' and where seemingly affective bonds can be placed above the usual instrumentality of corporate relations. Furthermore, drawing on shared symbolic repertoires and seasonal idealizations, including dressing, eating, and even playing various Christmas games together (Hidegh and Primecz, 2020), they help renew solidarities and relations of mutual identification between colleagues and the organization writ large.

For those charged with organizing them, there seems to be an emerging view, however, that they are becoming more trouble than they are worth, especially when it comes to their potentially negative impact on organisational reputation. Early concerns about such events emerged during the 1990s based on the fact that given they ostensively celebrate a predominantly Christian festival in what are increasingly multi-cultural workplaces[5] they are not only insensitive but potentially divisive. More recently, concerns have also started to focus on issues of workplace sexual harassment and how Christmas parties are increasingly reported as something of a hotspot for such problems (McGuinness, 2013; Hancock and Tyler, 2017).

This has led to organizations such as the UK's *Chartered Institute for Personal Directors*, the professional body for HR managers, providing specialist training on how to 'manage' Christmas celebrations in the workplace (Meves, 2017). At the same time, independent advisory and legal firms are increasingly offering procedural guidelines for employers during the festive season. Characteristic of such advice is reminding managers that their staff remain subject to company regulations and the law during such events and that anybody contravening them should be subject to regular disciplinary action. Other less punitive suggestions include prohibiting alcohol at events or running them as family occasions, encouraging partners, spouses, and children to attend. In 2019 accountancy firm BDO even started to provide senior managers as 'sober chaperones' at its departmental parties in London (Brown, 2019).

Certainly, having attended training events on this subject myself, I have experienced the seriousness with which employers increasingly take these events as a potential threat to corporate reputations. The dangers of social media usage, primarily through photographic apps, are particularly stressed at such gatherings, with HR managers advised that any photographs taken not only at, but on the way to and leaving such parties, should not be posted on such media and to do so should be considered a disciplinary offence. While it was difficult to ascertain how many of the HR managers present would really wish to oversee or implement such a policy, there was a clear sense that while Christmas parties might indeed have once fulfilled a critical integrative function, they have become increasingly unattractive to many organizational leaders requiring, as they do, what seems to be an extension of more formal and visible disciplinary practices that would effectivity undermine any existing cultural benefit they possess.

Seasonal Work and Festive Conditions

There is, of course, far more to the relationship between work and the organization of Christmas than workplace parties, important as they might be. In those countries where Christmas is officially celebrated, and increasingly in those where it has become an unofficial event, the season represents a period of intense workplace activity not only for those already in employment but also for a large reserve army of seasonal workers. Moreover, while this impacts all sectors, nowhere is this truer than in retail. In 2021, for example, the UK's largest supermarket chain *Tesco* (Williams-Grut, 2021) looked to employ an additional 30,000 staff across the country to see them through the Christmas period, many of whom would find themselves adorned in t-shirts covered in Christmas decorations and featuring festive slogans such as 'Christmas? Bring it on!' (Figure 4.1).

At the same time, online retail giant *Amazon*[6] created 20,000 seasonal jobs across the UK while offering one-off bonus payments of between £1,000 and £3,000 to existing and potential employees. Furthermore, a similar pattern can be seen across many other countries with, for example, over half a million seasonal positions purportedly created each year in the US, particularly in retail and distribution.[7]

High demand for temporary staff is also common in industries such as hospitality, especially in bars and restaurants, that depend on buoyant Christmas trading. Here seasonal staff often work long hours right throughout Christmas facing frequent exposure to the worst that the industry can throw at them in the form of impatient, rude, and often inebriated customers (Stephens and Stephens, 2016) and increased levels of well-established workplace problems such as sexual harassment (McDonald, 2012). Yet despite this, several discussions I have had with such seasonal employees over the years have also suggested more of an ambivalent attitude towards the opportunities and challenges thrown up by such work. For while being quite aware that the work is particularly taxing and often characterized by intoxicated patrons who are overly demanding, if not downright aggressive or intimidating, they seem generally happy to endure this not only because of the ready availability of work and money but also, it would appear, the camaraderie amongst staff that often emerges at this time of year.

FIGURE 4.1 Supermarket employee in a Christmas t-shirt. Photograph by the author.

As one student who regularly works as a waitress over the Christmas period told me:

It can be pretty manic, and customers can be very petty and sometimes quite nasty. But it's a time when everyone I work with seems more up for a laugh.

Even the manager's a bit more laid back. Of course, we have to get stuff right, but it seems to be done with more of a smile on everyone's face. It's fun.

Furthermore, each year the popular press runs numerous articles on those who are required to work, especially in the retail and service sector, during or over the run-up to Christmas (Wallop, 2015; Bakar, 2019), exploring the demands and pleasures of working on the festive front line. While many of these workers report less favourably on particular seasonal demands, from the additional emotional labour often required to appear in the required Christmas spirit (Edwards, 2017) to coping with unpleasantly low temperatures as retailers leave external doors open to entice in extra custom from the even colder outside (Gadd, 2014), again many also find it to be a time when workplace camaraderie and the spirit of the season can help mitigate its worst excesses (Wallop, 2015).

A noticeable change in UK retail that has had something of an impact on the seasonal workforce is the increasing popularity of pre-Christmas discount events such as Black Friday. While many of the more sensationalist stories reported about such events in the mass media – particularly tales of assault and injury[8] – are not reflected in my own discussions around this subject; there is no doubt that such events add additional stress for some of the retail employees I spoke with. Even with, according to a 2019 survey by auditors *PWC*, 49% of UK shoppers claiming not to be interested in such events or not believing the deals are genuine,[9] descriptions of such discount days I encountered ranged from 'crazy' to 'a bit scary', with a general feeling of annoyance evident among employees that shoppers seem to use such events to excuse behaviours and a lack of concern for others that they would normally consider unconscionable.

Nonetheless, retail workers I spoke to noted that such events are short lived and that everything quickly returns to the 'normal', if still somewhat challenging, pre-Christmas panics and pressures that customers often project onto staff, particularly as the big day gets nearer. This is reflected in a somewhat off-the-cuff comment by one store worker I spoke with who observed, almost gleefully, that 'it's quite funny to see the fear in some their eyes when you tell them we won't have this or that in again before Christmas'. Once again, therefore, despite the intensification in work and other pressures the season can bring, some workers continue to find their festive pleasure where they can.

This pleasure in Christmas work is also reflected in one of the most interesting academic studies of working in the run-up to Christmas, Bozkurt's (2015) participant research into work on a UK supermarket delicatessen counter during the Christmas season. From it, she derives a telling insight into both the pains and pleasures of customer-facing labour during the festive season. As already observed, Christmas is a significant time of the year for retail, especially in supermarkets. Requiring a combination of both increased hours for part-time employees already in situ and the employment of temporary, seasonal staff,

Bozkurt documents how Christmas in this particular supermarket required not only longer and far busier working hours but also greater flexibility in the kinds of duties undertaken by staff. This was especially true in terms of the additional expectations surrounding product knowledge and delivery skills, as well as the enhanced practices of emotional labour required when dealing with both fellow employees and customers and who were often under immense strain due to working longer hours while trying to prepare for the festivities themselves.

The research also identifies, however, the increased meaning that she and many of her colleagues derived from the enhanced operational discretion that Christmas working allowed them due to increased pressure on the chain of command. For example, in the case of reducing the prices of certain items as they reached the end of their shelf-life, often supervisors would delegate this responsibility to whoever was on hand such that, as Bozkurt (2015: 489) observes:

> the extreme work of Christmas was, while difficult, frustrating, and at odds with other seasonal obligations, greeted largely with enthusiasm by the deli counter workers, like a temporary upgrading of the significance of their jobs.

This increased sense of meaning and identification with their jobs was also enhanced, in a similar vein to the attitudes and experiences I identified earlier, by an increase in the relative camaraderie in everyday workplace interactions and the opportunities that Christmas provided for more significant social interactions. Furthermore, it extended well beyond the boundaries of the immediate workplace and encouraged staff to interact with colleagues through parties and more informal gatherings that contributed to a sense of seemingly, at the time, communal fun and a sense of a shared endeavour.

However, not all work that takes on an additional dimension at Christmas is as evident as that in major retail outlets such as supermarkets. Nor are the extra demands made during Christmas always greeted so enthusiastically. While not an area of employment that receives much coverage during the festive season, women working in the sex industry, for example, paint a very mixed picture when it comes to working at Christmas. Some, it would seem, do indeed report real advantages to working during the season, telling tales of Christmas bonuses, gifts, and other perks of the job, including being invited to Christmas parties and other seasonal 'events' (Kane, 2017; Fallowfield, 2021). However, for most, it can be a particularly challenging time of year.

With business traditionally quiet in January, as well as on Christmas Day itself, and with the financial pressures the same as for so many others at this time of year (Bishop, 2008), many working in the industry feel pressured to take on more clients in the run-up to Christmas. As a consequence of this, they feel less able to be selective to whom they offer their services (Jones, 2015), often putting them at increased risk from men leaving parties drunk or under the influence of other intoxicants and, as such, often prone to violence (MacNamee, 2017). Even when this is not a problem, at what can be a lonely time of the year, many clients reportedly need comfort and reassurance more than sexual release (Chester, 2020). This often places workers in a difficult situation, feeling ill-equipped to give the kind of advice they think their clients need. As one escort reported to the BBC (Mayfair, 2018):

> Christmas is an emotional time for lots of us – for an escort this means that there is a lot more emotional labour involved. Often, I end up hearing about a lot of failing marriages, loneliness and work pressures. Once, a client booked me for a few days before Christmas we went to a lovely hotel, had a few drinks and then he just broke down. He was going through a divorce and it was the first Christmas that he would be spending without his kids.

Add to this the personal loneliness and social isolation that often accompanies sex work due to the stigma still attached to it in most societies, and which is often exacerbated at Christmas (Graham, 2016; Brown, 2018), and one can understand why the season is far from necessarily a jolly affair for those working in this sector of the service economy.

Delivering Christmas

As I noted in the introduction to this chapter, it would be impossible to consider all those whose work helps make Christmas happen, either by being directly involved in some aspect of the delivery of seasonal goods and services, or by simply carrying out their day-to-day jobs. One occupation that has become indelibly linked with Christmas, however, and which is charged with bringing a little bit of seasonal cheer to many a household is that of the postal worker, especially those working in postal delivery who deliver cards and parcels throughout the season. As we know, one of the innovations during its Victorian resurrection was the popularization of Christmas cards and the introduction of an affordable postal system that ensured their timely and cost-effective passage from household to household (Golby and Purdue, 2000). Since then, these two developments have become closely entwined with the expectations and anticipations associated with the season. Indeed, one of the most recognized Christmas symbols, the red-breasted Robin, became popularized especially as a motif on Christmas cards due to its association with red-tunicked English postmen of the 1800s (Pimlott, 1978).

As the twentieth century evolved, Christmas cards were gradually joined by gifts and deliveries of all types, especially with the rise of catalogue shopping that began in earnest during the Edwardian era. By 1913, the number of cards and parcels had increased year on year, with the London Post Office alone having recruited an extra 10,500 staff over the festive period to meet demand (Armstrong, 2010). While many of these additional recruits worked in various sorting offices, the postal delivery staff bore much of the burden of the Christmas delivery schedules. Indeed, until delivery workers campaigned against this practice in 1960, a regular morning delivery was expected on Christmas Day itself. Not that opposition amongst the workforce should be all that surprising given the nature of some of the deliveries they were expected to make, with Johnes (2016: 190) noting how, at the time, it could even involve delivering Christmas dinner in the form of 'heavy turkeys' to impatient housewives. One can only hope, at least for the postie's sake, if not the turkeys, that they were already dead.

More recently, advances in sorting and logistical technologies, alongside the popularity of private global couriers and delivery companies, have somewhat eased the burden on traditional postal services at Christmas. Nonetheless, the overall trend remains one of increasing public demand. In 2016, for instance, the Royal Mail handled a staggering 750 million Christmas cards,[10] along with an additional 130 million parcels.[11] By 2018, to be able to manage this seasonal demand as well as opening additional sorting centres around the country[12] the Royal Mail had to employ around 23,000 extra Christmas workers who started between the end of October and the middle of November and worked through until the day before Christmas Eve. Furthermore, although the company may have engaged in questionable advertising by making promises such as the availability of "exciting parcels and letters" during the Christmas season, there is no indication that such seasonal employment is viewed unfavorably. In fact, based on reviews posted on relevant websites, it appears that only a minority of individuals who have worked for Royal Mail during the holiday season have expressed dissatisfaction with the work or its conditions.

Factory Work for Christmas

There is, of course, more to working at Christmas than retail and service work. Christmas is when demand for all kinds of manufactured goods increases, and, as we have already observed, if we are to consider the significance of manufacturing work to the organization of Christmas, it is to China and Southeast Asia that we must look, and the city of Yiwu, as mentioned previously in Chapter 2. Around 90% of the world's Christmas decorations and associated novelties are manufactured here, and to produce what many would consider the raw materials necessary for the Christmas season often requires long hours and uncomfortable working conditions for those employed in one of the city's 600 factories (Wainwright, 2014). Not only do these factories manufacture Christmas on an industrial scale, however, but they also depart quite dramatically from any image one might harbour of a real-life Santa's workshop (Chamberlain, 2016). For while the products might speak of magic, goodwill, and generosity, such values rarely seem to define the lives and experiences of those charged with making them.

For example, reports from the city, such as that by Oliver Wainwright (2014), have identified issues such as factory employees – mainly migrant labourers – being required to work over 12 hours a day for little more than £200 to £300 a month in what are often dangerously toxic conditions. Here they are described in 2014 by BBC journalist Tim Maughan (2014):

> Upstairs is the plastic moulding room, mainly staffed by young men, stripped to the waist because of the heat. The air here is thick with fumes, the smell of chemicals and warm plastic. The men feed plastic pellets from Samsung-branded sacks into machines to be melted down, and then pressed into moulds to make toy snowmen and Father Christmases. It's repetitive, and potentially dangerous, as the workers must constantly reach inside the large presses.

It is not just in Yiwu that such conditions are found, however. In 2007, the US-based *National Labor Committee* produced its report 'A Wal-Mart Christmas' that documented the illegal and dangerous working conditions faced by young people at the vast Guanzhou Huanya ornaments factory in the Guangdong province (Kernaghan et al., 2007). Here they found that the employees – often children – worked an average of 77 hours a week, rising to 105 hours in many instances. This was for rates of pay that were often half the legal minimum rate in China and under conditions that breached even the country's relatively lax safety laws.

The production of Christmas decorations and novelties only tells part of the story, however. Similar concerns have been raised about the working conditions of those producing most of the world's toys, another staple of the Christmas market. In November 2017, a report entitled 'The Dark Side of the Toy World' by the US-based NGO *China Labor Watch* identified a string of labour law violations and abuses of workers' rights, along with at least two suicides associated with working conditions. For example, Yang Zongfang, an employee of ten years in one factory, threw himself to his death having been fired for allowing other workers to use his factory entry card (*China Labor Watch*, 2017: 5). Wage levels were so low that workers were effectively forced to work illegal amounts of overtime to make ends meet, while unknowingly being exposed to dangerous levels of chemical pollution. In addition, dormitories made necessary by the long hours were reportedly overcrowded and unsanitary, while stories of excessively punitive disciplinary measures by factory management were standard.

Some factories have even been accused of utilizing slave prison labour to meet Christmas targets at low cost. For example, in 2019, a six-year-old girl in London opened a box of supermarket charity Christmas cards sold by *Tesco* to find that one of them had already been written in by an inmate of a Chinese prison (Humphrey, 2019):

> 'We are foreign prisoners in Shanghai Qingpu prison China', the message read in capital letters. 'Forced to work against our will. Please help us and notify human rights organization'.

Florence had accidentally stumbled on a chilling link between Christmas and Chinese human rights abuse, forcing the UK supermarket chain *Tesco* to immediately cancel all orders from such factories (Siddique, 2019).

As such, despite the image that many of us might wish to hold onto of happy elves fuelled by hot chocolate and nestled in a cosy, magical workshop somewhere in the Arctic, the reality could not be further from the truth. Instead, it is often one of desperate men, women, and children finding themselves at the sharp end of industrial mass production, undergoing hard labour in hot and often dangerous conditions and usually for a pittance of pay. All this to ensure that the world has its seasonal supply of shiny baubles, plastic toys and, somewhat perversely, goodwill to all.

Keeping the Christmas Show on the Road

Alas, few people who keep Christmas, even indirectly, are aware of or take any meaningful interest in the possible plight of such workers. Instead, and whether one approves of it or not, Christmas is considered by most who celebrate it as a carefree and indulgent time. It is a season of fun and, for those who can, of letting one's hair down and taking time out from the world, perhaps by visiting a Christmas show, enjoying a night out at a club, or visiting a festive event. Indeed, if there is one thing that often characterizes Christmas above all else, it is a time when we expect to be entertained. Moreover, for those creative workers employed in the entertainment industry, Christmas is also an important time of the year, albeit often for different reasons. It is when work is usually plentiful, and market forces work in their favour, increasing the demand for their services and the amount people are willing to pay.

Not that this is an entirely novel situation. As we have already seen, Christmas has long provided exposure and often lucrative returns for creatives and performers of all types. From the travelling entertainers of late antiquity and the Middle Ages, through the playwrights and actors of early modern times, to those performers we see today on stage, television, and in venues ranging from inner city cabaret clubs to village halls, it has long been a season when the sun may not always shine, but there is usually hay to be made.

In the UK today, one form of popular entertainment associated closely with Christmas, especially the ideal of a family-centred Christmas, that is impossible to ignore is that of the pantomime. In Chapter 2, I briefly alluded to the characteristics and importance of this theatrical performance style, particularly to the British Christmas. Despite what some might consider to be its somewhat formulaic and even dated style, for many families, visiting a pantomime over the Christmas period remains an essential seasonal ritual. Nor is it quite as parochial as I have just suggested. While remaining a predominantly British theatrical form, since the appearance of US television star and actor Henry Winkler as Captain Hook in a production of Peter Pan at the Liverpool Empire in 2006 (Carpenter, 2009), several US celebrities and stars, including Jimmy Osmond, David Hasselhoff, Pamela Anderson, and Mickey Rooney (Lee, 2014), have all joined British theatrical greats such as Sir Ian McKellen in treading the festive boards.

While this somewhat idiosyncratic combination of musical theatre, slapstick comedy, cross-dressing, double-entendres, and often topical politics is not to everyone's taste, its importance as a commercial art form that provides a significant income for many should not be underestimated. As Millie Taylor (2007), in her fascinating book, *British Pantomime Performance*, observes, while pantomime in the UK is generally dominated by large production companies such as *QDos Entertainment*,[13] both smaller operators and those shows put on by local theatrical repertoire companies continue to flourish across the country. As such, while a company such as *QDos* can invest up to around £500,000 in a production by seeing that investment recouped over several years as the show tours the country's major theatres, smaller operators and in-house productions thrive by utilizing a mix of lesser-known celebrities and local actors to draw in the audiences. Moreover, while for smaller theatres, pantomimes are not, as Taylor (2007: 27) observes, the cash cow they once were, they remain financially significant as by making a small profit or, if not at least only a slight loss, they commonly ensure the theatre's operational viability for the forthcoming year.

Pantomimes also provide employment opportunities for freelance actors, designers, and other performers at a time of the year when their incomes can be even more precarious than usual. Even those US stars mentioned above are, it is suggested, attracted to the top-end of the UK pantomime circuit as much as by the fact that they can earn five-figure sums for around six weeks of work in a traditionally slack time back home (Carpenter, 2009; Lee, 2014), as they are by being part of a British theatrical tradition. Certainly, for some jobbing actors and performers I have spoken to in the UK, December offers a stark choice between either appearing in pantomime, performing as a department store

Santa Claus, or watching the pennies even more closely than usual. Not that the work is itself easy. Performers and actors are still required to negotiate what are often demanding auditions for roles that increasingly require more of their applicants each year. As one acting website reminds would be panto stars:[14]

> Nowadays, you have to be an 'all-rounder' when working in pantomime. You have to act, sing, improvise and dance numerous routines not to mention the essential comic timing and spontaneity. The number of companies using specialist dancers seems to be decreasing year by year as budgets become tighter and the need to utilize a company to maximum effect becomes ever stronger.

As such, there are, as one performer I spoke to told me, fewer and fewer places to hide on a pantomime stage.

Nor is pantomime simply about those on stage. Theatres, especially the smaller provincial ones, also require additional staff throughout the season, particularly in front-of-house, to meet a hoped-for increase in demand for anything from show merchandise to drinks at the bar. Similarly, the creative work of often self-employed and freelance musicians and musical directors ensures these quintessentially Christmas events hit the right note. For one freelance musician I spoke to, pantomimes and Christmas events as a whole represent a significant component of their professional year. As both a keyboard player and musical director, he would expect to work on a pantomime from October, undertaking pre-production such as writing musical arrangements and producing backing tracks, sometimes right through until Easter, with often only one or two days off over the Christmas period itself.

Producing such backing, or 'click-tracks', can involve significant amounts of paid work, especially if the theatre 'orchestra' only consists of a keyboard player and a drummer. Interestingly, the increasing amount of work that often has to go into these accompanying soundtracks is considered to be a result of changed expectations amongst younger audiences in particular:

> If you go back to when I started doing panto over 15 years ago, it would be a drummer doing a 'badum tish' when there was a gag, or when the dame came on, you might play the dame music. Nowadays, because the kids are so used to watching cinematic entertainment, they're used to a bed of sound underneath everything ... So, putting that all together beforehand is quite a significant chunk [of work] and can be an earner.

Such an extended workload can also have its downsides, of course. While the continuity of work and the income associated with it is very welcome, it can be particularly restrictive in terms of one's own ability to enjoy or take anything from the season:

> For me, the kind of issue is when you're so busy working on a Christmas show that you don't have time to enjoy it … I don't even have time to prepare for it [Christmas]. And also, because you're creating this wonderful Christmas atmosphere for everybody else, I struggle to kind of feel that myself.

Alas, this kind of seasonal alienation, even amongst those who enjoy Christmas, is not an uncommon by-product of working intensively to entertain people during the build-up to the festivities. Certainly, having spoken to several gigging entertainers, musicians, and event organizers, a similar tale often comes to the fore. For example, one musician I spoke with explained that while Christmas is undoubtedly the most lucrative time of the year, with more work offered over a three to four-week period than they can accommodate, it can come at a cost. For while there is something special about, as they put it, the 'energy' of a Christmas gig that carries them along, the work of putting on two shows a day can also often detract from their own enjoyment in the build-up to the season which had traditionally always been what they looked forward to most about it. As they put it:

> It's very much a job, you're creating that magic for other people. You never receive that, you never get that kind of warm glowing feeling, certainly with what I do, I've never kind of experience that really.

Despite the absence of such a 'warm glowing feeling', as I have suggested above, the season is crucial for independent performers, as well as events promoters and organizers who also often experience a precarious professional existence. As such, the relative guarantee of work over the period, with entertainers of all kinds often combining significant corporate events with smaller-scale private and company parties, is welcomed (Figure 4.2).

Additionally, due to such demand often exceeding supply, a Christmas premium of often up to a third can be charged on top of regular rates, resulting in the season being described by one interviewee as a 'licence to print money'. Similarly, for many small venues and promoters, December can often account, as in retail, for around a third of their annual turnover – especially when additional corporate Christmas events and New Year's Eve parties are taken into account. As one promoter explained, while their monthly cabaret club nights attract steady custom throughout the year, the Christmas and New Year period is the one time when they can be confident that they will sell out their events.

However, such confidence also requires that a considerable amount of work be put in throughout the year. As the same promoter explained, bands and acts

FIGURE 4.2   Christmas events are an important source of income for many performers. Photograph: Clayton Hartley.

must be booked early in the spring to secure their services for Christmas. At the same time, regarding stand-alone corporate parties, for example, availability enquires are fielded throughout the year, sometimes starting as early as January. However, only around 20% of these will likely be converted into actual bookings, and things can go wrong. One tale recounted the story of a corporate party that had taken months of negotiations to set up, only for it to fall through at the last minute because it transpired that the company individual responsible had booked it on the wrong date. This situation represented a loss of income for the club and the company, which was liable for various cancellation fees, including those of the performers and caterers.

Furthermore, logistical and communication breakdowns are just some of the problems event organizers and promoters encounter at this time of the year. A heightened expectation amongst guests and revellers that at Christmas they 'must have a good time', while often leading to greater expenditure on food and expensive drinks, can also lead to, as one club security office politely put it, 'people acting like bigger idiots'. And while this often plays out as less of a problem on the evening itself, it can have repercussions after the event, especially considering the various social media outlets available for customer feedback. It was noted, for example, how feedback is often far more mixed after seasonal events, with guests often castigating aspects of a club from, for example, reasonable security measures put in place to keep customers safe to its décor or music policy, even when they had been openly advertised as integral to the styling of the venue or event.

While this is a challenge for smaller clubs and venues, for individual entertainers and performers, such expectations combined with excessive festive intoxication can often expose them to more than just negative feedback after the event, however, with rudeness, verbal abuse, and even physical assaults all being reported as more prevalent at this time of year. While some performers seem to take this in their stride, often accepting it as the price they must pay for the relative abundance of work on offer during the season, for some, and especially those whose acts bring them into particularly close contact with members of the public, it can be somewhat distressing. Combined with the general fatigue that often sets in during the season, a consequence of the intensive workload and the often excessively repetitive nature of the performance demanded – 'you've sang *Santa Baby* or *Have Yourself a Merry Little Christmas* so many times' – one experienced cabaret performer lamented the usually unrecognized emotional labour that goes into keeping up the Christmas cheer:

> You can have people pawing at you, pulling at you, and shouting at you, and swearing at you. And you know, 'if you don't do what I want you've ruined my fucking Christmas'. It's really hard to keep kind of smiling and say 'yes of course madam' while gritting your teeth. That's really hard.

Elf and Safety

Musicians and singers are only some of the creative workers for whom the demand for a magical Christmas experience is a significant opportunity to secure work. Another more unusual but seasonally ubiquitous example is that of performers who take on the character of Santa's helpers or Christmas elves. Generally involving either entertaining children and their parents or guardians as they queue to meet and greet Santa Claus in one of his many seasonal grottos, or attending private or corporate Christmas parties and events, this is a role immortalized in the written work of the American humourist David Sedaris (1999) and his *Santaland Diaries*. Regaling the reader of his Christmas spent working as an elf at *Macy's* department store in New York, Sedaris tells tales of his encounters with bullying parents, vomiting children and curiously flirtatious fellow elves, stories that reflect many aspects of my own discussions and interviews with such performers.

While I was aware that young men occasionally performed this role, as in Sedaris's case, most performers I encountered tended to be young women between their early 20s and 30s who were either drama students, jobbing theatrical performers, or semi-professional children's entertainers. Often employed by freelance agencies specializing in events marketing and public relations and, while not necessarily self-employed as many of the performers and musicians I spoke to are, they were also subject to equally precarious employment conditions (Kalleberg, 2009) characterized by relatively low wages and zero-hours contracts. An interesting exception to this, however, were those usually older women who, rather than portraying elves, performed as various incarnations of Mrs Santa Claus, a character far more commonly seen at Santa's side in the US and northern countries of continental Europe.

Indeed, the Mrs Claus performers I spoke to often tended to be married or partnered with the male Santa Claus performers with whom they worked. Interestingly, while the couples commonly perform as teams, there is a visible and functional distinction between the American, and UK and European portrayals of the characters. Perhaps the most immediate difference is in the style of dress.[15] The American Mrs Claus tends to present themselves in a somewhat glamorous manner, often peroxide blonde and bejewelled; they usually wear the same red velvet outfits and white fur as their male partners, albeit with a somewhat more fitted cut. Furthermore, they take on a more notably proactive 'Santa' type role, discussing possible gifts and quizzing children on their behaviour.

Indeed, those I spoke to consider their role to be one of replicating the activities of their male partners, albeit while adding a touch of glitz to the proceedings. In contrast, their UK and European counterparts adopt a more differentiated look and identity. Commonly appearing in cotton pinafore dresses replete with aprons and lace-trimmed bonnets, they present a far more traditional homemaker identity while being more inclined to discuss domestic matters with those they meet, such as how many gingerbread cookies they have to bake each year or how it is not easy to keep the North Pole tidy with all the elves running around. Often appearing at smaller private children's parties, these performers commonly consider their role to be a highly gendered one, namely of reassuring and placating children who might feel intimidated by Santa himself:

> Sometimes, younger children especially, are a little bit scared of Santa. I can step in and either distract or entertain them. It seems to reassure many of them that a kind lady is there as well as a big hairy man … however kindly he is.

The Christmas elves were something of a different festive character, however. Predominantly tasked with operational duties, their primary responsibility tends to be managing the throughput into large commercial grottos and entering children and other visitors as they wait to see a store or shopping mall-based Santa Claus. Naturally, this requires a high degree of flexibility and the possession of numerous skills, including magic and conjuring tricks, child pacification, and logistics. Many also have to keep an eye on the general quality of the experiential dimension of meeting Santa, requiring a degree of human resource management expertise. As one UK-based Elf performer explained in this respect, as well as managing the behaviour and expectations of the visiting children, sometimes, the Santa Claus performer they would be working with might also require 'encouragement' or 'guidance':

> Sometimes they're just old and sleepy, and you just have to keep them on their toes, literally, or you have to go in and wake them up before a child comes in if it's a slow day. Or sometimes they're just a little bit, well not as jolly as they should be. It has been known, somebody saying 'the presents aren't good enough' or 'I'm not going to give these out'. So, quite often we're a bit of a mediator and are talking to the client, and the children, and looking after Santa.

Nonetheless, most of these elfin performers I spoke to consider their work to be predominantly child-focused, ensuring that young visitors – and adults – reach Santa Claus both happy and prepared. Once again, this often involves dealing with both nervous and over-excited children, both of which can present definite challenges:

> You'll get one kid that you have to calm down because they are tearing around and threatening to jump on Santa when they get through the door, and the next is all tearful and quivering like he's off to the dentist or something. Yet your job is to try and get them both in the right frame of mind.

As is now evidently common to much service work, especially at Christmas, such activities involve aesthetic skills concerning self-presentation and copious amounts of emotional labour. This is because performers are required to manage not only their own emotional responses towards the children but also have a positive impact on the emotional state of all their visitors as well. As one performer told me, making children happy is usually a relatively straightforward task, while adults, on the other hand, can be somewhat more demanding:

> With parents, there can be such conflict because you can see when you're making a child happy, and you can make them the worst model balloon in the world, but they've really enjoyed seeing you make it and you giving them that attention, whereas a parent says 'No, no, I wanted the reindeer hats'.

Whatever the demands placed on the performers I spoke to in the UK, however, those faced by their counterparts who work in the kinds of specialist Christmas resorts found in places such as Rovaniemi and Saariselkä in Finnish Lapland were often even more intense. Like tourist centres worldwide, Christmas in Finnish Lapland relies heavily on the labour of relatively low-paid and usually young workers employed mainly on seasonal contracts of only one to three months (García-Rosell and Hancock, 2022). Once again, it is predominantly young women who are employed as elves and whose duties include meeting tourists at local airports, accompanying them back to the resorts, entertaining them throughout their stay, and acting as guides to the various activities on offer. Unlike their UK counterparts, however, this often requires a sustained performance that adheres far more closely to what is described in the official recruitment documentation as a 'magical' elfin identity, particularly in respect of the everyday use of a more childlike style of speech and an infantile demeanour and behaviour.

It was clear from the conversations I was able to have with some of these performers, however, that while they enjoy the opportunity to work in what they consider to be a somewhat novel physical and cultural environment, many found the work to be more physically and emotionally demanding than they anticipated, especially the need to always 'be on' or in character. Not that they should have been entirely surprised by this. As the following extract from a recruitment website[16] indicates that the performative demands of bringing Christmas magic to visitors cannot be taken lightly:

> Elves are only ever seen by our guests as Elves and not in any other capacity in order to keep the believability. This involves character work, endless energy and a love for Christmas magic. You must adhere to the Elf character at all times.
>
> A comprehensive and constant commitment to the Santa story is essential and a desire to make all our guests' dreams come true. Only committed and

responsible applicants with previous experience and training in acting, as well as a love of Christmas will be considered.

The intensity of such demands for emotional and aesthetic labour and to 'adhere to the Elf character at all times' is further compounded by the requirement to work for days at a time in sub-zero temperatures and an environment that is devoid of natural daylight and dealing with visitors who were often tired and disorientated from what was a 5,000 km day trip. Then after Christmas, the amount of work and the need for seasonal workers inevitably decreases, and while a small elite of employees are kept on throughout the year, most of these young employees see their contracts end throughout the spring.

It is not only a precarious human workforce that is employed to perform the magic of Christmas, however. Such resorts also rely heavily on seasonal animals such as huskies and reindeer (Valtonen, 2009), which are also integral to the entertainment of visitors. While huskies especially play an essential role in Lapland tourism (García-Rosell and Tallberg, 2021), nothing is as popular with tourists as the presence of reindeer. Traditionally draught animals, they embody the combined magic of both the festive season and the arctic landscape. Being there to greet tourists as they arrive at local airports, taking them on sleigh rides, often to see Santa Claus himself, and being accessible for petting and feeding, they have become as central as snow and pine trees to the Christmas aesthetic of Lapland, entertaining visitors simply by their very presence.

However, no matter how important, this only protects some of these animals from an even more precarious existence than their human counterparts. Even though reindeer cultivation remains a vital ingredient of the indigenous economy of Lapland, there remains something distastefully curious about the fact that such animals are not only objectified, as indeed are their human counterparts (García-Rosell and Hancock, 2022), as objects of a tourist gaze (Urry, 1990) but also as material souvenirs of the experience. For while it is the skilled castrated male reindeer who become, for the tourists at least, the truly magical ones, smaller, and in particular female reindeer are reduced to another form of fleshy commodity. Often only briefly seen by tourists, these reindeer are quickly reduced to the utility of flesh, skin, and bone and converted to tourist souvenirs – such as the ubiquitous 'reindeer pelt – and a hearty evening meal of Poronkäristys or sautéed reindeer (see Hoarau-Heemstra, 2018).

The labour of entertaining the tourists and making Christmas magical does not end with death, therefore. Instead, in a manner reminiscent of the need for UK stores to encourage visitors to their Christmas attractions to purchase a bit of the seasonal magic to take home, tourists are encouraged, quite literally, to take a piece of this aspect of their Christmas experience away with them. So it is not wholly unusual, if no less uncomfortable, to see, for example, a happy family boarding their return flight with a large plush 'Rudolph' in one bag and several reindeer pelts in another.

Yet no matter how important the elves, reindeer, and other sources of entertainment might be to the Christmas experience, there is one character who retains a preeminent position when it comes to truly bringing the magic of the season, quite literally, to life. And it is to this character that I turn in Chapter 5, one that is not only the personification of the work and organization that goes into the season but of Christmas itself.

Notes

1 www.tuc.org.uk/news/more-1-million-workers-will-be-work-christmas-day-says-tuc
2 https://1hourlife.org/where-to-volunteer-on-christmas-day/
3 In Scotland, Christmas Day only became a public holiday in 1958, while Boxing Day was similarly recognized in 1974.
4 www.cartridgepeople.com/info/blog/christmas-party-statistics
5 https://peoplepointhr.co.uk/blog/equality-diversity/workplace-diversity/
6 www.bbc.co.uk/news/business-58954976
7 www.statista.com/topics/991/us-christmas-season/
8 www.bbc.co.uk/news/uk-30241459
9 www.pwc.co.uk/industries/retail-consumer/insights/black-friday-cyber-monday.html
10 www.postaltechnologyinternational.com/news.php?NewsID=26510
11 http://uk.businessinsider.com/royal-mail-delivered-130-million-parcels-over-christmas-2016-1
12 www.royalmail.com/christmas-parcels-2016-thank-you
13 https://qdosentertainment.co.uk
14 www.actorhub.co.uk/301/pantomime-roles-and-auditions
15 In trying to explain this distinction to a colleague once, I contrasted the image of Mrs Claus being played on the one hand by Dolly Parton and on the other by Angela Lansbury. While both are American performers, I hope it conveys the requisite image.
16 https://res.cloudinary.com/dqc68ksfw/image/upload/v1/workaseason/media/1259/job-spec-workaseason-santas-lapland-elf-2017.pdf

References

Armstrong, N. (2010) *Christmas in Nineteenth Century England*. Manchester: Manchester University Press.
Bakar, F. (2019) 'People Working on Christmas Day Explain How They Make It Festive'. *Metro*, December 25.
Bishop, T. (2008) 'Christmas Under City's Red Lights'. *BBC News On-Line*, Accessed at: http://news.bbc.co.uk/1/hi/england/7786629.stm
Bozkurt, Ö. (2015) 'The Punctuation of Mundane Jobs with Extreme Work: Christmas at the Supermarket Deli Counter'. *Organization* 22(4): 476–492.
Brown, J. (2019) 'Employers Shy Away from Boozy Christmas Parties Amid Fears of Negative Fallout'. *People Management On-Line*, November 25.

Brown, R. (2018) 'What It's Like to Be a Sex Worker in Cambridge Over Christmas'. *Cambridge News*, December 18. Available at: www.cambridge-news.co.uk/news/cambridge-news/sex-worker-christmas-brothel-15519504

Carpenter, J. (2009) 'The Reason Why Hollywood Stars Love the British Pantomime'. *Daily Express*, December 3.

Chamberlain, G. (2016) 'The Grim Truth of Chinese Factories Producing the West's Christmas Toys'. *The Guardian*, December 4. Available at: www.theguardian.com/business/2016/dec/04/the-grim-truth-of-chinese-factories-producing-the-wests-christmas-toys

Chester, N. (2020) 'Sex Workers On the Three Types of Christmas Day Client'. *Vice*, December 22. Available at www.vice.com/en/article/akdjgz/sex-work-christmas-day

China Labor Watch (2017) *The Dark Side of the Toy World: Investigation into the Sweatshops of Disney, Mattel, Hasbro, and Walmart*. Available at: https://chinalabor.wpenginepowered.com/wp-content/uploads/2021/04/Toy-Investigation-Report-1127.pdf

Dickens, C. (2006) 'A Christmas Carol in Prose: Being a Ghost Story of Christmas'. In, R. Douglas-Fairhurst (ed.) *A Christmas Carol and Other Christmas Stories*. Oxford: Oxford University Press. Pp. 5–83.

Edwards, R. (2017) 'I Never Want to Hear That Mariah Carey Song Again': 6 Stories From Retail Workers at Christmas That Will Make You Question Humanity'. *Metro*, December 23.

Fallowfield, M. (2021) 'Christmas Escort: "A Man Paid for Me to Have Sex with His Wife as a Festive Gift"'. *Closer*, December 1. Available at https://closeronline.co.uk/real-life/news/christmas-escort-real-life-story/

Forbes, B.D. (2007) *Christmas: A Candid History*. Los Angeles, CA: University of California Press.

Gadd, S. (2014) 'The 14 Absolute Worst Things About Working in Retail at Christmas Time'. *The Daily Mirror*, November 28.

Gander, K. (2015) 'Christmas Parties: 39 Per Cent of Workers Have Sex at the Annual Do, with IT and HR Departments Most Badly Behaved'. *The Independent*, December 1.

García-Rosell, J.C. and Hancock, P. (2022) 'Working Animals, Ethics and Critical Theory'. In, N. Thomas (ed.) *Animals and Business Ethics*. London: Palgrave. Pp. 91–110.

García-Rosell, J.C. and Tallberg, L. (2021) 'Animals as Tourism Stakeholders: Huskies, Reindeer, and Horses Working in Lapland'. In, J.R. Rickly and C. Kline (eds) *Exploring Non-Human Work in Tourism: From Beasts of Burden to Animal Ambassadors*. Berlin, Boston: De Gruyter Oldenbourg.

Golby, J.M. and Purdue A.W. (2000) *The Making of the Modern Christmas*. Stroud: Sutton Publishing.

Graham, H. (2016) 'Sex Workers in Newcastle Facing Isolation This Christmas as They Battle to Survive'. *Chronicle Live*, December 20. Available at: www.chroniclelive.co.uk/news/north-east-news/sex-workers-newcastle-facing-isolation-12345647

Hancock, P. and Tyler, M. (2017) 'How to Avoid Sexual Harassment at the Office Christmas Party'. *The Conversation*, December 5. Available at: https://theconversation.com/how-to-avoid-sexual-harassment-at-the-office-christmas-party-88502

Harrison, M. (1951) *The Story of Christmas: Its Growth and Development from the Earliest Times*. Watford: Odhams Press.

Hidegh, L.A. (2015) *Critical Human Resource Management: The Reproduction of Symbolic Structures in the Organizational Lifeworld Through the Case of the Colonization of Corporate Christmas*. Unpublished PhD Thesis, Corvinus University of Budapest.

Hidegh, L.A. and Primecz, H. (2020) '"Corporate Christmas": Sacred or Profane? The Case of a Hungarian Subsidiary of a Western MNC'. In, J. Mahadevan, H. Primecz and L. Romani (eds) *Cases in Critical Cross-Cultural Management: An Intersectional Approach to Culture*. New York, NY: Routledge. Pp. 46–58.

Hoarau-Heemstra, H. (2018) 'A Life Worth Living: Reindeer in Nordic Tourism Experiences'. In, C. Kline (ed.) *Animals, Food and Tourism*. London: Routledge. Pp. 113–128.

Humphrey, P. (2019) 'Tesco Charity Cards "Packed by China's Prison Slaves"'. *The Sunday Times*, December 22.

Johnes, M. (2016) *Christmas and the British: A Modern History*. London: Bloomsbury.

Jones, N. (2015) 'As a Sex Worker, Christmas Is One of my Busiest – and Strangest – Times'. *The Independent*, December 22.

Kalleberg, A.L. (2009) 'Precarious Work, Insecure Workers: Employment Relations in Transition'. *American Sociological Review* 74(1): 1–22.

Kane, M. (2017) '5 Sex Workers Share Their Most Memorable Christmas Days'. *Metro*, December 25. Available at: https://metro.co.uk/2017/12/25/5-sex-workers-share-their-most-memorable-christmas-days-7024732/

Kernaghan, C., Briggss, B., Giammarco, J. and Hallock, A. (2007) *A Wal-Mart Christmas – Brought to You by a Sweat Shop in China*. New Your, NY: National Labor Committee.

Lee, V. (2014) 'US Stars in UK Panto: From David Hasselhoff to Jerry Hall'. *The Independent*, December 22.

Lemmergaard, J. and Muhr, S. (2011) 'Regarding Gifts: On Christmas Gift Exchange and Asymmetrical Business Relations'. *Organization* 18(6): 763–777.

MacNamee, G. (2017) '"I work because they are lonely": Sex workers describe the dangers of the trade at Christmas'. *The Journal*, December 23. Available at: www.thejournal.ie/sex-workers-christmas-3733596-Dec2017/

Maughan, T. (2014) 'Yiwu: The Chinese City Where Christmas Is Made and Sold'. *BBC Future*, December 18. Available at: www.bbc.com/future/article/20141218-the-hidden-home-of-christmas

Mauss, M. (1954) *The Gift: The Form and Reason for Exchange in Archaic Societies* (trans. W.D. Halls). London: Routledge.

Mayfair, M. (2018) 'Christmas Is a Really Busy Time to Be a Sex Worker'. *BBC Three On-Line*, December 21. Available at: www.bbc.co.uk/bbcthree/article/200ac945-f7bb-409f-b09b-90cd3481c289

McDonald, P. (2012) 'Workplace Sexual Harassment 30 Years On: A Review of the Literature'. *International Journal of Management Reviews* 14(1): 1–17.

McGuinness, K. (2013) 'Office Holiday Parties are Ripe for Sexual Harassment'. *The Guardian*, Friday December 13.

Meves, K. (2017) 'The Office Christmas Party: Dos and Don'ts for Employers'. *People Management On-Line*, December 8.

Mistry, P. (2017) 'The Evolution of Office Christmas Party: From Outlandish, Drunken Mixes to a Sombre, Unhurried Affair'. *The HR Digest*, December 1. Available at: www.thehrdigest.com/evolution-office-christmas-parties-outlandish-drunken-mixers-somber-unhurried-affair/

Pimlott, J.A.R. (1978) *The Englishman's Christmas: A Social History*. Hassocks: The Harvester Press.

Rippin, A. (2011) 'Ritualized Christmas Headgear or "Pass Me The Tinsel, mother: It's the Office Party Tonight"'. *Organization* 18(6): 823–832.

Rosen, M. (1988). 'You Asked For It: Christmas at the Bosses' Expense. *Journal of Management Studies* 25(5): 463–480.

Sedaris, D. (1999) *Santaland Diaries*. Phoenix: London.

Siddique, H. (2019) 'Tesco Withdraws Christmas Cards from Sale After Forced Labour Claims'. *The Guardian*, Sunday December 22.

Spicer, A. and Cederström, C. (2014) 'Working Over the Holidays? You're Not Alone' *The Conversation*, December 22. Available at: https://theconversation.com/working-over-the-holidays-youre-not-alone-35740

Stephens, C. and Stephens, J. (2016) 'I Worked in Hospitality for Five Years, and What I Witnessed at Christmas Parties Was Horrifying'. www.mamamia.com.au/hospitality-workers-christmas/

Struthers, J. (2012) *The Book of Christmas: Everything We Once Knew and Loved About Christmastime*. London: Ebury Press.

Taylor, M. (2007) *British Pantomime Performance*. Bristol: Intellect Books.

Thompson, E.P. (1967) 'Time, Work-Discipline, and Industrial Capitalism'. *Past & Present* 38 (December): 56–97.

Urry, J. (1990) *The Tourist Gaze: Leisure and Travel in Contemporary Societies*. London: Sage.

Valtonen, A. (2009) 'Small Tourism Firms as Agents of Critical Knowledge'. *Tourist Studies* 9(2): 127–143.

Wainwright, O. (2014) 'Santa's Real Workshop: The Town in China That Makes the World's Decorations'. *The Guardian*, Friday December 19.

Wallop, H. (2015) 'What's It Like for the 900,000 Working on Christmas Day?'. *The Telegraph*, December 22.

Weightman, G. and Humphries, S. (1987) *Christmas Past*. London: Sidgwick & Jackson.

Williams-Grut, O. (2021) 'Tesco and Royal Mail Take Christmas Hiring Spree to 100,000 Amid Fears Firms Could Struggle to Fill Roles'. *Evening Standard*, October 8. Available at: www.standard.co.uk/business/tesco-royal-mail-amazon-sainsburys-morrisons-john-lewis-christmas-hiring-staff-b959495.html

5

HERE COMES SANTA CLAUS

Introduction

Santa Claus is the embodiment, both figuratively and literally, of Christmas. Already encountered at various junctures throughout this book, he bestrides the season like some red and white colossus. To cite Harrison (1951: 206), 'he is Christmas' and, as such, deserves particular attention. And while many things make him special, his uniqueness is found in the fact that unlike other childhood fictional characters, such as the Easter Bunny or the Tooth Fairy, each Christmas, through the creative labours of a worldwide army of performers, he is made 'real'. Every year at parties and in commercial venues worldwide, he appears as more than simply a character in a story or an image on a billboard, but rather as a tangible, fleshy human being: someone who meets and talks with excited children and just as often, enthusiastic adults, discussing their most intimate Christmas hopes, dreams, and, of course, wishes.

However, for this to happen, there must be men who are both willing and able to 'be' Santa: Performers who can not only adopt the role but identify with it to such an extent that they can win over the most demanding and inquisitive of all audiences, young children. At the same time, there needs to be something to perform, a recognized set of traits and values associated with the name and man himself, providing a template and a set of expectations to adhere to. After all, if this were not the case, each year grottos would simply be inhabited by portly gentlemen with a beard and a somewhat questionable relationship to fur. But as we know, thanks perhaps to one Francis Pharcellus Church and his reply to Virginia O'Hanlon's 1897 letter to the *New York's Sun* newspaper, there is indeed a Santa Claus,[1] and he remains someone that children of all ages are eager to meet.

DOI: 10.4324/9781315637969-6

To be Santa is a challenging feat to achieve, however. Santa Claus is a complex and multifaceted character. Both a historical and a very modern figure, most of the time he is a paragon of virtue who personifies a generosity of spirit, goodness, and unconditional love. At other times and places, however, he can be a far darker and more disciplinarian figure, one prepared to not only reward the good but also mete out often violent punishments to the unruly. Moreover, on a perhaps earthlier plane, he is also a businessman and a brand ambassador for thousands of different products, services, and organizations, having fronted advertisements for everything from children's dolls to condoms and firearms. He represents both charity and unselfish generosity while, according to one account, having an estimated commercial value of more than $1.6 trillion.[2]

In order to do this seasonal figure justice, in this chapter I first consider some of the mythologies that underpin our contemporary understanding of his character and origins. This is not only as the contemporary figure of Christmas benevolence we know today but also, as alluded to above, the ancient and sometimes misanthropic agent of organized fear and discipline that continues to haunt him. From there, I then explore the evolution of the modern and more benign Anglo-American Santa Claus, replete with his supercharged sleigh, team of magical reindeer, and a rigorously prepared sack of presents, charting his journey from gift giver to a contemporary icon of international advertising and commerce.

Second, I explore, mainly through their own words, the creative labour and organizational skills of those men who, each year, bring the character and magic of Santa Claus to life. In doing so, I describe their work and how through it they subsequently experience 'being Santa'. Furthermore, I also reflect on why they choose to do it and the potential costs and consequences of such a vocation. In doing so, I place the creative labour of performing, or 'being' Santa Claus, not only at the forefront of how Christmas is made to happen as both a cultural and economic phenomenon, but how the role itself contributes to the self-organization of these performers' sense of identity and personal esteem.

Santa before Santa

Most accounts of the origins of Santa Claus commence with the Christian saint, Nicholas. A fourth-century bishop in what was the Greek city of Myra, during his life Nicholas was renowned for acts of generosity and care. Perhaps the most well-known of these concern him delivering gold in the night to a family whose father was unable to pay wedding dowries for his daughters, saving them from a life of slavery or prostitution, and his resurrection and rescue of a group of students who when out searching for food had been murdered, dismembered, and pickled by a desperate innkeeper (Sansom, 1968). As they became more widely circulated, these stories sowed the seeds of his legend; that of a miraculous nocturnal bringer of gifts and a protector of children and the young. After his death and subsequent adoption as a saint,[3] Nicholas's Saint's Day of December 6 was increasingly celebrated by local clergy and other civic leaders making costumed visits to the houses of well-behaved children at night, and leaving small gifts in his name.

However, Saint Nicholas also had another side to his character for those children reportedly ill-behaved. For while a saint, he was no angel and was indeed known for having something of a temper. In 325 AD, for instance, he reputedly struck an Egyptian bishop at the first Council of Nicaea over a theological disagreement, while in death, he was said to have descended from the afterlife to beat a Dutch abbot simply for having refused to allow his monks to venerate Saint Nicholas in song (Siefker, 1997). And it was this somewhat more robust side to Nicholas that seemed to legitimize the treatment of those children deemed too naughty for gifts, with beatings purportedly being a typical response by those acting out the winter visit of the saintly bishop when confronted by such children,

As stories of such annual visits spread, however, this disciplinary aspect of his performance became something of a source of embarrassment to Church officials. After all, how could a saint, especially one associated with the care of the young, also be associated with inflicting violence on children, especially when some were reportedly carrying out this aspect of his character with a little too much zeal? At the same time, however, both church and parents welcomed the positive impact on behaviour and compliance a visit from Saint Nicholas's could have, helping keep the often unruly young in line. The answer to this problem, or so it turned out, was for storytellers to reach back into pre-Christian mythology and find Saint Nicholas a companion; one who could fulfil these disciplinary duties alongside him.

Santa's Naughty Helpers

European folklore is replete with tales of bedraggled, bearded half-men who roam remote areas only to encroach on human settlements mid-winter when it is dark and cold and food is scarce (Husband, 1980). Fortuitously, as it turned out, some of these characters were ideally suited to be companions for Saint Nicholas, empowered by the Godly saint for one night of the year to punish on his behalf. In the Germanic regions of Europe, for example, these companions were often horned and cloven-hoofed with names such as *Pelznichol*, *Bellesnickle*, and *Knecht Ruprecht*, depending on the area in which one lived (Sansom, 1968). Charged with accompanying Saint Nicholas on his wintertime visit, these wild men were given holly licence to administer anything from a beating to the spiriting away, purportedly into the depths of hell, to any misbehaved children they might encounter.

FIGURE 5.1 Saint Nicholas and Krampus visiting a family home.

Nor was it just in the Germanic countries that such creatures were let loose. In France, for example, the role was played by a similarly bedraggled *Père Fouettard* – delightfully translated into English as 'Father Whipper', or in the low countries by *Zwarte Piet*, a Moorish slave[4] who often continues to accompany Saint Nicholas in this part of Europe during his appearances on December 5 or 6. Today, however, perhaps the most horrific, and thanks mainly to Hollywood, most well-known of Saint Nicholas's companions is the Alpine character of *Krampus* (Hawkins, 2013). A truly 'domesticated demon' who has an enthusiastic proclivity for thrashing naughty children, throwing them off cliffs and even eating them for 'Christmas dinner', he has increasingly become the definitive embodiment of Saint Nicholas's evil companion and alter-ego (Figure 5.1).

Gradually freed from his association with Saint Nicholas, Krampus now in fact often appears as an independent character, a wintertime devil charged with tracking down and tormenting those who have misbehaved throughout the year. As well as appearing in a series of Hollywood gore-fests such as Jason Hull's 2013 film *Krampus: The Christmas Devil* and, in 2015, Robert Conway's *Krampus: The Reckoning*, amongst others, today's events celebrating the character continue to be held in Alpine countries such as Austria,[5] and even in North American cities such as Los Angeles, where hordes of drunken Krampuses frequently intimidate and harass residents and tourists alike during annual Krampus parades.[6]

Moreover, the Santa Claus we know today is not solely a derivative of Saint Nicholas but also has many of his origins in similar dark characters and stories. For example, in *Santa Claus, Last of the Wild Men*, Phyllis Siefker observes how 'our Santa is one of the last descendants of a long line of dark, sooty, hair-covered men, the remnant of a pre-Christian god of awesome power' (Siefker, 1997: 5). And while this might be a slight exaggeration, it helps contextualize not only the existence of such festive accomplices but how Santa himself appears and behaves. For Hawkins (2013), one figure that immediately stands out as relevant in this respect is the Germanic God *Wodan* (or *Odin* in Norse). Wodan, legend has it, would lead a demonic hunting party across northern winter skies while becloaked in red and astride his eight-legged flying horse Sleipnir. On those nights, children would leave gifts of food in exchange for sweet treats, while those deemed unworthy could find themselves spirited away and forced to join his supernatural hunt for all eternity.

In Scandinavian lore, the evil spirit *Nuuttipukki*, who became today's winter totem *Joulupukki*, or Yule goat, would similarly reward good children while beating or again devouring the naughty (Hawkins, 2013). Finally, in England, there was *Robin Goodfellow*, or *Puck* as he is also known. While more of a mischief maker, Goodfellow was nonetheless a regular defiler of women, and occasionally men, whom he considered to have crossed him. Eventually sanitized in the form of the *Green Man* and combined with the northern tales of Wodan, he reappeared in the sixteenth century as *Father or Sir Christmas*, the spirit of winter cheer (Siefker, 1997) and a clear forerunner of today's Santa Claus.

In addition to their festive associations, what is particularly interesting about all these figures, including Saint Nicholas, is their role in reinforcing predominantly hierarchical social relations. For not only were they a metaphor for the often genuine dangers prevalent during the dark and cold of the season but rather, like so many cultural tales of the evil that awaits in the night, such as those of hobgoblins and bogeymen, such figures were extensions of parental and often societal authority (Warner, 2000): an authority concerned with deterring the young from straying too far into that dark lest they should indulge in mischief and wrongdoing out of sight of village elders or other sources of authority. Nor was it just the young that were subject to such a disciplinary focus. According to such stories, women, if their behaviour was considered less than appropriate, were just as likely to face nocturnal visits and punishments from such seasonal and clearly patriarchal enforcers. As Hawkins (2013: 86) observes, for example, one tale of Wodan's winter hunt describes how 'loose, sinful women were tormented with hot burning nails, penetrating their buttocks and thighs in punishment for their "sensuous lechery"'. Similarly, popular images of Krampus were, and indeed are, just as likely to portray him taking his righteous anger out on grown women as on young, frightened children. And while suitably tempered for more modern audiences, this disciplinary orientation continued to inform the character of Santa Claus as it first emerged in the US during the nineteenth century.

Is Zat You, Santa Claus?

While an amalgamation of many of the characters discussed above and a host of other more benevolent European Christmas gift givers such as the German *Weihnachtsmann* and *Christkindl* there is, as Belk (1993) acknowledges, something about the Santa Claus we know today that is uniquely American. In fact, Santa Claus owes much of his identity to the same nineteenth-century group of liberal New York artists and intellectuals associated with the *New York Historical Society* referred to previously. Again inspired by Washington Irving, these men popularized a version of the Dutch story of Saint Nicholas in the hope that it would contribute to their efforts to promote their vision of a more family-oriented Christmas (Nissenbaum, 1997). Even so, while the idea that Saint Nicholas was a figure who would visit good American, or at least East Coast children, grew over the first two decades of that century, it was not until 1821 that someone more recognizable as Santa Claus first made an appearance.

That year, a poem, possibly written by Arthur J. Stansbury, was published in New York. *The Children's Friend: A New-Year's Present to the Little Ones from Five to Twelve* featured a character called 'Santeclaus' for the first time, and was also, by virtue of its lithographic illustrations, the first to depict him wearing a fur hat while seated inside a gift-laden sleigh drawn by a single reindeer (Nissenbaum, 1997, Bowler, 2005). Santa, however, had not entirely abandoned his ecclesiastical roots at this stage. The hat remained reminiscent of a mitre, while his name is considered a variation on the Dutch for Saint Nicholas, Sint Nikolaas, abbreviated in turn to *Sinter Klaas* (Nissenbaum, 1997). Another strong connection he retained with the bishop of Myra, and his sidekicks of old, was his advocacy of physical punishment for those deemed to be naughty or disruptive. For while the poem extolls Santeclaus's joy in 'love and peace' by the time we reach the final verse he is urging parents not to spare the rod on the misbehaved, very much as Saint Nicholas might once have done:

> *But where I found the children naughty,*
> *In manners rude, in temper haughty ...*
> *I left a long, black, birchen rod,*
> *Such as the dread command of God.*

It was only a year later, however, that another poem would do even more to establish this new Santa Claus for an American audience. Clement Clarke Moore's *A Visit from Saint Nicholas*[7] appeared in 1823, and while adopting the saintly bishop's name, it further established several characteristics of the modern Santa Claus mythos that endure to this day. These included the idea that he delivers 'toys' to children on December 24 (rather than on Saint Nicholas's Day), flies a magical sleigh pulled by eight named reindeer, and gains access to the house via a chimney. Equally importantly, Santa was described as a jolly and harmless character, albeit an elf, giving the poem's young narrator 'nothing to dread'. No more was there a threat of actual physical punishment or judgement, therefore, allowing this new St Nick to be placed at the centre of an increasingly idealized 'snug family centred holiday' (Bowler, 2005: 41).

As Santa Claus further evolved and his story travelled back to many of those countries from which its origins sprang, he did take something of his old disciplinary ways with him, however. Nevertheless, this was not so much based on physical punishment but instead on what the likes of nineteenth-century philosopher and reformer Jeremy Bentham (1995) originally described as a panoptic form of control (Hancuff and O'Connor, 2010). As such, rather than being threatened with physical punishment or restraint for parentally reported transgressions, children were told that they were constantly under surveillance by Santa or one of his magical helpers. Thus, they were encouraged to monitor and regulate their own behaviours less they risked having their Christmas gifts withheld by the big man.

By the mid-twentieth century, having shaken off his elfin stature and other various aesthetic and ethical idiosyncrasies, including a few dalliances with militaristic images and actions,[8] Santa's identity, as we know it today, was finally settled. Gone were the overly punitive associations to be replaced with that of a peace-loving and child-centred personality complemented by a broadly standardized physical appearance and gift-giving modus operandi. In the UK, for example, while most people continued to transpose the medieval title of Farther Christmas onto this new seasonal gift giver, he had become largely indistinguishable from his US counterpart. Similarly, across continental Europe, while Santa still had to compete with some of his old-world ancestors such as the *Christkindl* in Austria and parts of Germany and, most notably, *Saint Nicholas* in the low countries, by the 1950s the American Santa Claus had become the preeminent symbol of the season. Indeed, there are few figures today who are as instantly recognizable to children and adults around the world and for whom the preservation of their myth is pursued with such commitment.[9]

Selling Santa

Today, berobed in red and white, with a luxurious white beard and a kindly demeanour, Santa Claus has become the avuncular patriarch who is tasked with making the hopes and dreams of children the world over come true. It is not only children's hopes and dreams that Santa can make come true, however. The same could be said for the men and women of commerce who rely on his image to sell services and goods worldwide, not only at Christmas but often throughout the year. So, while Ebenezer Scrooge might have justified his lack of interest in Christmas partly by alluding, via Jacob Marley, to being 'a good man of business' (Dickens, 2006: 28), as I have already demonstrated, Christmas today *is* business, and big business at that, and no figure is a more unquestioning advocate of the ability of consumer capitalism to grant Christmas wishes than Santa Claus.

While, as we saw in Chapter 2, for many, it was *Coca-Cola's* use of Sundblom's illustrations that not only helped to define Santa's global image (Charles and Taylor, 1992) but also established him as an international marketing icon. His commercial importance to advertisers, especially in the US was, however, already well recognized by then. Indeed, the rival US soft drink and mixers company *White Rock* had already, several years before Sundblom's images appeared, advertised their own products with a similar red and white clad Santa enjoying a bottle of their ginger ale in both his office and in the homes of those he was visiting (McKay, 2008).

Even earlier than this, however, as Bowler (2005: 115) observes, Santa's first known commercial advocacy role was in the guise of Saint Nicholas when a New York jeweller printed a flyer in the 1820s claiming that 'St Nick' had been 'seen in his shop checking out the merchandise'. Since then, Santa's image has gone on to advertise and sell almost everything imaginable While more traditional endorsements, such as the 2011 TV campaign for Apple iPhone 4S featured Santa using the device to navigate his way from home to home on Christmas Eve while keeping in touch with Mrs Claus, others often appear somewhat incongruous even in at a time when advertising relies more and more on shock tactics to reach an increasingly desensitized public. At the more humorous end of this spectrum, for instance, is a poster that appeared on the London Underground in 2019 advertising male erectile dysfunction medication featuring a sunglasses-wearing Santa excitedly pointing to the strapline, 'Order Online, Deliver in Bed'.

A harder-hitting illustration was the 2011 TV campaign by UNICEF that ran in Sweden. Featuring a disgruntled Santa, the advert had him declaring that he does not 'do poor countries' when faced with the idea of delivering medical supplies to children in need as a substitute for individual gifts. And while a mainstream organization such as UNICEF must tread carefully when reappropriating Santa in this way, more radical advertising campaigns such as those led by the *Occupy Movement*, and organizational collectives such as *Adbusters*, have sought to further parody and undermine Santa's credentials, stressing the role the character arguably now plays in culturally legitimizing envy, debt, and environmental despoliation.[10]

Perhaps one of the more unique virtues of Santa Claus as a sponsor of various goods, services, and causes is, however, that he can step off of the advertising hoarding or television screen and interact with potential customers not simply as a representation but as 'Santa' himself. This is especially true in those places where so much Christmas consumption often still occurs, such as department stores or shopping malls. As we saw in Chapter 4, such outlets increasingly invest large sums of money in their Christmas activities and attractions, operating them at an ever-increasing level of sophistication. Utilizing interactive technologies and the like, they endeavour to manufacture a 'magical' atmosphere that, it is hoped, will encourage increased consumption throughout the season. Nevertheless, whatever the technology available, even today, the most critical feature of such attractions to those who finance and benefit from them remains the quality of the interaction between Santa Claus and children and adult visitors alike, and it is to this subject that I now turn.

Being Santa

As we saw previously, the earliest appearance of a Christmas grotto replete with Santa Claus can be traced back to the mid or late 1800s (Connelly, 1999; Bowler, 2005). Nonetheless, whatever the specifics, since the early twentieth century, grottos, where shoppers and their children can meet Santa Claus, have become an annual fixture in most department stores and malls. While initially somewhat basic, they have developed into elaborate seasonal displays and 'bazaars' in their own right and, as such, require a more polished and believable Santa Claus to attend them. As such, theatrical and PR agencies, alongside photographic companies, today compete to put their performers in such grottos worldwide.

Furthermore, this has also led to Santa training schools appearing in the US and spreading to the UK and Europe. Supported by books such as Nick Kelsh's (2001) *How to Be Santa Claus* and Connaghan's (2010) *Behind the Red Suit: The Business of Santa Claus*, they explain not only the intricacies of how to perform the role but also how to start up one's own 'Santa business', including the organization of contracts, marketing, and insurance. Nevertheless, at the heart of this is the message that authentic performers must always live up to conveying Santa's status as an exceptional individual. More than a man, but a figure of almost transcendent goodness, patience, and generosity, it is their responsibility to ensure that they must not sully this identity in any way, especially as that would be bad (business) for everybody (Butchart, 2003).

What exactly constitutes authenticity when it comes to Santa Claus is something of a grey area, however. As Michael Pretes (1995) observes, one might, given his multiple points of origin, consider Santa to be an example of what French sociologist Jean Baudrillard (1983) would describe as a simulacrum,

FIGURE 5.2   Santa Claus performers attending the annual World Santa Claus Congress, Klampenborg, Denmark. Photograph by the author.

a copy of that which there is no definitive original. However, despite this, there is a surprising degree of consensus amongst performers themselves, based on the kinds of legends and stories discussed earlier, as to the values and attributes that underpin an authentic portrayal of the seasonal gift giver. Moreover, nowhere was this made more evident than during my visit to the *World Santa Clause Congress*. Dating back to the 1950s, the event is held annually at the Bakken Amusement Park, Klampenborg, just outside Copenhagen in Denmark (Figure 5.2). Attracting Santa Claus performers not only from Europe but from as far afield as the US, Russia, Hong Kong, and Japan, it is an event where professional and semi-professional performers gather together to entertain, parade, and even network. And while regional and national traditions are apparent with, for example, the occasional Dutch Saint Nicholas or Russian Father Frost in attendance, the relative uniformity regarding of Santa's global identity is notable.

Nor is it a role that appears open to much in the way of diversity when it comes to who is considered appropriate to perform it. Given his traditional portrayal as an older white man, it is an industry that has tended to strictly adhere to such an ideal when hiring performers for the role. In the US, there are examples of Black performers being employed in major department stores and at events, as well as more general representations of Black Santas being displayed, but this in itself has been highly contested at both ends of the political spectrum (West, 2020). More recently, the 2022 film by Nick Sweeny, *Santa Camp*, has reported on a Santa training camp in New Hampshire in the US where an emphasis is placed on the need for, and the positivity of, more diverse portrayals of Santa Claus including a transgender, a Black, and a physically disabled performer all of whom share their experiences and aspirations (Valentish, 2022). Nonetheless, the role remains largely the domain of male, white, mobile, and predominantly rotund men.[11]

In the UK, the most high-profile work is undertaken by an elite corps of such performers who are often working or semi-retired actors or entertainers. Having interviewed and spoken with a number of this creative workforce, I found they were usually registered with various theatrical or promotional agencies that arrange work each year with large commercial enterprises, including department stores, shopping malls, and major businesses, such as banks, that employ performers for Christmas parties and promotional events. Occasionally, they also attend private events usually organized by some of the wealthier international residents domiciled in particular areas of London, which, they told me, can be some of the more lucrative Christmas gigs they are offered.

A key defining feature of this workforce is that its members consider the faithful portrayal of Santa Claus to be more than just a job but claim it is a moral responsibility that brings joy to the children and, just as often, the adults they meet, wherever it takes place. Often demonstrating a significant personal investment in the role, they undertake historical research into the myths and stories surrounding Santa Claus, invest in high-quality costumes and accessories, and attend training and social events associated with the character.

Furthermore, despite the money they can make from such performances, their motivations for taking on this role often seem less than pecuniary. Not that getting paid is wholly unimportant to many of the performers I spoke with. As one light-heartedly reminded me, 'the reindeer still have to be fed'. Nonetheless, for the majority, the money appeared far less significant than the pleasure they took in performing the role. This is a view summed up succinctly by one interviewee who exclaimed to me, rather animatedly, that:

I love it. I love it and would do it if I didn't get paid, but I do it and get paid. Deduct from that as you wish!

As I spoke with more of them, what became increasingly clear was that what appeared to underpin such enthusiasm for the role was an even deeper-seated relationship to the work than I had suspected, and what it might offer the individuals who performed it. In fact, what became evident was that for the majority of those I spoke to, the job is more akin to something resembling a gift relationship, or perhaps what Bolton (2005: 139) might refer to as emotional philanthropy in that it is more of 'a sincere performance' than a workplace contractual exchange, it being something they wanted to 'give back' to the world as they, in most instances, entered their twilight years.

As the likes of Mauss (1954) have recognized, however, even a gift relationship is rarely unconditional and usually expects some degree of reciprocity, be it through a gift in return or the acknowledgement of the giver's status and generosity. Not that these performers intentionally placed any such expectation on the children they met, apart from perhaps in the case of the children nominally 'being good'. Nevertheless, while the children they met were gifted the attention of a larger-than-life icon and a hoped-for source of forthcoming indulgence, the performers did indeed suggest a desire for another form of reciprocity, namely that they were held in high esteem, or *recognized*, as the authentic embodiment of the values and ideals associated with Santa Claus.

Interestingly, the significance they placed on securing such recognition through their work reflects similar concerns in both social philosophy (Taylor, 1994; Outhwaite, 2009) and increasingly work and organization studies (Hancock, 2008; Islam, 2012; Tyler and Vachhani, 2021; Hancock, 2022) about the importance of understanding how feeling recognized can be vital for a person's sense of identity and psychological health. Drawing primarily on the work of the contemporary German philosopher and critical theorist Axel Honneth (cf. 1995, 2007, 2012), recognition theory, as it has come to be known, focuses in particular on how our desire for recognition and the sense of *self-confidence, self-respect,* and *self-esteem* it can lead to, might be enabled or thwarted by forms of social, economic, and political organization.

To unpack this, for Honneth to desire recognition, that is a secure sense of practical self-identity and worth, is to desire what he terms love, respect, and esteem from those around us and to feel valued as legitimate members of society at large; desires we must also, it should be said, be prepared to fulfil for others. Described as something we aspire to and, hopefully, achieve through a number of stages, the first stage is the achievement of a sense of self-confidence that develops through a relationship of trust grounded in the 'felt assurance that the loved one will continue to care even after he or she has become independent' (Honneth, 1995: 107), or as Honneth describes it, love. Such confidence enables us to express our needs without fear of rejection or abandonment. The second is the achievement of a sense of self-respect, and is a product of our experience of formal institutional recognition encapsulated in those universal rights and responsibilities ascribed to us by society and significant organizations, particularly the state. Through such recognition we are able to partake fully as members of a society or organization. Finally, the type of recognition that is perhaps the most relevant here is self-esteem. Emerging through opportunities to 'relate positively' to our own and others 'concrete traits and abilities' (Honneth, 1995: 121), such esteem reflects both a social and inter-subjective acknowledgement of the value of our skills, character attributes and capabilities and the contribution we can make through these to society and the lives of others.

For these performers, recognition was not simply courted on account of their ability to convincingly act the part of the character of Santa Claus as one might expect, although, as we shall see, that remains vitally important. Rather, it was sought through an almost flawless identification of the performer with the virtues and magical capabilities associated with the character. In other words, the sense of self-esteem they derive from their work does not so much arise simply from a sense of doing a good job. Instead, it is from a sense of actually embodying the virtues of Santa Claus himself and being recognized as such by others. Let us return to the categories devised by Honneth to illustrate this more broadly.

So, when it comes to a desire for love, it is the unquestioning adoration of young children of Santa Claus – and, as I must keep qualifying, some adults as well, that means so much to these men. This was encapsulated by one performer who told me how:

> These kiddies sit there with open mouths, and they're looking up at you, trusting little things like little chicks, and you think, 'This is just wonderful!' I love it.

Likewise, although we may not typically associate Santa Claus with a heightened sense of respect and universally recognized rights, several individuals I spoke with perceived certain privileges and advantages when portraying him. Usually, this was a relatively benign recognition of their right to be greeted with heightened courtesy and excitement befitting their identity. On one occasion, however, I was extolled with a story that points to something even more dramatic in terms of how such respect can, in certain situations, manifest itself as a form of legitimate authority. The story revolved around one performer successfully requiring the Diocese's Bishop to pay to enter a church Christmas fete, despite his initial refusal. The tale concluded with the performer explaining how:

> Once that costume is on you, it's an authority. With that I could tell the Bishop off because he didn't pay. It may not have been the Bishop but, you know, somebody. If not the Bishop, it could have been just a priest, but I can tell him 'You didn't pay!' But if I was an ordinary person, I'd get a smack on the hooter.

However, when we started to discuss the question of self-esteem and the social recognition that bestows it, it was then that I began to fully understand that these men sought a form of almost transcendent recognition. For each performer

I spoke to about this issue stressed, to a lesser or greater extent, the importance they placed on being recognized, first and foremost, for what they considered to be an authentic embodiment of the values of generosity, kindness, and patience associated with Santa Claus. In some cases, this was expressed as a desire for the recognition of qualities they felt they could never claim in real life. One interviewee lamented, for example, that while he needed to believe he had the virtues of Santa while being him, he knew that, in reality, he 'wasn't quite good enough'. Yet it was not despite, but rather because of such a self-understanding among the performers I met that each seemed to share a deeply held conviction that Santa Claus was a performance like no other. To recollect what was perhaps the most memorable of statements during my research in this area, 'you don't do Santa, you have *to be Santa*', and to be Santa was to possess those virtues that he, and only he, embodies.

Lest we get too carried away with this idea, however, it is worth reminding ourselves that these men are still performers and that while their ambition is to transcend being seen to simply act the role, to achieve the recognition they desire still comes with a need for significant planning and execution on their part. Moreover, as it became clear throughout this research, their ability to transcend imitation relies not on some magical transfiguration but instead on adherence to several organizational techniques and the hard work that defines the interactive labour process they undertake. While not entirely homogeneous, my time with these men suggests that such efforts can be encapsulated by three relatively distinct but very much interrelated sets of working techniques and practices. For relative ease, I will describe them here as the *performative*, *epistemic*, and *ethical* dimensions of what I call the Santa Claus labour process.

The Santa Claus Labour Process

The idea of a labour process is traditionally associated with how industrial production is analysed from within a predominantly Marxist framework (Marx, 1939; Braverman, 1974) and refers to how labour, or paid work, is valorised and regulated. For example, this could be in manufacturing, whereby human activity comes to bear on raw materials to turn them into, say, a table or a motor car, and then sold at price based on various factors, most notably an abstract calculation of the amount of work that went into making it. What is known as Labour Process Theory is concerned, therefore, with developing a critical understanding of how such labour is undertaken, managed, and experienced. Furthermore, since the 1990s, the concept has been extended to help make sense of various non-industrial occupations and working practices, particularly interactive service work (Sturdy et al., 2001).

By utilizing analytical concepts such as emotional (Hochschild, 1983; Bolton, 2005; Lewis and Simpson, 2009) and aesthetic labour (Hancock and Tyler, 2000;

Pettinger, 2004; Cutcher and Achtel, 2017) to understand how value is generated and the labour force organized, labour process scholars have explored a range of interactive service jobs ranging from flight attendants (Tyler and Abbot, 1998) and retail workers (Williams and Connell, 2010) to stand-up comedians and musicians (Butler and Russell, 2018; Hancock et al., 2021). And what I argue here is that to create the magic of the encounter by 'being Santa', there also exists an identifiable labour process. Moreover, this is one that, while reflecting practices often characteristic of creative and interactive service work more generally, offers in combination a relatively unique insight into the work of these performers and how it creates particular value in the form of a living, seasonal mythology.

Performative Labour

Alan Bryman (2004: 4) coined the term *performative labour* to describe the affective combination of emotional and aesthetic skills that are increasingly considered to be 'part of the labour involved in service work' at Disney theme parks. Here, I use the term to describe a similar affective combination amongst the Santa Claus performers I met, focusing on the importance of their physical appearance and how they seek to embody the Santa Claus identity through their aesthetic and emotional presentation of self.

The Aesthetic

Santa Claus is instantly recognizable due to his stature, jolly demeanour, bearded appearance, and costume, and for all the performers I met, attention to the details of their appearance and the work that goes into creating it is considered integral to their ability to be Santa Claus. In fact, several of the more experienced performers I interviewed insisted on donning their costumes before our meeting as they felt it was the only way they could fully articulate what the role meant to them, explaining that 'as soon as I put that costume on, I am Santa'. Moreover while this might appear something of a charming eccentricity, it illustrates the commitment of these performers to the idea that when wearing the costume, a non-negotiable commitment to the identity of Santa Claus is expected. This was something encapsulated by one performer's analogy of a police officer:

> You *can't* come out of character. I suppose it's like putting on a police uniform. You *become* a policeman as soon as you put the uniform on.
>
> *(Emphasis added)*

Throughout all my encounters, with one exception that I will return to in a moment, the importance and capacity of an appropriate costume to ensure a performer's ability to embody Santa Claus was never questioned. Many of those I spoke to had made a significant personal investment, between £1,000 and £2,000, to make their costumes rather than wear standard agency or store ones. At the same time, artefacts such as spectacles and gloves were also often purchased as they were deemed to play a vital role in their transfiguration, for example, in the latter case hiding any distinguishing features on one's hands. They could also use other material resources, such as a 'magic' key tied to the belt to explain how Santa could achieve domestic access in the absence of an open chimney stack, to add to the experience of 'meeting Santa'. Most performers also ensured that they used their own make-up to whiten eyebrows and redden noses and cheeks, while issues such as personal hygiene were scrupulously attended to, with the greatest taboo being the odour of alcohol or cigarettes.

A further significant investment in the embodied identity of Santa Claus made by many of the performers was the growing of a suitable beard. While in the US, what are known as 'Real Bearded Santas' can earn upwards of 25% more than their theatrically bearded counterparts (Connaghan, 2010), in the UK while having a natural beard brings with it a degree of aesthetic upkeep it offers little noticeable financial benefit. Nonetheless, for those who had one, it enhanced a self-belief in their ability to achieve the desired level of recognition. As one of my more magnificently hirsute interviewees confided:

> When Santa arrives at a job with a real beard, you can just tell. It's a big difference ... Although our costumes are brill and our beards are brill, when they get a real beardy bloke it's like 'wow', they see you *as* Santa.
>
> *(Emphasis added)*

Interestingly, possessing a Santa-like beard also challenged the notion that one actually had to be in costume to be Santa. For while several bearded performers acknowledged that they received second looks while out in civvies – as they liked to put it – one performer explained how for him it established an embodied identity that he could never entirely escape. Frequently approached by young children who would express either their excitement or indeed puzzlement that Santa might be out, say shopping, or on holiday, he explained to me how, when approached, he tried to respond in a consistent manner that stayed true to his seasonal identity:

> I just talk to the child and say 'Whatever you do, don't tell anybody that you have seen me. I'm only here early because I'm just checking is everybody nice. I've got my magic book with me. Can you see the book?' They say no. I say 'Well, it's a magic book. You can't see it, but I'm writing everything down'.

And while aesthetic concerns constitute a central aspect of the performer's performative labour, this interview extract also demonstrates how equally important it can be for these performers to self-manage their emotional commitment to the character. In this instance, it is by being prepared to suspend everyday life to reassure a child as to their authenticity and, in doing so, reaffirm the child's emotional investment in the character.

The Emotional

Given the mythos surrounding him, it is probably no surprise that the most apparent emotional commitment any performer can make to 'being Santa' is performing an unfailingly jolly demeanour. Yet this is often more difficult than one might suppose. And while disruptive children, or indeed adults, can present a challenge to such a presentation, what tends to pose the greatest difficulty is encountering children experiencing significant illnesses or impairments or recounting upsetting tales of family break-ups or deaths. It was moments such as these that, the performers confessed, often required substantial amounts of emotional labour on their part to maintain the integrity of their identity. For example, a performer working at a multi-Santa Christmas-themed park recounted meeting a young boy with a severe life-limiting illness. While the performer made it through the actual encounter, as soon as the child and his family left, he had to suspend his session to compose himself 'backstage'. Tellingly, he also described a situation reminiscent of Marek Korczynski's (2003) notion of 'communities of coping' whereby those experiencing shared emotional demands in the workplace would take time to listen to and support each other:

> There's a back door you can go outside and stand in the winter sunshine, if there is any amongst the trees, and just have two or three minutes. Quite often you'll see there's another Father Christmas from the hut further up and he's also listening to the birdsong, you know, and you shuffle over and say, 'How's it going?' 'Oh, okay. I've just had one of those'. 'Oh, right'.

While this example suggests a degree of communal support, described by one performer as 'Santa solidarity', in response to emotionally trying encounters with children presenting special needs or personal traumas, most performers saw it as their responsibility to absorb such experiences and 'take the child somewhere else' before moving on to the needs of the next visitor.

Perhaps one of the most difficult scenarios reported to me was when a child would ask a performer to either convene with, or actually resurrect, deceased family members. One performer's recollections, for example, focused on the highly distressing experience of meeting a young girl who had brought a teddy bear along to 'meet Santa', asking him to talk to it as it had belonged to her recently deceased younger sibling but again noting how, even in the face of such meetings:

> I've never lost it. It hits you in the heart [and] you've got tears coming down your face, but you're still being merry, do you know what I mean?

Epistemic Labour

Of course, Santa Claus is more than just a bright red coat and a consistently jolly demeanour. There are also a set of somewhat more intellectual or even scholarly expectations that need to be respected by the performers if they are to achieve the recognition they desire. To be Santa, therefore, the performers are also required to undertake a form of what I will call here, *epistemic labour*. This involves not only knowing all that Santa should know about his own life and history but also being able to demonstrate a magical knowledge of, for example, whether a child has been 'naughty or nice' or mundane details such as the names of their siblings and friends or what their likes and dislikes are. As such, the performers have to ensure they are both fully aware of the mythology surrounding the character while at the same time develop techniques and practices that enable them to acquire sufficient knowledge about individual children, their siblings, and significant others to ensure them of their authenticity.

Knowing Santa

While the Anglo-American Santa Claus story is both multifaceted and, thanks primarily to Hollywood, an evolving one, as Belk (1993) notes, it also contains established 'facts', the knowledge of which needs to be exhibited by those who lay claim to his identity. Indeed, a key element in the Santa Claus training events I attended was helping to establish a shared historical narrative for the performers in attendance. Sessions, for example, helped to ensure that each performer knew the names of Clement Moore's original flying reindeer, that Santa lives with his elfin helpers and Mrs Claus in Lapland or the North Pole, depending on local customs, and, more generally, that they knew how to answer questions patiently and, in a manner, befitting Santa Claus. How performers responded to these sessions could then impact on whether they were subsequently hired by those agencies either running or in attendance at these events. One attendee, for example, explained to the other attendees how he liked to discuss his favourite alcoholic beverages with children (rather than a glass of milk) but pointed out that he told them that he had to be careful not to get 'sleighed' (sic). He was then somewhat put out because he was not selected to work by this particular agency that year.

Despite such an occasional aberration, however, most of the performers I met considered such knowledge central to their ability to be Santa, especially when challenged by children or mischievous parents. Indeed, it was considered a significant failing by most of them if someone did not have all the relevant 'facts' to hand, with several that I interviewed in their homes eager to show me their collection of books on the history and traditions of Santa. As one performer explained to me:

> You need to know this stuff in case a kiddie asks. Some Santas I have worked with haven't even known the name of his reindeer or where he lives, which I find really, well disappointing.

Knowing the Customer

The second and equally important aspect of the performers 'epistemic labour' was not so much based on such scholarship, however, but more on their supposedly magical credentials. Considered to be very much part of the experience of meeting Santa was the ability of the performers to demonstrate intimate knowledge about their young visitors, including their name, age, and personal information such as the name of any pets or siblings, thus helping them to replicate Santa's reputation for omnipresence. In reality, of course, this depended on the collection and manipulation of this data, either at the point at which they encountered the children or even weeks if not months before. Nonetheless, it very much hung on the performers' ability to make convincing use of it.

In many ways, this has been made far easier by the emergence of online booking systems that can gather personal information, such as the names of siblings, friends, and pets, often well in advance of a meeting. According to one of the performers, this enhanced their ability to inhabit the role and 'exceed the expectations' that accompanies it:

> [Having read the briefing] I'll say something such as 'Well, I thought your friend William was coming with you. Is he not coming today?' The fact that you even know William is quite a shock. The fact that he's perhaps younger than them or older than them or has a bike that they'd like, which you could introduce, they think is amazing.

Where such systems were not available, however, practical in-situ techniques continued to be utilized by the performers that would elicit similar information. These would often take advantage of the performer's aforementioned 'helpers' or 'elves' who might act in collusion with amenable parents or guardians. The most common technique was for those working on the door to the grotto to ask a child's name, age, and other specific details and then repeat it loudly so the performer inside would hear it. This would enable them to subsequently greet the child by name and possess sufficient details about their background to initiate a knowledgeable conversation.

The performers also used this perceived omnipresence to help militate some of the potentially distressing emotional situations described earlier. For example, as I mentioned earlier, it was not uncommon for children to request the return of dead parents or siblings as Christmas gifts. In such instances, the performers often reassured the child that they did not need to worry or be lonely as Santa 'knows' that these significant but absent others are well, happy, and watching over them.

Ethical Labour

The final and perhaps most challenging form of labour the performers felt they had to undertake is what I term ethical labour. This is a response to the expectation that, as Santa Claus, they must embody an almost unimpeachable virtuousness and moral responsibility upon which is built, in the eyes of those who believe, his unquestionable trustworthiness and authority. While many of the performers I spoke with often found this to be a difficult aspect of their work to articulate, it was clear that whenever they were being Santa Claus, they felt an overriding ethical responsibility for the happiness and well-being of the child they were with:

> Santa is about children and caring for children, you know? For those few minutes I'm with each one of them, I'm kind of responsible for not just their happiness but their belief in Christmas, which at that age means the world.

For some, this resulted in an almost dismissive attitude towards parents and carers in favour of children whereby, as another told me:

> I'm sorry. Children have the experience in here. This is for them. Some of the parents are bloody rude. And, you know, it's the kid wants to see Santa … I won't put up with any nonsense from the parents. I put them in their place.

Occasionally this could also mean that performers would have to mediate between the demands of parents or guardians when Santa was asked to encourage, or as in this case, discourage, particular behaviours by their children:

> They bring the dummies in and all that and they say … I mean obviously they try and make a sort of game of it really and say, 'We've just got a little

present for you Father Christmas', and then, you know, if they say, 'What do you do with the old dummies?' – 'I give them to the elf babies', you know, and that sort of thing'.[12]

While several of the performers were not happy when such expectations were placed on them, reminiscent as it was of older ideas of a more punitive Santa, others attempted to draw the children into such exchanges in a way that they became part of what one described as a 'conspiracy with Santa Claus'. One performer gave the following example of trying to take such an approach:

it could be, 'Tell him to go to bed at night and when he goes to bed, stay in it!' [and I say] 'You know, you've got to be careful about this business of wandering around, you know. Mum might think or dad might think it's burglars!'

Interestingly, such moral authority and the ability to exercise it were not always confined to the performers' interactions with children. Throughout the interviews, we often discussed, for instance, how the recognition they achieved as Santa enabled them to counsel accompanying and seemingly receptive adults against, for example, drinking and driving or overeating during the festive period. And while this willingness to recognize the authority of Santa Claus is perhaps illustrative of Robert Cluley's (2011) account of Santa's popularity with adults as an example of a narcissistic performance of identification aimed at children, such a relationship of recognition could still manifest itself even where children were not present.

One experienced performer, for example, explained to me how young couples had visited him on several occasions and how, for example, a young man had proposed to his girlfriend while requesting 'Santa's blessing' while another recounted the somewhat melancholy tale of a young man who, at a large corporate Christmas party, took the opportunity to unburden himself of his personal woes:

This lad later on in the evening, he came in on his own … I did the usual thing 'Have you been a good boy this year?' and 'What do you want for Christmas?' and he said, 'I'd like a flat', and I did my usual gag of 'Well, that's a big difficult to get on the sleigh. I've tried it before and, you know, it just unbalances the sleigh' I said, 'But why a flat particularly?' He said, 'Because I've just split up with my girlfriend and I'm living on someone's floor', and he just poured it all out to me, a complete stranger in a beard and wig.

It's Not All Ho-Ho-Ho

While the above has explored how each performer worked to ensure that any meeting with Santa was as authentic and memorable as possible and, in doing so, maximize the recognition they might achieve through this, things did not always go as planned. As with any interactive service role, challenges and dangers can arise, usually due to poor resourcing or conflicting organizational interests (Kalia, 2021) or simply because of the indeterminacies that occur when working with members of the general public in such an intimate manner. As one performer was at pains to tell me:

> You tend to think that being Father Christmas is just being ho-ho-ho and very nice … [but] there's all kinds of problems.

Often, such problems would arise from a need for more alignment between the endeavours of the performers to 'be Santa', and the commercial values and priorities of the organizations, such as department stores, to whom they report while in character. The most common example of this is found in the failure of many clients to provide basic facilities for the performers, such as comfortable and private changing areas. Often this means that performers must arrive and take any breaks they are allowed while in full costume or otherwise run the risk of being seen changing, threatening the integrity of the performance and the character. Even where facilities are provided, they are often minimal, as one performer angrily observed:

> One of the worst things about this job? It's the grotty facilities you get to change. [At one store] we change in the security changing room, which is the filthiest bloody cupboard hole that you've seen. Down at [another place], you're screened off in this marquee which has got a water container … So, you're basically changing in mud.

Others described being left to change in a car park or publicly accessible toilets – often trying to duck or hide when children and parents entered in order not to shatter the magic of any subsequent encounters.

Performers also talked about the working discomfort created by long shifts, inadequate breaks, poor ventilation, and the like, while another significant concern was the simple overload of visitors many faced and the rate at which each performer was often expected to see them, especially at events such as large corporate parties:

> It is hard. Sometimes they have parties where there's maybe 400–500 children and you are in a little booth, so to speak, with lights and everything and you have one helper, and you have to see all those 500 children in 4 hours and that is some going. All the time they're saying 'Hurry it up! Hurry it up! Hurry it up!'.

Reminiscent of the worst excesses of the rationalized assembly line or the demands of what has been referred to as a customer-orientated bureaucracy (Korczynski, 2001) that often combines an irreconcilable requirement to follow formal procedures while meeting the particular demands of customers and clients, it is at this point which the contradictions between the child-centred ethics of the performers and the predominantly commercial priorities of the client are most stark. And while these can be reconciled if enough children are themselves keen to move through the actual Santa encounter quite rapidly, if not, the majority of performers were unwilling or simply unable to comply with what they considered to be an inappropriate instruction to speed up when faced with a child who clearly desires their attention:

> I'm aware of the commercial aspect, but I'm child based. I mean if you're only doing it for money, if you're only doing it as a commercial aspect, you can't really portray the character fully and you have to believe in him in order to do so.

Abusing Santa

Alongside such tales of their work's managerial and supervisory intensification, there were also distressing stories of performers facing harassment, bullying, and even physical assaults. Frequently, performers reported finding themselves subject not only to rude children but also abusive parents and guardians who might be unhappy with, for example, the size or quality of the gift they might have received as part of the admission price or the photography arrangements on offer, neither of which are under the control of the performer but upon whom they vent their frustration:

> [They start arguing] saying, 'I don't like that. I don't like that one'. 'Well, let's take another one'. 'No. Look, he's not smiling'. 'No, he's got his head the wrong way'. And this can go on like 10, 15, 20 times ... and you're only supposed to take no more than 3 photos, but if they insist, you can't say no. But you do get very pushy mums who are trying to get the ultimate picture.

Typically, however, the performers reported feeling relatively safe within a grotto environment where there is usually an assortment of CCTV cameras, panic buttons, and helpers present to dissuade or diffuse any potentially threatening or violent encounters. However, there are other environments where such safeguards are only sometimes available.

'Walkabout Santa' roles, for example, generally involve roaming around stores or shopping malls, speaking to children they meet or, for those working in alternative settings such as corporate parties, moving from table to table. Unlike the relatively secure environment of the grotto, this arrangement often leaves performers feeling especially vulnerable. This is notably true at corporate events, especially when they are solely adult occasions. As one highly experienced performer reflecting on several City (of London) parties he had attended over the years told me:

> the worst ones are when you go to firms' dinners and there's no kids there. It's companies and they've been on the lash and they're taking the piss out of you.

Fortunately, reports of physical violence against performers at such events were relatively rare, although one cannot say the same for those required to roam commercial and public spaces.

These even more extensive walkabout roles, while generally unpopular due to the physical demands they place on performers who usually have to work over multiple levels in stores or malls, often in excessive heat while in costume, clearly present a host of threats both to their ability to maintain the integrity of the character, as well as to their physical and emotional well-being. This is illustrated by the following extended tale of a performer working on the ground floor of a provincial department store:

> In came a group of 14, 15-year-olds. 'You alright, Santa? There's no such person'. I just got a handful of sweets and I said 'Here guys, this little girl believes in Father Christmas. If you don't that's up to you'. Next minute they're all surfing on the edge of the escalator lying on the black band going up the side and suddenly there was a yank on the back of my costume, and it really jerked me back up and at the same time somebody grabbed the beard and yanked the beard off. I didn't know where I was for a minute.

Perhaps seven more harrowing was the experience of one performer left alone and vulnerable while tasked with seeing children in an open sled in a London shopping mall. During an informal conversation he described the experience of being threatened with what he assumed was a knife and being told to hand over his 'wallet and phone' while children were queuing to see him. While he managed to diffuse the situation by calmly remaining in character and explaining to the young man that, 'like the Queen', Santa doesn't carry money or need a phone, he clearly remained traumatized by the encounter several years after the event.

Tainted Identities

While these are somewhat extreme examples, nearly all the performers I spoke to expressed at least some concerns about the emotional and physical challenges they face regarding their well-being and their ability to 'be' Santa Claus. 'It's bloody hard being Santa when some parent or teenager is giving you grief', as one performer told me. Nonetheless, this differs from the work's most taxing or distressing aspect in that many of the performers felt an increasing need to be alert for pre-meditated threats to what they consider to be the reputation and propriety of the character, threats that they think are becoming increasingly commonplace.

The majority of these, perhaps unsurprisingly, tend to focus on a cultural reassociation of the character not with magic or care but with a form of exploitative or predatory male sexuality, what one interviewee described as the 'dirty old man thing'. In an age in which several high-profile revelations about the activities of a handful of middle-aged and older men, especially in the UK where police operations such as Yewtree[13] have investigated allegations of child sexual abuse mainly by individuals working in the UK entertainment industry, and a scandal-obsessed tabloid press has collided, it is felt that Santa Claus is increasingly a target for those wishing to capitalize on this contemporary moral panic (Cohen, 2011).

This illustrates a further commonality between the work of these performers and many other interactive service workers in that it carries with it what one might call a tainted evaluation. Taint has largely, although not exclusively, been associated with the activities of those who undertake what is referred to as 'dirty work' (Hughes, 1951; Perry, 1998; Ashforth and Kreiner, 1999; Tracy and Scott, 2006; Simpson et al., 2012). This usually refers to jobs that deal in some way with 'matter out of place' (Douglas, 1966) and carry a quality of physical, social, or moral shame, with the work being, say, physically disgusting, such as in servicing toilets or symbolically degrading, such as selling fast food. Alternatively, it might be deemed anti-social or morally questionable in some way, such as with sex work (Hughes, 1951). Of course, these various forms of taint can often be interrelated, with many occupations experiencing taint across 'multiple dimensions' (Ashforth and Kreiner, 1999: 415).

In this instance, the primary taint feared by these performers is predominantly a moral one in respect of their own reputation and, if not more so, that of Santa Claus himself. Moreover, it is this risk of being ascribed what the sociologist Erving Goffman (1963) might have described as a stigmatized identity that is something that weighs on these performers' minds, requiring them to adopt particular working practices to negate the risk of being falsely accused of something inappropriate and facing an ascription of moral taint that is entirely at odds with their self-understanding and desire for recognition. Nevertheless, despite the issue's assumed prominence, broaching it with most performers I spoke to was difficult. Indeed, it was clear that when I raised the issue, usually adopting the discourse of 'child protection' as a way of introducing it, a heightened level of suspicion about my research and motives quickly became apparent. Addressing the issue with one events manager, for example, he replied:

> This is not an area we talk about an awful lot because too much is made of it, but there is a slight, I think, nervousness because everyone has this fear in their mind that everyone who's an old bloke is a pervert in some ways. So … when the media ring up anyway, I just change the subject immediately. I go 'Rubbish!'.

Unfortunately, for most performers, such bravado is not always possible. One veteran performer who was forthcoming in respect of his feelings on the matter made it perfectly clear how he felt:

> You're scared stiff. You really are. You've got to watch what you do all the time. I'm a really tactile person. I've got a lovely son and I've always, you know, given him lots of love and I teach drama …. But you've just got to 'Whoa!' – stand back from it.

While all the performers I spoke to in the UK are required to have a Disclosure and Barring Service check (formerly Criminal Records Bureau) to be employed, such checks merely represent a formal record of past status. In addition, the employing agencies and the performers tend to use several organizational and personal tactics to protect the moral integrity of Santa Claus and the encounter with the children. First and foremost, the institutional norm in all settings in the UK, and increasingly elsewhere, is that a second member of performing staff, a helper or 'elf', is always present in the room to act as an independent third-party witness to all interactions. As I observed in Chapter 4, such performers are usually female, and it was subsequently explained to me that the reason for this is that it is generally believed, correctly or not, that a woman is unlikely to collude with a male performer in any inappropriate or possibly abusive acts. For the Santa Claus performers, alongside the role they play as entertainers, the protective function of their elves or helpers is crucial. Indeed, as one recalled, when this condition was not met, it could cause significant concern, if not distress:

> You need those female elves. They're a sort of insurance policy really because, you know, one girl one year left me in the grotto with the family and the kids and when she came back, I was really angry and I said, 'You must never do that again'. I said, 'One of the reasons you're here, no matter how bored you are, one of the reasons you're here is to protect me because if one of those adults says I touched their kid inappropriately, I only have your word, and mine obviously'.

Secondly, children in the UK are rarely permitted to sit on a performer's knee but are required to sit on a stool or seat at his side, avoiding all physical contact. Not that this form of spatial distancing is entirely unproblematic for the performers. For example, it puts children in a much better position to physically inspect the performer's appearance and notice any on-the-day errors, such as a slightly ill-fitting beard. Moreover, it also causes problems indirectly when parents or other attending adults are either ignorant of such rules or deliberately choose to ignore them. This usually involves children being physically forced onto Santa or the child or children being allowed to hug or even jump on him, resulting in performers having to choose between the rules or what they consider to be their ethical reasonability towards the child 'as' Santa Claus.

In most instances, however, this is a rare occasion when matters largely have to be resolved in favour of the rules to the point that children are turned away by some performers, despite parental sanction, as a consequence of both the implicit cultural taboos and the explicit regulations under which they work:

> People come in with a baby and they go 'Here you are, Santa!' and I say, 'No, I'm sorry. I'm terribly sorry' (always in character) 'I'm not allowed to have your child on my lap. They can sit there, but I cannot have them on my lap'.

Not all performers accepted what they felt were formal impediments to their ability to develop a significant relationship with each child, however. Indeed, some clearly believe that such rules and regulations stunt their ability to be Santa Claus and to offer children the attention and magical experience they deserve:

> As a very young boy, if your aunt or your uncle or your mum or dad took you into a department store and you met Santa in his grotto, you'd probably sit on his lap and he'd give you a cuddle. You're not allowed to do that. That's very much the way now, but that, I'm afraid, is a sign of the times that we live in.

Another performer explained that he regularly rejected the instruction to wear white gloves, designed to avoid flesh-on-flesh contact and make it easier to see where his hands are, as a compulsory part of the costume. This was because, for him, this diluted the importance of being able to hold Santa's hand:

> Now children hate white gloves. Well, they hate gloves. They don't like it. If you hold a hand you want to, you know, hold a hand; you don't want to hold a glove.

Not that this performer had any evidence that children did not like holding a gloved hand. Instead, as we spoke, I got the sense that he felt, more than anything, that the gloved hand was itself almost an admission of something 'unnatural' in the role and the relationship he had with the children he met. As he later confided, 'there's an element of it being sinister, and I would hate to think that Santa Claus or the image of Father Christmas is sinister at all'.

Another matter that also seems to haunt a number of these performers, and the managers and supervisors looking after them, are the activities of unscrupulous journalists and media outlets looking to generate stories that deliberately propagate suspicion of the character and the men that perform him. Several performers and agency and store managers described what they considered to be examples of attempted press entrapment they had experienced over the years. And while there were no reports of these directly involving stories of inappropriate sexualized encounters with children, the aim seems to have been to help generate a general sense of discomfort about the character's sexual integrity.

Usually, such reported attempts to tarnish the character of Santa took the form of attempting to manipulate the performers to pose for an inappropriate photo or surreptitiously placing packets of, for example, cigarettes or even condoms in a photo shoot. In one of the most shocking incidents told to me, an unfortunate duty manager who offered to act as a stand-in Santa was cajoled into having his photo taken with a young woman sitting on his knee, only to find the next day that he had appeared on a full page of a leading daily UK tabloid newspaper because, as the marketing manager subsequently realized: 'she was a ringer, basically, and there's a shot of her lifting her top up showing her breasts, with Santa going "Aaah" in the background [and] he couldn't see that because he's behind her'.

Santa's Moral Economy?

At first sight, it might appear strange that anybody would seek to besmirch the good name of Santa Claus in such a way. Nevertheless, as we have seen, Santa is not in actuality the benign figure one might necessarily think, having played many roles that might not endear him to all, being the administrator of adult and patriarchal discipline, military propagandist, pedlar for global consumer capitalism, and, it should not be overlooked, the source of perhaps the biggest lie many of us ever tell our children (Johnson, 2015). It is doubtful, of course, that acts such as those described above, designed to discredit both the men who perform him and the character of Santa Claus himself, are underpinned by any such well-thought-through objections. Instead, they express much that is characteristic of lowest common dominator journalism and a puerile appetite for the salacious that is probably as old as Santa Claus himself.

Nevertheless, as all deities throughout the centuries have discovered, they tend to experience greater moral scrutiny than their mortal counterparts.

Today Santa Claus has become a precarious arbiter caught in the contradictions between his own magical, moral economy, and a life defined by the realities of a Christmas marketplace and driven by an annual passion for accumulation that exceeds even capitalism's usual rapacious tendencies. A paragon of truth built on lies, generosity built on greed, and an ethic of care built on what is often a lack of respect for those who cannot afford to partake in the indulgences of the season. Santa is perhaps a more complicated performance to convincingly pull off than one might realize.

However, these performers' work and organization occur at the juncture of these contradictions. Aware of the cultural and economic environment in which their performance happens, their desire for recognition is driven by the belief that it is only by being Santa that they can offer anything other than a caricature of the values and ideals they believe they owe not only those they meet, but the character himself. Their labour is the labour of not only being Santa Claus, therefore, but of resisting being a bishop or a huckster and being something that transcends the strictures of both faith and market.

The fact that they seek recognition suggests a not entirely disinterested generosity on their part, of course. However, recognition must always be mutual and intersubjective. Furthermore, their performances continue to embrace a belief that Christmas is a season in which anything might be possible. Be it the appearance of a much wished-for toy at the end of the bed to the possibility that, if only for a few weeks of the year, one might become better and more worthy of recognition than usual, even if it has to be by 'being Santa'.

Notes

1 For the story behind this, see www.villageschoolma.org/pdf/YesVirginiathereis aSantaClaus.pdf
2 https://brandfinance.com/press-releases/jingle-sells-jingle-sells
3 Nicholas was recognized as a saint before the Roman Catholic Church standardized canonization in the late tenth century – www.stnicholascenter.org/who-is-st-nicho las/real-saint
4 A representation that has, quite rightly, provoked increasing opposition both at home and across Europe, see Chini (2019).
5 www.salzburg.info/en/salzburg/advent/krampus-percht
6 http://krampuslosangeles.com
7 The authorship of *A Visit from Saint Nicholas* remains contested, with some crediting it to Henry Livingston, Jr. For background to this debate, see Westover (2015).
8 See, for example, Westover (2016).
9 In 2021, for example, Bishop Antonio Stagliano of the Noto diocese in Sicily generated public uproar when he told children at a local Christmas festival that Santa Claus did not exist (Associated Press, 2021). Similarly, I recall having to undertake protracted discussions before speaking on a BBC radio academic affairs programme about how I would refer to the Santa Claus 'performers' I had recently interviewed so as not to upset children who might be listening. Finally, I had to settle on describing them as 'Santa's helpers' so as not to bring the BBC into disrepute.

10 www.facebook.com/Occupy-Christmas-236907349699891/wall/
11 It should be noted, however, that grottos are themselves becoming more attuned to the needs of visitors with physical disabilities including, for example, in 2022 a UK grotto especially designed for children with a vision impairment – www.guidedogs. org.uk/blog/guide-dogs-is-launching-the-uks-first-ever-inclusive-christmas-grotto
12 Although it is worth noting that in some mainland European countries, particularly around Scandinavia, collecting children's dummies, or pacifiers, is considered an honourable duty of Santa Claus.
13 www.operationyewtree.com

References

Ashforth, B. and Kreiner, G. (1999) 'How Can You Do It? Dirty Work and the Challenge of Constructing a Positive Identity'. *Academy of Management Review* 24(3): 413–434.

Associated Press (2021) 'No Ho Ho: Italian Church Apologises Over Bishop's Claim About Santa Claus'. *The Guardian*, Saturday December 11.

Baudrillard, J. (1983) *Simulacra and Simulation* (trans. P. Foss, P. Beitchman and P. Patton). Los Angeles, CA: Semiotext(e).

Belk, R. (1993) 'Materialism and the Making of the Modern American Christmas'. In, D. Miller (ed.) *Unwrapping Christmas*. Oxford: Oxford University Press. Pp. 75–104.

Bentham, J. (1995) *The Panopticon Writings* (ed. M. Bozovic). London: Verso.

Bolton, S.C. (2005) *Emotion Management in the Workplace*. Basingstoke: Palgrave.

Bowler, G. (2005) *Santa Claus: A Biography*. Toronto: McClelland and Stewart Ltd.

Braverman, H. (1974). *Labor and monopoly capital: The degradation of work in the twentieth century*. London; Monthly Review Press.

Bryman, A. (2004) *The Disneyization of Society*. London: Sage.

Butchart, E. (2003) *The Red Suit Diaries*. Grand Rapids, MI: Fleming H. Revell.

Butler, N. and Russell, D. (2018) 'No Funny Business: Precarious Work and Emotional Labour in Stand-up Comedy'. *Human Relations* 71(12): 1666–1686.

Charles, B.F. and Taylor, J.R. (1992) *Dream of Santa: Haddon Sundblom's Vision*. Washington, DC: Staples & Charles.

Chini, M. (2019) 'What's the Issue with Zwarte Piet?'. *The Brussels Times*, December 4. Available at: www.brusselstimes.com/81413/sinterklaas-who-is-zwarte-piet-belg ium-the-netherlands-december-blackface

Cluley, R. (2011). The Organization of Santa: Fetishism, Ambivalence and Narcissism. *Organization* 18(6): 779–794.

Cohen, S. (2011) *Folk Devils and Moral Panics: The Creation of the Mods and Rocker*. London: Routledge.

Connaghan, T. (2010) *Behind the Red Suit: The Business of Santa*. Riverside, CA: The Kringle Group.

Connelly, M. (1999) *Christmas: A Social History*. London: I.B. Tauris.

Cutcher, L. and Achtel, P. (2017) '"Doing the Brand": Aesthetic Labour as Situated, Relational Performance in Fashion Retail'. *Work, Employment & Society* 31(4): 675–691.

Dickens, C. (2006) 'A Christmas Carol in Prose: Being a Ghost Story of Christmas'. In, R. Douglas-Fairhurst (ed.) *A Christmas Carol and Other Christmas Stories*. Oxford: Oxford University Press. Pp. 5–83.

Douglas, M. (1966) *Purity and Danger: An Analysis of Concepts of Pollution and Taboo*. London: Routledge and Keegan Paul.

Goffman, E. (1963) *Stigma: Notes on the Management of Spoiled Identity*. New York, NY: Simon and Schuster.

Hancock, P. (2008) 'Embodied Generosity and an Ethics of Organization'. *Organization Studies* 29(10): 357–1373.

Hancock, P. (2022) 'Employee Recognition Programmes: An Immanent Critique'. *Organization*. doi: 10.1177/13505084221098244

Hancock, P. and Tyler, M. (2000) 'The Look of Love: Gender and the Organization of Aesthetics'. In, J. Hassard, R. Holliday and H. Willmott (eds) *Body and Organization*. London: Sage. Pp. 108–129.

Hancock, P., Tyler, M. and Godiva, M. (2021) 'Thursday Night and a Sing-along "Sung Alone": The Experiences of a Self-employed Performer During the Pandemic'. *Work, Employment and Society* 35(6): 1155–1166.

Hancuff, R. and O'Connor, N. (2010) 'Making a List, Checking It Twice: The Santa Claus Surveillance System'. In, S.C. Lowe (ed.) *Christmas: Philosophy for Everyone*. Pp. 104–113.

Harrison, M. (1951) *The Story of Christmas: Its Growth and Development from the Earliest Times*. Watford: Odhams Press.

Hawkins, P. (2013) *Bad Santas, and Other Creepy Christmas Characters*. London: Simon & Schuster.

Hochschild, A.R. (1983) *The Managed Heart: Commercialization of Human Feeling*. Berkeley, CA: University of California Press.

Honneth, A. (1995) *The Struggle for Recognition: The Moral Grammar of Social Conflicts* (trans. J. Anderson). Cambridge: Polity Press.

Honneth, A. (2007) [2000] *Disrespect: The Normative Foundations of Critical Theory* (trans. various). Cambridge: Polity Press.

Honneth, A. (2012) *The I in We: Studies in the Theory of Recognition* (trans. J. Ganahl). Cambridge: Polity Press.

Hughes, E. (1951) 'Work and the Self'. In, J.H. Rohrer and M. Sherif (eds) *Social Psychology at the Crossroads*. New York, NY: Harper. Pp. 313–323.

Husband, T. (1980) *The Wild Man: Medieval Myth and Symbolism*. New York, NY: Metropolitan Museum of Art.

Islam, G. (2012) 'Recognition, Reification, and Practices of Forgetting: Ethical Implications of Human Resource Management'. *Journal of Business Ethics* 111(1), 37–48.

Johnson, D.K. (2015) *The Myths That Stole Christmas: Seven Misconceptions That Hijacked the Holiday (And How We Can Take It Back)*. Washington, DC: Humanist Press.

Kalia, A. (2021) 'Even the Reindeer Were Unhappy: Life Inside Britain's Worst Winter Wonderlands'. *The Guardian*, Monday December 13.

Kelsh, N. (2001) *How to Be Santa Claus*. New York, NY: Stewart, Tabori & Chang.

Korczynski, M. (2001) 'The Contradictions of Service Work: Call Centre as Customer Oriented Bureaucracy'. In, A. Sturdy, I. Grugulis and H. Willmott (eds) *Customer Service: Empowerment and Entrapment*. London: Palgrave. Pp. 79–101.

Korczynski, M. (2003) 'Communities of Coping: Collective Emotional Labour in Service Work'. *Organization* 10(1): 55–79.

Lewis, P. and Simpson, R. (2009) 'Centering and Engendering Emotions in Service Work'. *International Journal of Work Organisation and Emotion* 3(1): 56–64.

Marx, K. (1939) *Capital: A Critical Analysis of Capitalist Production (Vol. 1)* (ed. and trans. D. Torr). New York, NY: The International Publishers Co.

Mauss, M. (1954) *The Gift: The Form and Reason for Exchange in Archaic Societies* (trans. W.D. Halls). London: Routledge.

McKay, G. (2008) 'Consumption, Coca-colonisataion, Cultural Resistance and Santa Claus'. In, S. Whiteley (ed.) *Christmas, Ideology and Popular Culture*. Edinburgh: Edinburgh University Press. Pp. 50–67.

Nissenbaum, S. (1997) *The Battle for Christmas: A Cultural History of America's Most Cherished Holiday*. New York, NY: Vintage Books.

Outhwaite, W. (2009) 'Recognition, Reification and (Dis)respect'. *Economy and Society* 38(2): 360–367.

Perry, S.E. (1998) *Collecting Garbage: Dirty Work, Clean Jobs, Proud People*. New Brunswick, NJ: Transaction Publishers.

Pettinger, L. (2004) 'Brand Culture and Branded Workers: Service Work and Aesthetic Labour in Fashion Retail'. *Consumption Markets & Culture* 7(2): 165–184.

Pretes, M. (1995) 'Postmodern Tourism: The Santa Claus Industry. *Annals of Tourism Research* 22(1): 1–15.

Sansom, W. (1968) *Christmas*. London: Weidenfeld and Nicolson.

Siefker, P. (1997) *Santa Claus, Last of the Wild Men: The Origins and Evolution of Saint Nicholas, Spanning 50,000 Years*. Jefferson, NC: McFarland.

Simpson, R., Slutskaya, N and Hughes, J. (2012) 'Gendering and Embodying Dirty Work: Men Managing Taint in the Context of Nursing Care'. In, R. Simpson, N. Slutskaya, P. Lewis and H. Hopfl (eds) *Dirty Work: Concepts and Identities*. Basingstoke: Palgrave Macmillan. Pp. 165–181.

Sturdy, A., Grugulis, I. and Willmott H. (eds.) (2001) *Customer Service: Empowerment and Entrapment*. Basingstoke: Palgrave.

Taylor, C. (1994) 'The Politics of Recognition'. In, A. Gutmann (ed.) *Multiculturalism: Examining the Politics of Recognition*. Princeton, NJ: Princeton University Press. Pp. 25–73.

Tracy, S. and Scott, C. (2006) 'Sexuality, Masculinity and Taint Management Among Firefighters and Correctional Officers: Getting Down and Dirty with "America's Heroes" and the "Scum of Law Enforcement"'. *Management Communication Quarterly* 20(6): 6–38.

Tyler, M. and Abbott, P. (1998) 'Chocs Away: Weight Watching in the Contemporary Airline Industry'. *Sociology* 32(3): 433–450.

Tyler, M. and Vachhani, S. (2021) 'Chasing Rainbows? A Recognition-Based Critique of Primark's Precarious Commitment to Inclusion'. *Organization* 28(2): 247–265.

Valentish, J. (2022) 'Why Should Santa Be White or CIS? The Camp Where Anyone Can Learn to Be Father Christmas'. *The Guardian*, Friday December 9.

Warner, M. (2000) *No Go the Bogeyman: Scaring, Lulling, and Making Mock*. London: Vintage.

West, E.J. (2020) 'Black Santas Have a Long and Contested History in the US'. *The Washington Post*, Wednesday December 23.

Westover, J. (2015) 'The Controversy of Who Wrote a Visit from St. Nicholas'. *Merry Christmas.Com*, October 22. Available at: https://mymerrychristmas.com/the-cont roversy-of-who-wrote-a-visit-from-st-nicholas/

Westover, J. (2016) 'Santa Claus at War'. *Merry Christmas.Com*, August 25. Available at: https://mymerrychristmas.com/santa-claus-at-war/

Williams, C.L. and Connell, C. (2010) '"Looking Good and Sounding Right": Aesthetic Labor and Social Inequality in the Retail Industry'. *Work and Occupations* 37(3): 349–377.

6

HOME AND THE GENDERED ORGANIZATION OF CHRISTMAS

Introduction

Christmas has long been considered a time best enjoyed when families celebrate it together at home. For many, the season is seen as a time to reconnect with loved ones and see the old year out together while looking forward to the next. It is also an important time to celebrate the home itself. Indeed, few images be they on a Christmas card, the cover of a magazine, or these days a downloadable computer wallpaper, suggest Christmas more immediately and sympathetically than that of a festive home, usually featuring an open fire, a begarlanded mantelpiece and a richly decorated tree surrounded by presents. Rarely, of course, do these soft-focus pictures reflect the reality of the season, but that, as they say, is to miss the point. Rather, they present a cultural idealization that increasingly shapes and organizes our perceptions of what Christmas is and what it ought to be. They are an invitation that is not only seductive but almost sublime in its perfection and, as such, always seemingly just out of reach.

Indeed, as Gaston Bachelard (1994) writing in 1958 might have had it, at Christmas home is at its most poetic. It evokes personal and emotional responses that are often intimately tied to memories and fantasies of either being a child or raising children, and that leaves one, if only for a few days of the year, feeling securely oriented in space and time (McAndrew, 2017). Such memories and dreams are not simply conjured from thin air, however. Instead, for homes to become both the repositories and, indeed, factories of such Christmas ideals once again requires the organization of many, often competing, resources. However, unlike the shopping malls and tourist destinations considered elsewhere in this book, they are seldom glamorous locations. Rather, they are where the most

DOI: 10.4324/9781315637969-7

mundane activities associated with the season take place, the festive coalface, if you will, where not only do the celebrations never entirely end but neither does the domestic labour and organization that makes them possible.

Not only does Christmas at home involve organization and hard work, however. It also generates a workload that is often unevenly distributed, particularly in respect of the gendered division of labour. For despite a growing awareness that Christmas represents a time of intensified work and stress that is not only unpleasant but disproportionally threatening to women's mental health (Collins-Sharp, 2014; Nolsoe, 2019; Rodsky, 2019), it is on women that the majority of the burden associated with Christmas continues to fall. This includes shopping for gifts, preparing food, decorating the house, and other tasks typically associated with the season. Moreover, as well as pursuing their organizational duties, Christmas seems to generate additional pressures on women as they are expected to adopt, or perform, a particular gendered identity in order to fulfil these. This is one that is required to be both highly rational and organized and yet, at the same time, almost hyper-feminine in its attention to acts of care and empathy.

In this chapter, I consider the proposition that for Christmas at home to be experienced as a unique or magical time, it is creatively, if disproportionally, organized primarily by women. It commences with a discussion of the historical development of the family home as the primary organizational unit of the festive season and the significance of the gendered division of domestic labour in its emergence. Next, it explores how this has also generated an abundance of resources that promote the incorporation of organizational ideas and practices that would typically sit outside the sphere of domestic relations, particularly in such a way that they specifically target a female readership and promote a form of gendered agency. Finally, I argue that these not only provide an organizational template for how women should go about organizing 'the most magical' of domestic Christmases but also how, in doing so, they play a broader role in helping to organize and structure the performance of women's gendered identities not only within the festive home but also beyond.

Home for Christmas

Seventh in a list of the UK's most played Christmas songs (Bemrose, 2019), Chris Rea's 1988 release of *Driving Home for Christmas* captures what, for many, is the importance of reaching a place called home in time for the holidays. Recounting a 250-mile Christmas Eve drive from London to his hometown in the northeast of England, Rea sings of a widespread yearning for the safety and comfort of home and the joy that can be found only amongst family and friends at this time of year. It is the musical equivalent of those movies discussed in Chapter 3, such as It's *a Wonderful Life* or *National Lampoon's A Christmas*

Vacation, in which, whatever the challenges and travails of the season, the familial love and companionship of home will ensure the spirit of Christmas endures.

It is, of course, a pop song and, like such films, a product of the kind of feel-good Christmas culture industry discussed earlier. Moreover, it shares this message with many other musical hits of the season. Songs such as Bing Crosby's original 1943 recording of *I'll Be Home for Christmas*, or Darlene Love's 1963 'Wall of Sound' classic, *Christmas (Baby Please Come Home)*, all offer a highly idealized and somewhat saccharine image of the enticements of a Christmas spent at home amongst and the love and warmth to be found there. Nonetheless, and perhaps because of this fact, each year, such songs remain a powerful and symbolically rich reminder of the centrality that the idea of a place called home plays at Christmas.

The truth is, of course, that home can be experienced very differently and mean very different things, even during the festive season. For some, it might indeed represent a place of comfort and sanctuary, a familiar place to shelter from the deprivations of mid-winter and the stresses and demands of everyday life. For others, however, it can just as easily become a place of disappointment, sadness, and regret, not to say one of threat and even violence. While family arguments and the grey cloud of disgruntled teenagers are common, if reasonably harmless features of many a Christmas at home, more serious matters such as cases of domestic abuse, for example, commonly increase over the festive period as financial pressures and the often-close proximity afforded by the season appear to provide further licence to perpetrators to act abusively (Verney, 2021). Moreover, as for the homeless or those on the margins of society, the idea of a home might seem like an even more unattainable dream at this time of year, one perhaps no less fantastical than that of the Christian nativity itself.

Whatever the realities, however, Christmas continues to perpetuate a very particular idealization of the domestic sphere as an alternative 'world' or 'reality' in which 'family values are generalized to everybody' (Kuper, 1993: 171). At Christmas, home is portrayed not only as a unique and wholesome place but also a permeable one, private and closed and yet joyously public and open. It is the focal point for intimate family celebrations and an arena for extended gatherings and entertainment that welcomes family and friends alike. It is also a site where the magic of Christmas is most visibly, but also inequitably brought into being through work and organizational practices that are highly gendered, falling predominantly, if not exclusively, on women. Indeed, as one homemaker told me, for her, home is the 'ground zero of Christmas'. It is where multiple expectations, hopes, and dreams collide and interweave but where they can just as quickly descend into a ferment of resentment and conflict if not managed deftly by the woman of the house as they 'try and keep everyone happy'.

According to Weightman and Humphries (1987: 76), it was, like so many aspects of the season we know today, 'the Victorians who made Christmas the festival of the family and created the compulsion people still feel today to get home'. However, as we have seen, the season's roots are far more ancient. Having originated in a far older response to the privations of winter, it is not beyond reasonable speculation to suggest that it was the shelters that we eventually came to call homes where this celebration of light, warmth, and life's reaffirmation first took place. In this sense, Christmas, or Yule, or whatever one wishes to call it, has most likely always centred on a place of shelter and safety during the long, cold, and darker mid-winter evenings. Then certainly by the time Christmas was established as the main winter festival across most of Europe, while far from confined to such spaces, festivities were widely recorded as taking place not only in the homes of the powerful but even in more modest domestic dwellings, drawing families, friends, and dependents together to share warmth, companionship, and often safety during the season (Hutton, 1996; Harrison, 1951). So, while Christmas undoubtedly spilt out into the country lanes and eventually urban streets, often much to the dismay, as we have seen, of the great and the good, from the off it had a long and vital relationship with a notion of home and homeliness that coexisted with more communal and public forms of celebration.

Having said this, whatever its earliest origins, it is fair to say that today's valorization of the home and a highly domesticated form of Christmas does indeed owe much of its character to the ideas and innovations of Victorians on both sides of the Atlantic. Moreover, as with many other aspects of the Victorian Christmas, such views were firmly rooted in an albeit romanticized and somewhat wistful vision of Christmases past that served as a possible template for the future (Archer, 2016). Key to perpetuating this vision were those writers we have already encountered, such as Scott, Dickens, and Irving, and their fantasy of those idyllic, peaceful, and charitable Christmases of years and centuries long gone. Turning to folk memories and tales of the domestic hospitality and largess of the landed and wealthy of the English Middle Ages, in particular, these Victorians nurtured a vision of the home at Christmas that was an antidote to the turmoil, inequities, and harshness of an industrializing society, yearning, as they did, for a more peaceful and 'safer' social settlement (Hutton, 1996: 133).

Considered to be an extension of ancient seasonal inversions of social hierarchy if not an act of political self-interest, the idea of opening one's home at Christmas to the less fortunate was, therefore, a touchstone for nineteenth-century representations of the season (Nissenbaum, 1997). An early illustration of this can be found in an extract from Walter Scott's renowned poem of 1808, *Marmion: A Tale of Flodden Field*, which celebrates his idea of a rural and what today we might describe as an inclusive English Christmas during the sixteenth century:

> The hall was dress'd with holly green;
> Forth to the wood did merry men go,
> To gather in the mistletoe.
> Then open'd wide the Baron's hall
> To vassal, tenant, serf, and all.
>
> (Scott, 1888: 174)

While an open home was one thing, however, if Christmas was to indeed act as a counterweight to the more dire and anomic consequences of an industrial age, then something more was also required: namely, a vision of an ordered and devout family at the heart of that home.

Not that this was a challenging notion to justify. After all, one only had to look to the Christian nativity and the 'Holy Family' of Mary, Joseph, and Jesus for a model of what was to become an increasingly nuclear vision of the idealized family unit comprising of 'parents and young children with mother at the centre, as housekeeper' (Leach, 1968:42). At the same time, and on a more secular level, it was also helped by the increasingly global popularity of the 'other' holy family, the British royal family whose own enthusiasm not only for Christmas but the virtues of family life in general has already been touched on (Hutton, 1996). Indeed, by the mid-1900s, even a cursory glance at the images and representations of the season demonstrates how quickly an idealized middle-class family unit had become established as the primary organizational setting for, and arguably the object of, this mid-winter celebration. Moreover, many of these pictures are clearly based on similar images of British royalty, especially that now somewhat iconic family scene found in the *Illustrated London News* of 1848 of Queen Victoria and Prince Albert and their young family at Windsor Castle (Figure 6.1).

As such, from Dickens's festive reflections on the love and solidarity of the Cratchits and, indeed, Scrooge's own extended family, through Henry Coles' now immortalized image of his family sitting down to a seasonal dinner, Christmas, home and family increasingly became entangled in both the popular imagery of the season as well as the Victorian imagination (Pimlott, 1978).

By the arrival of the twentieth century, Christmas had become almost inseparable from the practices and fortunes of both the nuclear and, indeed, extended family. Moreover, while this had been a largely middle-class concern of the 1800s, with the increasing popularization of the notion that Christmas should be a time predominantly for and about children and that the family home provided the best environment within which to raise them, the working classes were also rapidly bought into the fold. As I have already noted, for this

FIGURE 6.1   Christmas tree at Windsor Castle.

to become possible, however, the material conditions, say through the extension of official holidays, were also required and were often a long time coming. Nonetheless, by the early twentieth century, the idea that Christmas is best celebrated as a family event and that, in particular, it should favour children was increasingly ubiquitous, even if not everyone that shared this belief also possessed the resources to partake in it.

Indeed, for a working-class family at the turn of the century, Christmas celebrations were often only possible through year-long personal sacrifice and the use of annual savings plans to finance Christmas spending. Originating in the US, these saving schemes became known as Christmas clubs after, in 1909, Merkel Landis, who was treasurer of the *Carlisle Trust Company*, purportedly started the first known Christmas savings fund in that country.[1] However, the idea quickly spread to the UK, enabling working families to save and budget for the family Christmas enabling some to push the boat out at least once a year. The following account by the son of an iron moulder from Lancashire in England from just before the First World War gives something of a flavour of this:

> Christmas would be an especially gay day with presents such as dolls, toys, sweets, games and even once a watch. 'We always had a good Christmas dinner. A joint of pork or a fowl. In the afternoon Aunties and Uncles would come in for high tea and we'd have a party ...'
>
> *(Thompson, 1992: 66)*

Nonetheless, only by the mid-twentieth century did large and extravagant family gatherings become as common amongst working-class families as they were amongst their more comfortably off counterparts (Weightman and Humphries, 1987).

The Value of Home

In addition to its social significance, the idealization of the family home at Christmas was equally salient to those seeking to harness the season for more political and economic ends. As Johnes (2016: 41) observes at the opening of his own chapter on the 'family Christmas', the idea that the family remained the foundation of social stability, order, and indeed deference, was perceived to be an important bulwark against social unrest and any radical agitation. The writers of King George V's third annual Christmas Day broadcast in 1935, for example, described Christmas as the 'festival of the family' before portraying the British Empire as a home that effectively bound together an inter-continental 'family' in deference and loyalty to its sovereign.

Similarly, the home and family values it purportedly nurtured were no less significant for those concerned more with profiting economically than politically from Christmas. Advertisers, particularly in the US, quickly realized that few festive advertisements ccould be better set than in a festively decorated household. From Sundblom's illustrations of Santa for *Coca-Cola* to everything from a new family firearm to a steam iron, the home at Christmas provided the perfect backdrop to the pleasures of seasonal gift-giving and consumption.

A further, and perhaps less frequently considered, reason for the desirability of and identification with the home at Christmas during the twentieth century was the impact of two world wars that took so many young men and women away from those they loved and the relative security that many had known as children. As several authors have acknowledged (Golby and Purdue, 2000; Marling, 2001; Perry, 2010), for troops serving on all sides in such conflicts, Christmas represented a particularly poignant reminder of their separation from home and loved ones and the knowledge they may never see them again (Richards, 2020).

Not that the celebration of Christmas at home was quite what it was during times of peace. Particularly during the Second World War, occupied Europe had far less to celebrate either about or with, while in the UK, Christmas 'on the home front' was also characterized by increasing shortages of food and seasonal goods, while the constant threat of aerial bombardment and the predominance of a 'make do and mend' culture especially when it came to children's presents predominated (Brown, 2004; Taggart, 2017; Archer, 2020). Not that this always resulted in inferior celebrations or even gifts, especially if family members had the requisite skills and materials. As one young girl from the north-east of England recalls (cited Taggart, 2017: 180):

> My grandfather worked as a boilermaker in the shipyard, and he had a friend who was a carpenter. He made a farmyard and a crane for my brother and a set of doll's house furniture for me – all painted shipyard green. My brother said Father Christmas must have had a lot of green paint.

Whatever the realities of life away from the frontline were, however, swathes of the fighting population continued to value home as a place of security and comfort, and no more so than at Christmas, and this was an ideal that was to help embed this relationship even more deeply in the cultural memory of generations to come, particularly, it must be said, the menfolk.

However, while it was men that may have, in large part, carried such idyllic values of home and hearth at Christmas back with them from the battlefields of the world, it was the women who were, and arguably still are, charged with making them a reality, and it is the question of the relationship between gender, the home, and Christmas that I turn to in the next section. For as I have already observed, while Christmas is supposed to be a time in which we escape the demands of work, as Adam Kuper (1993: 171) observes, it is also when 'women work harder than ever', something obscured by the fact that as with much domestic labour, it is excluded from formal calculations of value creation and the recognition that accompanies it.

Christmas as a Domestically Gendered Affair

While cultural memory is integral to perpetuating the idea that Christmas is experienced best at home, it is also underpinned by a mass media that unrelentingly reinforces that same message. Much of this can be traced back directly to the world of commerce in general and advertising in particular. From press advertisements and magazines to television and the internet, we are constantly reminded that Christmas is a time to consume either in the home, for the home, or as compensation for not being home. Home is where gifts should be exchanged and bring pleasure, especially to children, and where familial loyalties are reaffirmed through communal acts of consumption and celebration. At the same time, festive slogans such as 'All Hearts Come Home for Christmas' or 'Home is the Heart of the Holidays' can be found emblazoned across signs, t-shirts, banners, and other seasonal artefacts that go on sale seemingly earlier each year. Finally, the kinds of films and popular songs discussed previously are equally integral to spreading the word that either being at or getting home for Christmas is the most crucial aspect of the season and home, preferably dressed for the season, is where Christmas should ideally be spent (Figure 6.2).

As such, home, either real or imagined, is a place that one cannot entirely escape at Christmas. Even children, when visiting Santa, rarely find that his grotto is simply a quickly converted garden shed or something resembling a polystyrene igloo anymore. Instead, behind the lights, the animatronics, and the giggling and cavorting elves, today they are more likely to encounter an extensive facsimile of a Santa-styled home replete with domestic furnishings, Christmas decorations and, of course, his own immaculately dressed tree. Furthermore, if one were to ask visiting children just who keeps Santa's house in such order and so exquisitely decorated, few, I suspect, would answer 'Santa' or even refer to his elven workforce. Instead, the overwhelming answer would be more likely to be 'Mrs Claus'.

Not that this should come as a surprise. After all, children are inclined to say what they see, and despite cultural and indeed economic patterns and practices shifting towards greater gender equality, women worldwide continue to be responsible for the majority of domestic work (McMunn et al., 2019). Moreover, at no time of the year is this expected more than at Christmas and nowhere is this more evident than in the plethora of festive adverts, where women are regularly targeted as the season's prime consumers and domestic managers. Indeed, even when a 2012 television advertisement for the UK supermarket

FIGURE 6.2   An 'ideal' home dressed for Christmas.

Source: Photograph by the author.

ASDA featured a clearly overworked and unsupported mother preparing for the season concluding with the tagline, 'It doesn't just happen by magic; behind every great Christmas, there's mum' received more than 600 complaints to the *Advertising Standards Authority* for being sexist, not one of these complaints was deemed worthy of upholding. This, one can only assume, was due to its perhaps albeit unfortunate accuracy. (Sweeny, 2013).

Women's Work at Christmas

Two facets of the domestic organization of Christmas for which women are held particularly responsible are the purchasing of seasonal gifts and the preparation of food. In respect of the former, while men do shop at and for Christmas, women tend to start shopping much earlier and buy far more gifts throughout more excursions to the shops (Laroche et al., 2000), or, one would increasingly assume, online. That gift shopping at Christmas is something that is still largely considered an area of female expertise and is 'real and important work' for a woman to undertake (Fischer and Arnold, 1990: 342) is, in part, due to its association with an expression of care; something that continues to be viewed as a predominantly female attribute. As Carrier (1993) observes, Christmas shopping for gifts and presents is often seen as a way of mediating between the intimacy of home and the commercial imperatives of the external world and is one that remains associated with a particular notion of femininity. However, Christmas shopping does not simply involve the physical act of gift buying. As she goes on to note, it is not just about the purchasing presents, but rather it can also involve weeks, if not months, of unrecognized emotional labour and the paying of close attention to the desires and needs of family members and friends to try and ensure that such gifts are both wanted and, hopefully, cherished.

Both Anne Shordike and Doris Pierces's (2005) and Valarie Wright-St Clair et al.'s (2005) study of women's practices involved in the organization and preparation of food similarly speak to how undertaking certain seasonal activities are often considered integral to the enactment of particularly gendered identities at Christmas. As Jenifer Mason and Stewart Muir (2012) point out, family Christmases are about introducing new ways of celebrating while simultaneously ensuring the maintenance of established and often long-standing traditions of how to 'keep the season'. For the women in Wright-St Clair et al.'s (2005) study, this is exemplified by an ongoing balancing of the reproduction of established values and rituals associated with food preparation handed down by previous generations of women, while responding to new entrants into the family and changing circumstances through adapting dishes and even introducing new ones. Furthermore, this is more than simply a seasonal necessity or ritual these women feel required to undertake. Instead, it is also experienced and expressed as a source of pride and identity affirmation, marking out everyone involved as a woman who is a 'skilled cook and homemaker' (Wright-St Clair et al., 2005: 348).

The work that women put into creating a home-centred celebration at Christmas is often far more than about simply providing the material ingredients of the celebration, such as gifts and food, however. As Wright-St Clair et al. (2005: 342) observe, the women involved in their study of food preparation are also:

> mindful of the needs of everyone present and do things so each one feels valued and part of the family occasion. The proceedings are orchestrated so young children don't get too tired, have something to entertain themselves with, or eat first so the adults can stay on and talk without much interruption. Serving each family member's favourite foods ensures they cater for individual uniqueness and choice.

Referred to by Alison Daminger (2019: 610) as 'cognitive labor', and entailing 'anticipating needs, identifying options for filling them, making decisions, and monitoring progress', this is a dimension of women's work at Christmas that often goes unseen and yet is integral to how Christmas is successfully reproduced year in year out. Especially on the big day itself, this is the backroom organizational activity that matches timings with hunger, the desire to open presents with the need to rest, the attractions of the television schedule with family rituals and traditions, and so on. Nevertheless, at the same time, such cognitive endeavours must also be combined with the additional physical labour the season generates and the additional emotional labour or work (Hochschild, 1983; Bolton, 2005) that accompanies it. For, as I have previously noted, no matter how much work is put into it, the family Christmas is often as much an emotional tinderbox as it is an oasis of familial love and generosity.

This aspect of Christmas, and the further demands it can place on women, is discussed at some length in an article in *The Guardian* newspaper by Laura Bates (2018), founder of *The Everyday Sexism Project*.[2] For Bates, drawing on both Hochschild's (1983) concept as well as that of what Susan Quilliam reportedly refers to as the 'emotional choreography' of Christmas, Bates explores the extent to which many women are required to manage both their own and others' emotions in order to preserve domestic harmony and the 'spirit' of Christmas. In doing so, she cites the experience of one woman who was introduced at a relatively early age to the idea that a woman's identity and the role she plays in managing the emotional demands of Christmas are intimately entwined:

> When I was 15 or so at my secondary school, we had an hour-long assembly on how a woman should run Christmas – and how her job is to make sure the family and husband enjoy their day. I think attitudes like these are the reason women especially run around shops going to extreme measures in order to make sure their families have the best days without thinking of themselves.

The Christmas Imperative

That such ideas are far from isolated is brought to the fore in perhaps the most extensive empirical study of such a gendered reproduction and organization of Christmas, Leslie Bella's (1992) book, *The Christmas Imperative*. Here, she defines such an imperative as a combination of a 'compulsion to reproduce Christmas' along with, drawing on Veronica Beechey's (1986) work, a dominant familial ideology that Bella (1992: 17) succinctly defines as 'the belief that the nuclear family, with a father in the workforce and mother at home, is both normal and preferred'. Throughout Bella's book, we see how Christmas is perpetually reproduced through work that is commonly associated with an idealized female gender identity or performance, while the home itself is where the idea of an orthodox nuclear family is itself brought into being through the annual reiteration of a series of seasonal expectations and practices. And while her account does not explicitly refer to the Anglo-American qualities of this imperative, what she describes as the feminization of Christmas is a process that she identifies and illustrates as commencing with the accession of Victoria to the British throne and her popularization 'as a role model on both sides of the Atlantic' (Bella, 1992: 94); one that only grew as the popular media of the age increasingly portrayed woman as the natural carriers of many a rediscovered Christmas tradition.

An interesting historical illustration of Bella's ideas can be found in Dulcie Ashdowns's (1976) anthology of Christmas articles from a selection of British nineteenth-century magazines. Here, periodicals of the age, some with telling titles such as *The Woman at Home*, or *Cassell's Family Magazine*, clearly illustrate the increasingly pivotal role women were expected to play in reproducing the ideal Christmas at home, especially in the form of such cognitive and emotional labour. For example, the advice and guidance in an undated article from *Cassell's*, entitled 'How to Entertain at Christmas', is directed solely at the female 'hostess' whose organizational responsibility, she is told, is not only to decide how long such entertainments should be planned for but, amongst other things, to 'preserve the general harmony' of such gatherings and determine what presents to give and 'how best to make the giving a source of pleasure' (Ashdown: 1976: 42–43).

Since the 1900s at least, therefore, the idea that it is predominantly the responsibility of women to reproduce the magic of the domestic Christmas has been handed down through generations of women via advertising and the media, as well as in the form of household rituals and cultural expectations that are often embedded within popular Christmas tales of both then and now. Indeed, Bella's (1992) own study is replete with interview extracts to this effect, with women continually aspiring, often futilely, to reproduce the ideal Christmases they liked to recall from their own childhoods and for which they held their mothers or other female relatives, almost solely responsible for. As one of her interviewees put it: 'Everything would appear magically, and who makes it appear? Mother!' (Bella, 1992: 23).

Nor have things changed all that much since Bella's interviews recounted their tales of gendered inequities at Christmas. Take, for example, an albeit light-hearted if somewhat telling piece by Shane Weston (2021) that appeared in the UK newspaper the *Daily Telegraph*. In it, he observes how there are many things that women, as the 'organizers of Christmas' as they are described, seemingly do not want to hear from men at Christmas including, 'I've just got a bit of work to finish up', or 'Did we remember to pick up the pie', knowing full well that 'we' here constitutes a very clear and direct 'you'. Moreover, in my own discussions with both men and women throughout the research for this book, similar stories and reflections emerged, albeit even where they were not primarily the focus of my questions and interests. While many men, for example, spoke about their run-up to Christmas as being busy at work, they would often then quite casually refer to the actual business of preparing Christmas as the implicit responsibility of a female spouse or partner. For example, as one heterosexual and married musical performer told me:

> Christmas is definitely my busiest time of the year for work coming in, and that means I don't get time to join in or prepare for it in any way, shopping, present buying, all that kind of thing. By the time it comes around and all the work's done I'm ready to just collapse on the sofa with the family.

The fact that Christmas often merely serves to highlight the asymmetrical and highly gendered character of domestic labour, while not universal, is not always entirely lost on those who generally benefit from it, however. While clearly there are men whose annual contributions in terms of cooking and other domestic duties come to the fore at Christmas, even if only in respect of their speciality function such as preparing a roast dinner, for many it still appears to be a time of year they find frankly daunting. As I was told by one of the Santa Claus performers we met in an earlier chapter:

> Yes, Christmas can get really busy, especially if I've got several gigs going on. Fortunately, my wife takes care of all the other stuff, presents, food, cards, and all that. I do what I can, but to be honest I find all that stuff a bit overwhelming.

While there appears to be at least some implicit acknowledgement here that organizing Christmas is not only work but potentially hard or even 'overwhelming' work, there also seems to be an assumption that it is something that the wives and partners in question can take in their stride. As such, replicating what appears to be established expectations surrounding a woman's responsibility and, indeed, aptitude for domestic work more widely (Oakley, 1974; Thébaud et al., 2021), gendered assumptions about it being the primary responsibility of women to organize and coordinate complex holiday arrangements continue to widely hold sway.

At the same time, there is no shortage of recognition by women themselves that organizing Christmas is an often complex and potentially overwhelming endeavour. While often, as observed by both the likes of Bella (1992) and Sheena Vachhani and Alison Pullen (2011), portrayed as something of a badge of honour and the crowning glory of the year's domestic endeavours, the arrival of Christmas can as often manifest a sense of ambivalence, if not trepidation, that is summed up by a now, as she put it, retired homemaker I spoke with:

> While we all loved Christmas, it was always something that I had to steel myself up for. Every year there always seemed to be more and more to do, and it never got any easier with practice.

This particular account of one woman's feelings towards the season reveals that even though it holds a special meaning for her, and its organization is something she repeated annually, it never became entirely mundane. Rather, each year it seemed to reinvent itself as demands to celebrate it in new and possibly more exciting ways, such as in the form of more sophisticated presents, foodstuffs, and entertainments were advertised and heralded. All of which, of course, had to be consciously measured against, and blended with, traditional expectations and rituals.

Given market capitalism's unnerving ability to extend its axial principles, such as quantification, efficiency, and competition, into every aspect of our daily lives (Hancock and Tyler, 2004), turning life into what has been referred to in some quarters as a social factory (Terranova, 2000), this is perhaps not surprising, of course. As anyone who celebrates the season will know, every year, the demand is for a measurably better Christmas than the last, with all the possibilities for this tied up with the purchase of new decorations, new gifts, and new ways of spending time together. And nowhere is this demand more evident than in the body of quasi-lifestyle magazines and instruction manuals that annually appear not only to caution women of the perils of not being thoroughly organized for Christmas but also to hold out a gentle, if resolute, guiding hand when purchasing and managing those essential seasonal ingredients for what will be 'the best Christmas ever'.

Gendered Guides for a Perfect Christmas

Lifestyle magazines have long played a prominent role in reinforcing a woman's perceived responsibility for the domestic organization of the home. This is even more true at Christmas, with such publications charging their predominantly female readership with the additional imperative of ensuring that 'this year' will be a Christmas never to be forgotten. Combining the virtues of Christmas consumption with a set of blueprints for the season's perfect execution that, if followed to the letter, will ensure that the woman of the house will make 'this Christmas more magical than the last' (Freeman and Bell, 2013: 341), each winter hundreds of thousands of such magazines continue to sell in the UK alone. While characterized primarily by commodity-driven feature articles that showcase various picture-perfect Christmas homes, replete with the prices and outlets for all the goods on show, underpinning their appeal is a discourse of female technical expertise that offers a form of gendered recognition (Honneth, 1995), bestowing on their readership the promise of esteem and respect by virtue of their unique organizational capacity to reproduce what should be a flawless family Christmas.

As I observed above, however, women's publications containing Christmas stories, features, and advice on everything from Christmas gift-making to hosting a festive soiree are nothing new and can be traced back to their popularization during the late 1800s.[3] Nonetheless, these magazines had developed a far more cross-class appeal by the twentieth century, especially at Christmas. For example, titles such as the mass circulation *Woman's Weekly*, first published in the UK, in 1911, quickly developed an annual Christmas edition with the 1912 December publication featuring, for example, a series of 'Christmas Reminders' including how to wrap Christmas presents in coloured paper and how to chop mincemeat for the perfect 'hot', mince pie (*Woman's Weekly*, 2014: 8).

In their comparative and systematic study of a selection of British women's magazines from the 1930s and the 1990s, Brewis and Warren (2011) have been able to chart both the developments and continuities that characterize such publications. Common to magazines from both periods, for instance, is the continued importance of consumption, alongside a preoccupation with the centrality, as mentioned earlier, of women as the primary selectors and purchasers of Christmas gifts. This is not only for family members and friends, however, but also other significant contacts, particularly a husband's or partner's work colleagues. Underpinning this is a portrayal of women not only as more emotionally attuned to the needs and desires of others than men, but as a gender positioned as naturally wanting to please and receive recognition from others through giving gifts that are both appropriate and wanted.

In contrast to this continuity, however, they also find evidence of a divergence between the earlier and later publications, with an increasing emphasis in the magazines from the 1990s on the need to apply a more rationally planned approach to the season. Acknowledging that Christmas is a potentially stressful time of year for the woman of the house, they recognize that, unlike their counterparts from the 1930s, many of their readers will now be juggling paid work with homemaking. Therefore, for women to depend on their purportedly intuitive skills and expertise as 'housewives' may no longer be sufficient. As such, these magazines promote what can be described best as a more strategic approach to organizing Christmas. This includes acknowledging that, for example, shortcuts might have to be taken in purchasing and preparing food for the big day but only, of course, when it allows the woman of the house to fit in more of those 'personal little touches' such as 'creating handmade place settings for the Christmas dinner table' (*Good Housekeeping* Magazine, cited Brewis and Warren, 2011: 758).

More latterly, Freeman and Bell's (2013) social semiotic exploration of such magazines looks explicitly at the stress they place on ritual food preparation and how women are both positioned as organizers while, at the same time, being organized in and through such Christmas activities. Published in 2010 in the UK and Australia, while these magazines appear to acknowledge the competing demands placed upon women in an age where more are economically active outside of the family, they nonetheless continue to showcase resources that not only sustain a woman's role in reproducing Christmas but also, in doing so, reproduce the dominant conception of women as both homemakers and Christmas carers. However, what Freeman and Bell (2013) also observe is the increasing presence of a new class of Christmas expert, the male celebrity chef. While the influence such chefs might have on social competencies has been a subject of wider critical scrutiny (Rousseau, 2012), as Freeman and Bell observe, they occupy an interesting position, particularly viz-a-viz the preparation of the Christmas Day 'feast'. Leaving to one side the commercial advantages a celebrity feature brings to a magazine by their presence, they introduce a new gender divide whereby women who had traditionally at least been considered the experts at preparing the Christmas day meal now became subservient in the kitchen to the expert authority of men.

Indeed, looking at both the examples cited by Freeman and Bell and more contemporary examples of such magazines, it is certainly noticeable that while women still feature heavily in such features, they are now predominantly illustrated as serving the food, not preparing it. Thus, while remaining the ones who most likely organize and cook the meal in the real world, they are now seemingly even denied recognition as the experts their mothers and grandmothers were, with that esteem now symbolically bestowed upon a supposedly more technically literate male who is represented as the actual source of their skill and expertise (Freeman and Bell, 2013: 347).

Having said this, while Freeman and Bell's research is empirically convincing, this supplanting of the kitchen's female expert appears to be something of an outlier in the broader scheme of things. Throughout such magazines, directed as they are at a predominantly female audience, women continue to occupy centre stage in nearly all other aspects of putting together the big day and beyond. Moreover, it is not simply in the role of Christmas cook, hostess, or gift buyer that women's magazines traditionally offer guidance and instruction. Christmas is, for example, a time when more than ever, the imperative is for women to not only play the part of the perfect hostess but also to look it.

Returning to Christmas issues of the *Woman's Weekly* (2014), for example, in 1912, readers are instructed how to make time away from domestic preparations to achieve 'that touch of dainty freshness so coveted by every woman'. By 1951 time must be found to add 'those little touches to make you sparkle', while during the 1990s, women were reminded not to scrimp on those festive 'magical makeovers'. Perhaps not surprisingly, by the time we get to what might be considered the racier end of the market, the advice becomes even more intimate as magazines such as *Cosmopolitan* extend their festive instructions into the bedroom, providing, for example, '21 Christmas sex ideas for the festive season' (Gulla, 2020).

The Christmas Specialist

Today, while such special Christmas editions of more generic women's titles continue to be popular, they have also been joined by the annual appearance of both specialist Christmas magazines and increasingly festive-orientated websites. Such publications have often gone to what might be considered the next level in terms of offering their female readership a thorough and detailed guide to achieving the 'best-ever' or 'most-magical' of Christmases at home. Examples such as The Christmas Magazine, currently the UK's top-selling festive publication, are becoming just as important as television listings magazines as readers plan their seasonal activities while deploying highlighter pens and other indelible markers to plan out their Christmas preparations based on the content and guidance they provide. In short, such magazines now define the trajectory and content of many a family's Christmas preparations. Moreover, in providing a work schedule for the domestic manufacture of the perfect Christmas celebration, this new breed of magazines also increasingly adopts a language that might appear more at home in a contemporary organizational management textbook than a guide to the most wonderful time of the year.

Reflecting what has been identified as a broader tendency amongst lifestyle magazines to feature largely quantified and instrumental resources for readers in search of a sustainable yet contemporary sense of self (Giddens, 1991; Hancock and Tyler, 2004), Christmas magazines typically tend to offer their readers what is in effect a seasonal planner. One that, if followed to the number and letter, will, they claim, ensure the most perfectly executed Christmas ever. This tendency is perhaps most obviously expressed in what appears to be the frequent reduction of Christmas, and its successful celebration, to a series of numbers or calculations reminiscent of a broader tendency towards the emergence of an increasingly quantified notion of the efficient self (Moore, 2017). As such, we are offered '990 ideas and tips of a perfect Christmas' (Kelsey Media, 2021) or '645 festive ideas' (Classic Christmas, 2021), all of which are usually accompanied by planners and tick boxes to ensure that these essential tasks and jobs are completed on time. Moreover, despite the increasing emphasis placed on 'affordability', or the relatively low-cost and more sustainable options of handcrafting or recycling decorations and the like, throughout these magazines, numbers in the form of the prices of everything from festive garlands to items of seasonally appealing furniture adorn most, if not every page, ensuring that the mindful woman of the house can closely calculate expenditure on not only on necessities but those festive dreams as well.

Yet even if one looks beyond the numbers, the language that features in these magazines is equally replete with organizational imperatives to plan, be efficient, and maximize resources. Monthly planning guides, usually starting around September or even earlier, provide instructions on investing in a stress-free, efficient Christmas. And while these often vary from magazine to magazine, the core ingredients are fairly universal. In 2021's *The Christmas Magazine*, for example, alongside its '990 ideas and tips for a perfect Christmas' the reader is guided through the perfect pre-Christmas itinerary with the shopping starting in September, the party planning in October and the baking in November. A more micro-managerial approach then kicks in with the arrival of December. With weeks one and two focused on ordering food, preparing party playlists, and decorating and finalizing one's Christmas wardrobe, week three becomes a frantic last-minute dash to wrap presents, pre-prepare foods for the freezer, and stock up on drinks all before the final big night when it should all 'finally come together'. Additional advice is also generously provided by experts in their field, with it being quite literally a field when it comes to picking the perfect Christmas tree, or perhaps closer to home in the case of professional crafters, issuing guidance on how to make that once in a lifetime Christmas table centrepiece.

Similar things can also be said of those largely enthusiast-led online resources that have also appeared over the last 20 years or so. Sites such as *TheOrganizationHouse.com*,[4] or *TheOrganizedHome.com*,[5] for example, both have dedicated Christmas sections, while those that focus solely on preparing for the big day 265 days of the year, such as *ChristmasOrganizing.com*[6] and *OrganizedChristmas.com*[7] set out to furnish even the most disorganized celebrants with free preparatory advice, techniques, and tools. For instance, to ensure that each Christmas is perfect, they also tend to advise the implementation of 'planning strategies',[8] ranging from simple shopping and cooking schemes to full-on Christmas journals in which one should write down one's 'dreams, desires and disappointments in respect of Christmas' as well as one's weekly 'focus assignments', all of which are geared towards helping the reader 'Calm the Christmas Chaos and take your Christmas from Stressed to Blessed'. Nor does it all end when Christmas does. For even once January beckons, just as it is for the department store buyers and the Christmas imagineers encountered in earlier chapters, it is then time for the organized woman of the house to commence the festive 'debriefing and storing of decorations' in order to ensure they get 'a good start on the next year's celebration'.[9]

Christmas Organizing Gender

Even though women now enjoy a more significant presence in the public sphere of paid work, as Sarah Thébaud et al. (2021) observes, all the evidence points to the fact that they continue to undertake most of the housework and domestic management across the bulk of households. And while the reasons for this are complex and include a host of interconnected factors, including the persistence of gender role ideologies, gendered differentials in income and national and regional labour market policies (Lachance-Grzela and Bouchard, 2010; Mandel et al., 2020), nonetheless, the persistence of such inequalities, even when economic and labour positions are accounted for, remains striking.

Even so, as the likes of Fischer and Arnold (1990) and Bella (1992) have observed, at Christmas, there is something about the extent to which traditionalist or even essentialist ideas about gender roles reassert themselves which is especially arresting. This is particularly evident in those discourses of care and service that extend the widely held expectation for women to be carers and to put the needs of others before their own (Finch and Groves, 1983). Indeed, nothing appears to characterize the 'Christmas imperative' more than an encouragement to women to attend to the domestic atmospherics of the event as a seemingly unavoidable extension of their womanly skills and attributes:

> The secret of successful entertaining lies in providing your guests not only with good food and attractive surroundings, but also with an atmosphere of warmth and charm.
>
> *(Halle, 1952, cited Waggoner, 2009: 89)*

Thus, to 'create a warm and welcoming environment for friends and family' (Classic Christmas, 2021: 142), or to perhaps take time and 'create a comfy place for guests to sit down and take off their boots … [making it] extra cosy by adding some festive cushions and a throw' (Your Home, 2020: 28) is presented as central to helping 'women find ways to spread happiness' at Christmas (*Woman's Weekly*, 2014: 2).

To argue that the organization of Christmas is a highly gendered affair, especially when it comes to the home, tells perhaps only part of the story, however. Paralleling the considerations of previous chapters, it is also necessary to consider how Christmas is not only organized but also an organizing event itself. In particular, and consistent with the subject matter of this chapter, it is perhaps worth thinking about, therefore, how Christmas helps bring not only forms of economic activity and social relations into being but also gender identities as well. There is, after all, an increasingly prominent notion that gender is not only a social rather than a biological phenomenon but also what has been termed a performative one (Butler, 1990; Lloyd, 2007). Furthermore, it has also been deftly argued that such performativity is organized and subject to the influence of fundamentally organizational practices and logics (Tyler, 2020).

The idea of performativity drawn on here, and developed most notably in the work of Judith Butler (1990, 2004) and those who draw on her work, is distinct from that earlier ascribed to Bryman (2004) in that it points to the idea that a person's gender identity is neither explained simply by nature or culture, but nor is it purely a conscious act, as say in the case of the Santa Claus performers I discussed in Chapter 5. Instead, it is considered the product of an ongoing performance that involves one actively 'doing' or 'being' a particular gender in largely unconscious or pre-reflective ways. As such, in the case of women, it is not simply that acting like a woman defines one *as* a woman, but rather that it defines *what* a woman is[10] through the perpetual reiteration of historically intelligible gendered practices, activities, gestures, and attitudes by those subject to them. These are then interpellated into an expected regime of gender performances or a 'repeated stylization of the body' (Butler, 1990: 45) that, in turn, comes to define and organize, to all extents and purposes, what it is to possess a recognized gender identity.

This is not to suggest, however, that one can perform one's gender in any way one sees fit; well, not easily anyway and particularly not if one is a woman. As I have observed, such performances are not entirely conscious or somehow premeditated. Instead, they reflect and reproduce historically constituted standards and expectations (Horkheimer, 1976) that must be considered intelligible if one is to be acknowledged as what Butler (1993: 232) would term a 'viable subject'; that is, someone who is socially recognized as possessing, and just as importantly displaying, what are viewed as the legitimate, and dualistic, characteristics of either a man or a woman. As such, the performance of gender both mimics and reproduces those signs and systems of signification that establish the very parameters of gender intelligibility and provide the context within which such performances come to be seen as natural or essential characteristics. As Butler (1990: 188) herself puts this:

> gender identity might be reconceived as a personal/cultural history of received meanings subject to a set of imitative practices which refer laterally to other imitations and which, jointly, construct the illusion of a primary and interior gendered self.

Not that this is to suggest that this mutual reproduction of context and outcome is an entirely stable or determined one, however. On the contrary, as Butler stresses, this relationship has a dialectical character that is profoundly negative (Adorno, 2008) or, as Lloyd (2007:19) refers to it, 'non-synthetic' in form. This means that neither gender identities nor the structures of signification that circulate their conditions of possibility are ever entirely stable, leaving albeit limited opportunities to renegotiate or even defy cultural norms and expectations. Nonetheless, despite any potential for provisionality and fluidity, this relationship and those identities, or subject positions (Foucault, 1978, 1980), that are formed through it are also, as Melissa Tyler (2020) notes, subject to processes of organization that, returning to Butler (1990:46), provide not only idealized gendered representations, but that actually 'seek to keep gender in its place by posturing as the foundational illusions of identity'.

Examples of such organizational processes are discussed, for instance, in Hancock and Tyler's (2007) study of highly gendered images of 'working' bodies that use various corporate recruitment brochures of the time to illustrate their case. These images of handsome and physically virile young people served, or so they argue, not only to signify organizational ideals about what a desired and desirable workforce should look like but, more significantly, also '*produce* organizationally legible and therefore viable subjects' (Hancock and Tyler, 2007: 521, emphasis added); subjects that would not only be young and beautiful, but fit, healthy, and ambitious in both practice and appearance. In doing so, these documents effectively restrict the gendered subject's scope to perform identities outside of a limited repertoire of intelligibility if they desire recognition as a potential organizational recruit. Unlike those men who annually perform the role of Santa Clause, however, while these men perform their roles are cognisant of both the repertoires and systems of signification they draw on and the part they play in reproducing them, what is at stake here is the emergence of specific identity positions whereby viability becomes internalized as a 'natural' and incontestable state of just being 'who you are'.

From this perspective, if we then return to say Bella's (1992) formulation of the Christmas imperative, we can therefore understand how, as a system of signification that appears annually in everything from Christmas magazines to supermarket advertisements, it produces a cultural framework that dictates not only how one should do Christmas *as a* woman but also what it should mean to be a woman at Christmas. So, just as one might constantly work on one's body by adhering to specific fitness regimes to be considered a sufficiently dynamic organizational employee, an act that, in itself, naturalizes the performative requirements to be such a person, Christmas requires an annual repetition of a range of performative gendered practices. These can range from festive self-adornment to what are effectively invisible acts of seasonal care that define and bring into being what it is to be a woman. And while these are by no means unique to the season, they are both keenly focused on and demonstrative of what constitutes the 'more' required to be a woman as both an ideal Christmas organizer and a generous and seasonally viable host. One who is not only enabled but summoned to become 'a sparklier, glowier version of oneself' (*Woman's Weekly*, 2014: 33).

And as the quote directly above suggests, this is precisely the message found within these kinds of magazines and websites in that one's claim to be recognized as a woman at Christmas is intimately bound up with an ability to unreflexively perform a gendered identity; one that is at the heart, both literally and figuratively, of domestic festivities, be it as a domestic goddess (Lawson, 2014) or a Santa hatted Christmas home-organizer (Blair, 2021). For to embrace Christmas fully as a household manager, hostess, and carer is to be a woman, whatever other roles or responsibilities one might have, and where the message is to follow women like Clara, who, while an entrepreneur blogger, 'would rather have three months of Christmas than summer' as this is when she is is at her happiest being able to to 'decorate, invite people round and wrap myself up in Christmas' (Classic Christmas, 2021: 74).

In this way, such seasonal resources are, therefore, more than simply furnishing decorating plans and cooking instructions for the perfect Christmas at home. Instead, they offer their female readership a mimetic repertoire that must be adopted and performed as a naturalized expression of their gendered identities. Their organizational blueprint not only serves as a guide to create and shape the perfect domestic Christmas , but also establishes the performative parameters for a recognized and intelligibly gendered Christmas hostess, whether it be in the kitchen, sitting room or even, perhaps, the bedroom.

Notes

1 www.agfinancial.org/resources/article/christmas-clubs
2 https://everydaysexism.com
3 Although the first recorded appearance of a magazine for women can be traced back to 1693 and the 'short-lived periodical called the *Ladies Mercury*' (Stearns, 1930: 43)
4 https://theorganizationhouse.com/organized-christmas/
5 https://organizedhome.com/organized-christmas
6 https://christmasorganizing.com
7 http://christmas.organizedhome.com
8 https://christmasorganizing.com
9 https://christmas.organizedhome.com/house-holidays-plan
10 Rather than the Cartesian dictum of *cogito ergo sum*, I think therefore I am, consequently, it becomes *facio ergo sum*, or I do or create therefore I am

References

Adorno, T. (2008) *Lectures on Negative Dialectic* (trans. R. Livingstone). Cambridge: Polity.

Archer, A. (2020) *Wartime Christmas: British Celebrations During Two World Wars.* London: Imperial war Museum.

Archer, S. (2016) *Midcentury Christmas: Holiday Fads, Fancies, and Fun from 1945 to 1970.* New York, NY: Countryman Press.

Ashdown, D. (1976) *Christmas Past: A Selection from Victorian Magazines.* London: Arrow Books.

Bachelard, G. (1994) *The Poetics of Space.* Boston, MA: Beacon Press.

Bates, L. (2018) 'I Think My Husband Thinks Santa Does It All: Why Women Dread the Emotional Labour of Christmas'. *The Guardian*, Tuesday December 11.

Beechey, V. (1986) 'Familial Ideology'. In, V. Beechey and J. Donald (eds) *Subjectivity and Social Relations.* Buckingham: Open University Press.

Bella, L. (1992) *The Christmas Imperative: Leisure, Family, and Women's Work.* Halifax: Fernwood Publishing.

Bemrose, B. (2019) 'The UK'S Favourite Christmas Songs'. *PRS Magazine*, December 20. Available at: www.prsformusic.com/m-magazine/features/playlist-the-uks-favourite-christmas-songs

Blair, K. (2021) *Christmas Planning 101: Your First Step in Creating Your* Christmas Plan. Jackson, TN: Independently Published.

Bolton, S. (2005) *Emotion Management in the Workplace*. Basingstoke: Palgrave.

Brewis, J. and Warren, S. (2011) 'Have Yourself a Merry Little Christmas? Organizing Christmas in Women's Magazines Past and Present'. *Organization* 18(6): 747–762.

Brown, M. (2004) *Christmas on the Home Front*. Stroud: Sutton.

Bryman, A. (2004) *The Disneyization of Society*. London: Sage.

Butler, J. (1990) *Gender Trouble: Feminism and the Subversion of Identity*. London: Routledge.

Butler, J. (1993) *Bodies That Matter: On the Discursive Limits of Sex*. London: Routledge.

Butler, J. (2004) *Undoing Gender*. London: Routledge.

Carrier, J. (1993) 'The Rituals of Christmas Giving'. In, D. Miller (ed.) *Unwrapping Christmas*. Oxford: Oxford University Press. Pp. 55–74.

Classic Christmas (2021) *Classic Christmas: Everything You Need for a Magical Celebration,* Bath: Future PLC.

Collins-Sharp, B. (2014) 'Say "No" to Holiday Stress'. *U.S. Department of Health and Human Services, Office on Women's Health*, December 17. Available at www.women shealth.gov/blog/no-holiday-stress

Daminger, A. (2019) 'The Cognitive Dimension of Household Labour'. *American Sociological Review* 84(4): 609–633.

Finch, J. and Groves, D. (eds) (1983) *A Labour of Love: Women, Work and Caring*. London: Routledge.

Fischer, E. and Arnold, S. (1990) 'More Than a Labor of Love: Gender Roles and Christmas Gift Shopping'. *Journal of Consumer Research* 17(3): 333–345.

Foucault, M. (1978) *The History of Sexuality, Volume 1: An Introduction*. New York, NY: Random House.

Foucault, M. (1980) *Power/Knowledge: Selected Interviews and Other Writings*. New York, NY: Pantheon Books.

Freeman, L. and Bell, S. (2013) 'Women's Magazines as Facilitators of Christmas Rituals'. *Qualitative Market Research: An International Journal* 16(3): 336–354.

Giddens, A. (1991) *Modernity and Self-Identity: Self and Society in the Late Modern Age*. Cambridge: Polity.

Golby, J.M. and Purdue A.W. (2000) *The Making of the Modern Christmas*. Stroud: Sutton Publishing.

Gulla, E. (2020) '21 Christmas Sex Ideas for the Festive Season'. *Cosmopolitan*, October 28.

Hancock, P. and Tyler, M. (2004) '"MOT Your Life": Critical Management Studies and the Management of Everyday Life'. *Human Relations* 57(5): 619–645.

Hancock, P. and Tyler, M. (2007) 'Un/doing Gender and the Aesthetics of Organizational Performance'. *Gender, Work & Organization* 14(6): 512–533.

Harrison, M. (1951) *The Story of Christmas: Its Growth and Development from the Earliest Times*. Watford: Odhams Press.

Hochschild, A.R. (1983) *The Managed Heart: Commercialization of Human Feeling*. Berkeley, CA: University of California Press.

Honneth, A. (1995) *The Struggle for Recognition: The Moral Grammar of Social Conflicts* (trans. J. Anderson). Cambridge: Polity Press.

Horkheimer, M. (1976) 'Traditional and Critical Theory'. In, P. Connerton (ed.) *Critical Sociology: Selected Readings*. Harmondsworth: Penguin. Pp. 206–224.

Hutton, R. (1996) *The Stations of the Sun: A History of the Ritual Year in Britain*. Oxford: Oxford University Press.

Johnes, M. (2016) *Christmas and the British: A Modern History*. London: Bloomsbury.

Kelsey Media (2021) *The Christmas Magazine*. Maidstone: Kelsey Publishing.

Kuper, A. (1993) 'The English Christmas and the Family: Time Out and Alternative Realities'. In, D. Miller (ed.) *Unwrapping Christmas*. Oxford: Oxford University Press. Pp. 158–175.

Lachance-Grzela, M. and Bouchard, G. (2010) 'Why Do Women Do the Lion's Share of Housework? A Decade of Research'. *Sex Roles* 63: 767–780.

Laroche, M., Saad, G., Cleveland, M. and Browne, E. (2000) 'Gender Differences in Information Search Strategies for a Christmas Gift'. *Journal of Consumer Marketing* 17(6): 500–522.

Lawson, N. (2014) *Nigella Christmas*. London: Chatto and Windus.

Leach, E. (1968) *A Runaway World?* London: The British Broadcasting Corporation.

Lloyd, M. (2007) *Judith Butler: From Norms to Politics*. Cambridge: Polity.

Mandel, H., Lazarus, A. and Shaby, M. (2020) 'Economic Exchange or Gender Identities? Housework Division and Wives' Economic Dependency in Different Contexts'. *European Sociological Review* 36(6): 831–851.

Marling, K.A. (2001) *Merry Christmas: Celebrating America's Greatest Holiday*. Cambridge, MA: Harvard University Press.

Mason, J. and Muir, S. (2012) 'Conjuring Up Traditions: Atmospheres, Eras and Family Christmases'. *The Sociological Review* 61(3): 607–629.

McAndrew, F.T. (2017) 'There's No Place Like Home for the Holidays – And That's What Makes the Pandemic's Winter Surge Particularly Devastating'. *The Conversation*, December 14. Available at: https://theconversation.com/the res-no-place-like-home-for-the-holidays-and-thats-what-makes-the-pandemics-win ter-surge-particularly-devastating-87575

McMunn, A., Bird, L. and Webb, E. (2019) 'Gender Divisions of Paid and Unpaid Work in Contemporary UK Couples'. *Work, Employment and Society* 34(2): 155–173.

Moore, P. (2017) *The Quantified Self in Precarity: Work, Technology and What Counts*. London: Routledge.

Nissenbaum, S. (1997) *The Battle for Christmas: A Cultural History of America's Most Cherished Holiday*. New York, NY: Vintage Books.

Nolsoe, E. (2019) 'How Does Christmas Impact People's Mental Health?'. *YouGov*, December 18. Available at: https://yougov.co.uk/topics/health/articles-repo rts/2019/12/18/christmas-harms-mental-health-quarter-brits

Oakley, A. (1974) *The Sociology of Housework*. New York, NY: Pantheon Books.

Perry, J. (2010) *Christmas in Germany: A Cultural History*. Chapel Hill, NC: University of North Carolina Press.

Pimlott, J.A.R. (1978) *The Englishman's Christmas: A Social History*. Hassocks: The Harvester Press.

Richards, A. (2020) *Wartime Christmas: British Celebrations During Two World Wars*. London: Imperial War Museum.

Rodsky, E. (2019) 'For Many Women, Christmas Is Just Hard Work. Here's How to Change Things'. *The Guardian*, Sunday December 22.

Rousseau, S. (2012) *Food Media: Celebrity chefs and the politics of everyday interference*. Oxford: Berg.

Scott, W. (1888) *Marmion: A Tale of Flodden Field*. London: Miller and Murray.

Shordike, A. and Pierce, D. (2005) 'Cooking Up Christmas in Kentucky: Occupation and Tradition in the Stream of Time'. *Journal of Occupational Science* 12(3): 140–148.

Stearns, B-M. (1930) 'The First English Periodical for Women'. *Modern Philology* 28(1): 45–59.

Sweeny, M. (2013) 'Asda Cleared Over "Sexist" Christmas Ad Despite More than 600 Complaints'. *The Guardian*, Wednesday January 30.

Taggart, C. (2017) *Christmas at War*. London: John Blake.

Terranova, T. (2000) 'Free-Labour: Producing Culture for the Digital Economy'. *Social Text* 18(2): 33–58.

Thébaud, S., Kornrich, S. and Ruppanner, L. (2021) 'Good Housekeeping, Great Expectations: Gender and Housework Norms'. *Sociological Methods & Research* 50(3): 1186–1214.

Thompson, P. (1992) *The Edwardians: The Remaking of British Society*. London: Routledge.

Tyler, M. (2020) *Judith Butler and Organization Theory*. London: Routledge.

Vachhani, S. and Pullen, A. (2011) 'Home Is Where the Heart Is?: Organizing Women's Work and Domesticity at Christmas'. *Organization* 18(6): 807–821.

Verney, C. (2021) 'Why the Increase in Domestic Violence Over Christmas?'. *DV-ACT* www.dvact.org/post/why-does-domestic-violence-increase-over-christmas

Waggoner, S. (2009) *Christmas Memories: Gifts, Activities, Fads and Fancies, 1920s–1960s*. New York, NY: Stewart, Tabori & Chang.

Weightman, G. and Humphries, S. (1987) *Christmas Past*. London: Sidgwick & Jackson.

Weston, S. (2021) 'What Women Want at Christmas (and We're not Talking About Presents)'. *The Telegraph*. www.telegraph.co.uk/women/life/women-want-christ mas-not-talking-presents/

Woman's Weekly (2014) *A Vintage View Christmas Special*. London: Time Inc.

Wright-St Clair, V., Hocking, C., Bunrayong, W. et al. (2005) 'Older New Zealand Women Doing the Work of Christmas: A Recipe for Identity Formation'. *The Sociological Review* 53(2): 332–350.

Your Home (2020) *Christmas Made Easy*. London: Your Home Style.

7

ORGANIZING CHRISTMAS

The Wrapping Up

Introduction

Multifaceted and multifunctional, Christmas is the global festival of the age. From the primordial mid-winter celebrations of Europe, it has evolved into an indisputable and indispensable thread in the fabric of contemporary life. It can bring a sense of continuity not only to one's everyday life but also to one's place in the flow of generations, a fixed point in time that 'feels indestructible, almost bulletproof' (Marsden, 2017: 62). And while it is a religious occasion of significance for some, during which even the most secular activities are understood to celebrate the birth of the Christian saviour, at the same time, for millions of others who celebrate it, Christmas is simply 'the holidays': A break or a pause in the formal cycle of production and a chance to catch their breath and rest, party, or just spend time with family and friends.

As I have argued, however, for it to be all these things and more, Christmas also demands hard work and the mobilization of a myriad of organizations and organizational resources, both human and non-human. For some people, this means working harder to make extra money to spend on seasonal gifts and luxuries. At the same time, for others, it might be more of a matter of making ends meet or even survival, with Christmas being a time of unhappiness as hardship and loss are felt more acutely than ever. Then there are those for whom Christmas is the season to organize and to plot, plan, and calculate in order to either just cope, or see the fruits of one's labours realized in 'the best Christmas ever': a time to set objectives, meet goals, and exceed expectations be it in the factory, retail store, restaurant, or home.

DOI: 10.4324/9781315637969-8

Nonetheless, whatever the demands and tensions that Christmas might bring, the season remains integral to how many people gauge not only the state of their everyday lives but that of the world around them. Indeed, as I write this concluding chapter, it is worth reflecting, albeit briefly, on the fact that developed nations are starting to emerge from the tragedy that was, and still is in many parts of the world, the COVID-19 pandemic. Yet while there was much to note during its darkest days, here in the UK, one thing that stood out was the role Christmas played as both a barometer of the national mood and a focal point for the population's hopes and fears. As it became increasingly apparent in 2020 that it would not be 'over by Christmas', the nation started seeing quasi-hysterical newspaper headlines declaring 'Christmas Cancelled' or that the pandemic was going to 'Wreck Christmas'. And even though the country, as did much of the world, made it through the season under lockdown, the rise of the Omicron variant of the virus in 2021 almost led to further restrictions once again throwing the nation into panic, if not uproar. The relief when the UK government eased restrictions on socializing over the festivities led, however, to equally impassioned declarations that 'Christmas is Saved' and that the UK population could 'Carry on Christmas' as the festive season became a clarion call to the country.

The significance of Christmas to people during such a crisis should come as no surprise, of course. While the economic impact of the virus was uneven during the winter, with particular sectors such as hospitality and entertainment hit severely (Office for National Statistics, 2022; Hancock et al., 2021), it was the human and cultural impact that was most keenly felt by many. For example, in addition to the deaths and human tragedies directly caused by the virus, even while government regulations were loosened in 2021, uncertainty and restricted socializing, especially with extended family groups, exacerbated a national and global decline in mental health over the season, especially among the young and elderly (Dale et al., 2021; Fancourt et al., 2022). Under such circumstances, as Christmas seemed to slip away, so it became even more important as a marker of hoped-for normality as well as an opportunity to reconnect with loved ones. At the same time, throughout both winters affected by the pandemic, many individuals and families in the UK and elsewhere also turned to Christmas to lift their own and their community's spirits. Often this was by illuminating and decorating their houses earlier than usual and leaving external illuminations up and lit well into the early spring. As such, not since the early years of the Second World War had Christmas seemed so important an event, as well as a focus of communal solidarity and shared struggles and aspirations.

However, while this is interesting in respect of once again foregrounding the importance of Christmas it is something of a digression from the series of objectives I set in writing this book. The first of these was to demonstrate that celebrating Christmas, particularly in its dominant Anglo-American form (Miller, 1993), is only possible due to the existence and functioning of various organizations and organizational practices. In doing so, I have attempted to illuminate the range of sites, techniques, and intentionalities that are at the heart of how Christmas is reproduced and experienced by people each year. From the stocking and staffing of shops and stores, through the presentation of seasonal entertainments, to something as mundane as putting a Christmas dinner on the table, I have endeavoured to explore these practices and their importance for the making and remaking of this December festival.

The second was to consider Christmas's role throughout its history as an organizing medium in society. Indeed, if, as Etzioni (2004) claims, we are what we celebrate, then more than any other celebration Christmas holds a mirror up to those societies in which it is observed. Moreover, however, it also provides what in sociological terms might be described as a nomos (Berger, 1967); that is, a framework of taken for granted behaviours and ways of organizing our daily lives that are not only of importance during the season but are normalized well beyond it. For example, the enduring centrality of the family unit and its reproduction to social stability, the virtue of mass consumption in a working free-market economy, and the maintenance of a suitably gendered division of domestic labour to a festive and, therefore, purportedly happy home, amongst others, all provide a constant thread that runs throughout the customs and values of Christmas and into the days, weeks and months that come both before and after it. Moreover, by exploring such ideas and practices, I have demonstrated how Christmas contributes to how we internalize and reproduce the organizational character of the world today, characterizing Christmas as an organizational nexus, a point of convergence of multiple institutions, practices and ideals that include religious organizations, governments, manufacturers and retailers, advertisers, families, and workforces of various hues, that are both organized and organizing of ways of acting, feeling, and, more broadly speaking, being.

The final of these objectives was to retain a critical dialogue with Christmas and its organizational features, particularly as they pertain to its commercial characteristics and their role in the reproduction of frequently inequitable social relations. Drawing primarily, although not exclusively, on ideas associated with the *Frankfurt School*, I have pinpointed, throughout the preceding chapters, sites at which certain contradictions of Christmas are revealed most starkly. As I stated in my introduction, my intention here has never been to simply damn Christmas. Nonetheless, from its reliance on exploitative employment relations, through its perpetuation of often unsustainable consumption practices and the accumulation of debt (Peachey, 2022), to its capacity to legitimatize inequitable gender relations, I have argued that Christmas cannot be celebrated unequivocally, however attractive a proposition that might be.

In saying this, I am aware, however, that I have provided perhaps less sustained evidence in respect of this latter objective than I would have liked.

As such, in this final chapter, I offer a more critical engagement with Christmas and its negative impact on our ability to live what I have described as a good life. In the first half, therefore, I explore a side of Christmas that is less written about. From environmental despoliation to its negative impact on those organizations charged with caring for our health and well-being posed by this season of merriment and indulgence, I consider both empirical evidence and political arguments that challenge the benefits of Christmas to society. Then, in the second, I conclude both the chapter and the book by asking if anything of value or meaning remains to be found in the festive season as we experience it today. In doing so, and drawing on the ideas of German philosopher Ernst Bloch (1976, 1986a, 1986b), I propose that despite its almost seemingly total incorporation into the commercial and organizational structures of life today, Christmas might yet retain a surplus of liberating ideas and values that remain relevant not only to how Christmas is organized but also to how we might genuinely nurture the joy and recognition that continues, even now, to legitimize this annual celebration.

The Challenges of Christmas

It would be hard to disagree with the proposition that the greatest challenge currently facing humanity and the planet is climate change and environmental despoilation. According to the *United Nations*, around 11.2 billion tonnes of solid waste is currently collected worldwide. The decay of the organic proportion of such waste contributes around 5% of global greenhouse gas emissions, while the electricity and heat we generate each year contribute around another 35%.[1] This has contributed to a degree of global warming that has seen a 1.1-degree rise in global temperatures since pre-industrial times; an increase that is already being held responsible for the growing impact of extreme weather events, including 'heatwaves, droughts, flooding, winter storms, hurricanes and wildfire'.[2] Given the levels of consumption associated with Christmas, it should come as no surprise, therefore, that the festive season is a notable contributor to the climate emergency facing the planet.

Leaving to one side Waldfogel's (1993, 2009) aforementioned claim that all seasonal gifting is intrinsically wasteful due to the deadweight loss it produces in the economy, Christmas undoubtedly results in the production of an excessive amount of material waste each year. Political ecologist Raymond Bryant (2010) has even gone as far as to suggest that Christmas is the world's largest annual environmental disaster, an image poetically captured by Powys (2010: 4) in his essay *The First Fall of Snow* when he observes how:

There are few things more depressing to look upon than a heap of soiled snow, several weeks old, banked up against a sidewalk. It is then, when one's eyes light up on scraps of human refuge projecting from the soiled mass, that one's imagination concedes with a shock the vision of the planet so radiant in itself being rapidly disfigured by the presence of an importunate, restless animal.

From thrown-away wrapping paper, leftover food, tin cans, and other containers, to toys and gifts that are broken and dumped before the New Year, Christmas is undoubtedly the season to discard like no other. Yet, while part of what has been termed a broader 'crisis of waste' (O'Brien, 2008), Christmas is also somewhat unique in that as a consequence of its association with production as a positive and joyous thing, the waste, destruction, and damage it leaves in its wake is something that is largely ignored or excluded from critical considerations of the season. This is illustrated in Carol Farbotko and Lesley Head's (2013) study of sustainable consumption at Christmas, finding as they did that even those individuals and families who typically considered themselves to be environmentally sensitive 'green consumers' tended to marginalize or play down environmental concerns at Christmas. Furthermore, this was especially true when it came to gift-giving, which they viewed as somehow external to the values they would typically adhere to in order to minimize their consumerist and carbon footprint.

Despite such seasonal myopia, the amount of waste material Christmas generates is regularly recorded by organizations from within the private, state, and third sectors, keen to record the season's wasteful nature and environmental impact. Take, for example, a report published and updated in 2021 by packaging company *GWP* (Dobson, 2022) which observes how in the UK, 30% more household rubbish is discarded each Christmas compared to the rest of the year. This is about three million tonnes of additional waste comprising, on average, 108 million rolls of wrapping paper, 125,000 of plastic packaging, and £42 million worth of unwanted Christmas presents.

Another significant source of Christmas waste is food. According to the UK government's *Department for Environment, Food & Rural Affairs*, homes across the UK annually throw away over 800,000 tonnes of potatoes and carrots, 100,000 tonnes of poultry, and enough gravy to accompany Christmas dinner for the entire UK.[3] Of course, it is not just the UK that contributes to such a festive waste mountain. The Anglo-American Christmas has a similar impact wherever it is celebrated. In Ireland, for example, households generated around 81,000 tonnes of packaging waste during the Christmas of 2020 (Browne, 2021), while in Australia, a third of the $554 million spent on extra food over the season finds itself in the bin while over 80,000 tonnes of used batteries are discarded at the same time.[4]

Furthermore, the disposal of such mountains of waste comes with economic as well as environmental costs. For example, in the UK, an estimated

£26 million is spent on disposing of Christmas waste each year, including a £1.2 million cost for decorations and £1.1. million for Christmas trees if they go into landfill (Dodds, 2019). Nonetheless, while the economic costs of waste disposal are real and significant, its environmental impact remains the primary concern for most organizations involved in monitoring such activities. Not that all of this is due simply to the waste produced at Christmas. As one might expect, the production, distribution, and usage costs of all those decorations, gifts, and other seasonal components cannot be taken lightly either. Moving away from the UK for a moment, a 2005 report by the *Australian Conservation Foundation* found, for example, that the $1.5 billion spent by Australians on clothing and related items over the Christmas period resulted in the production of an additional 720,000 tonnes of greenhouse pollution, the use of 38 gigalitres of water, and the disturbance of half a million hectares of land. Likewise, the manufacturing process of household appliances valued at $1500 million during that Christmas resulted in the emission of around 780,000 tonnes of greenhouse pollutants and the consumption of over a megatonne of materials (Australian Conservation Society, 2005).

And while these figures often try to factor in the additional transportation and supply chain costs, these are, however, notoriously difficult to calculate with any great precision. We know that around 90% of an organization's impact on the environment comes from its supply chains (Bové and Swartz, 2016), although how this translates directly to Christmas production, transportation, and consumption is hard to judge. Nonetheless, what is known is that both shopping and home deliveries produce a not insignificant carbon footprint at Christmas, and research suggests that the former is the most damaging option. A 2009 report, for example, found that in the UK an urban shopping trip by car for a specific item generates 4,274 grams of CO_2 per km while a successful first-time home delivery creates just 181 grams of CO_2 per km per parcel. As Cotton (2021) notes, however, while this report remains indicative, the gap has most likely widened further, given the higher investment in electric and green engine technologies by delivery firms compared to private individuals. Either way, home shopping remains the more environmentally friendly option, although neither is cost-free.

How individuals and families observe the season can also come with a high environmental price tag. In 2007, the *Stockholm Environment Institute* (SEI-Y) at the UK's *University of York* calculated that over the three days of Christmas festivities, celebrating can produce as much as a kilogram of carbon dioxide (CO_2) per average person, including 96 kg of CO_2 from Christmas car journeys and 310 kg of CO_2 from Christmas shopping.[5] Similarly, *Greenpeace* has calculated that the huge number of Christmas cards sent each year in the UK alone results in the destruction of roughly 200,000 trees, while it takes around 1.3 kg of coal to produce every 1 kg of wrapping paper, with the processes emitting 3.5 kg of CO_2.[6] Even within the home, the seasonal celebrations can result in something of a toxic atmosphere, and I am not just referring to when the relatives arrive. Pollutants associated with everything from scented candles and party poppers to simply cooking a turkey reportedly pose a statistically significant health risk to those exposed to them (Colbeck, 2016).

The above notwithstanding, however, the relationship between environmental costs and waste production remains perhaps the most significant impact associated with the season. While certain items associated with Christmas, such as cards, can be recycled, many other staples of the celebration continue to contribute to landfill and environmental pollution. In the UK, for example, celebrants dispose of approximately 4500 tonnes of contaminated tin foil and 125 tonnes of plastic packaging over Christmas (Jessop, 2022), while the rest of the waste packaging of toys and other gifts is dumped in around 100 million black bags every year. Furthermore, when it comes to Christmas trees, even real ones, once discarded, can give off up to a hundred thousand tonnes of harmful gases as they decompose, producing methane which is 25 times more damaging as a greenhouse gas than carbon dioxide (Hall, 2021).

Having said this, it should also be recognized that Christmas has also played its part as a campaigning tool in response to the climate crisis. Perhaps one of the most notable examples of this was the 2013 campaign by *Greenpeace* that attempted to raise awareness about the despoliation of the artic due to climate change and the advantage being taken of the melting ice by oil companies who are venturing further and further into this previously unspoilt wilderness. Entitled 'Save Santa's Home' (Figure 7.1), this integrated campaign used a combination of print advertisements, Christmas cards, social media and, in particular, a striking video featuring Santa played by UK actor Jim Carter, pleading for help in what looks like a hostage or 'found-footage' post.[7] And while the real-term effectiveness of such campaigns is often hard to measure, the use of Christmas and the image of Santa Claus, in particular, produced a hard-hitting message that resulted in global coverage and a reported one million signatures supporting the objective of creating a protective sanctuary around the arctic (Palmer-Sutton, 2014).

Animals and the Cost of Christmas

We can also interpret the natural environment we depend on more widely to include, for example, those non-human animals we share the planet with. In Chapter 4, I briefly alluded to the fates that meet certain reindeer in the Christmas tourist destinations of Finnish Lapland, where they are both exalted as magical and much-loved confidantes of Santa Claus while consumed not only as objects of the tourist gaze (Urry, 1990) but as flesh and bones in the form of souvenirs and food. While this has led to regional and organizational

FIGURE 7.1   Greenpeace campaign poster to save the Artic and 'Santa's Hone'.
© Greenpeace.

interventions, including the creation of a welfare charter for reindeer in the country,[8] concerns about animal welfare during the season are much more widespread. In the UK, organizations such as the *Royal Society for the Prevention of Cruelty to Animals* (RSPCA), for instance, annually run campaigns reminding the public of the costs and responsibilities of giving animals as domestic pets for Christmas with reports often emerging of around three pets every hour being abandoned over the festive period (Insley, 2010). Equally, one RSPCA inspector I was fortunate to speak with explained how another major problem they faced was that external Christmas decorations, especially electrical displays, could be particularly hazardous to wild animals, with many calls over the season reporting foxes, birds, and even deer caught up in, and injured by such features.

Furthermore, staying with the implications and dangers of Christmas for non-human animals, in 2016 the UK's Vegetarian Society made headlines with its 'True Cost of Christmas' report highlighting the cost to livestock animals during the festive season. It observed how around ten million turkeys are slaughtered each Christmas while many other animals, including pigs and geese, are farmed for the season in intensive and degrading conditions that cause both ill-health and psychological and emotional distress.[9] Such an approach to the production of meat in general, and Christmas meats in particular, represent a significant extension of instrumental and organizational rationality that results in the industrialization of death to such a scale that it is reported that the UK's largest turkey producer now slaughters around 100 birds a minute in the run-up to Christmas (Kuehnel, 2016). In Germany, in a not dissimilar campaigning vein, *The Animal Welfare Office* ran a TV advert entitled 'The Most Violent Time of The Year'. Featuring the Christmas story of an animated goose called Fibi, it charts his slaughter and consumption as a mass, mechanical act that lacks any of the joy and compassion associated with the season.[10]

Nor is it just a question of the welfare of non-human animals and a lack of compassion towards them that is at stake here. The impact of such intensive livestock-rearing practices is not only considered environmentally detrimental but can also have harmful implications for human health with the consumption of such animal products associated with everything from obesity to cancer and, increasingly, the growth in antibiotic-resistant bacteria (Horrigan et al., 2002).

Seasonal Health and Well-being

While Christmas is a season that can be highly detrimental to both animals and the planet, it can also prove, therefore, to be an immediate health hazard to people as well. While the human cost of overindulgence can undoubtedly be traced back to the season's formative centuries, the earliest reported harms caused directly by the contemporary Anglo-American Christmas can be most reliably traced back to the 1850s and include, for example, historical records of Christmas tree candles igniting the dress of young girl and a young boy eating holly berries until the was admitted to hospital in a death like trance (Morris, 2015). It was not only children who were at risk, however. For example, in 1876 a man reportedly contracted arsenic poisoning from painting large seasonal cards with bright green paint that contained copper hydrogen arsenite (Ferner and Aronson, 2020). From what I can tell, however, all survived to celebrate another Christmas.

Today, such minor festive health challenges, or 'Chrishaps' as Ursula Wild et al. (2021) refer to them, can range from Christmas tree allergies and damaged corneas due to a scratch of the eye from one of its branches to food poisoning from leftovers that have been left a little too long. Food poisoning can, of course, prove to be more severe than simply a Chrishap, with death being a possibility for more vulnerable individuals. Indeed, today Christmas is associated more generally with increased morbidity and mortality spikes (Phillips et al., 2010), with deaths in the UK between December 21 and January 19 significantly higher than during the rest of the winter months, up around 10% by Christmas Eve compared to early December. In addition to the increased prevalence of infection and death from viruses such as Flu and COVID-19, this is due in large part to the number of accidental deaths that increase over the season, including those involving, for example, traffic accidents, falls, and fire, as well as incidents due to environmental factors including exposure to cold (NHS Choices, 2012). Add to this research reported in the *British Medical Journal* that shows that Christmas Eve is the worst day of the year for heart attacks, with the risk increasing by nearly 40% (Mohammad et al. 2018), and Shofiq Islam et al.'s (2016) finding that assault-related facial injuries occur more frequently during the season of goodwill than at any other time, and it would seem that Christmas is not always a season of healthy good cheer.

Physical health is not all that suffers over Christmas, however. While the season can be particularly stressful for many people, for those who already suffer from mental health conditions or who have perhaps recently faced a bereavement, the season can be additionally demanding. According to a YouGov survey, 25% of the UK population claim that Christmas worsens their mental health with, as I noted in Chapter 6, women reportedly experiencing greater levels of stress and anxiety than men at this time of year (Nolsoe, 2019). As such, organizations concerned with mental health are wary of dismissing such concerns during the run-up to the season and emphasize its apparent knock-on effects into the New Year. For while the idea that during Christmas suicide rates rise itself is something of a myth (Hillard et al., 1981; Burton, 2012), with rates usually falling in most countries, it often peaks around New Year's Day, as Brendan Cavanagh et al.'s (2016) study in England indicates. In the UK, mental health charities such as *Mind* are therefore often busy campaigning to ensure that symptoms of mental illness and depression are not overlooked during the festivities and that common trigger factors, such as feeling frustrated by other people's views of a 'perfect' Christmas, especially if these do not match one's own experiences are recognized by others.[11]

Health and Social Care at Christmas

What all this often means for healthcare professionals, both for the reasons above, as well as the challenges of frequently working with reduced numbers of colleagues due to leave and seasonal illnesses, is that Christmas can be particularly challenging. As Adam Kay (2019: 2), in his humorous recollections of work as a junior doctor, puts it, in addition to all the everyday demands placed on emergency departments at Christmas, they can be:

> Busier than turkey farms, thanks to black eyes from carelessly popped champagne corks, fleshy forearms seated by roasting tins, and children concussing themselves by hurtling down the stairs in the box their Scalextric came in. Not to mention the fairy-light electrocutions, turkey bones trapped in tracheas, and finger amputations from careless parsnip chopping.

And while this is undoubtedly true, having spoken to many hospital workers and indeed worked as one of them in a previous professional life, the festive season can also present some of the ugliest of scenes of the year. From the often tragic consequences of drug taking and drunk driving incidents, through domestic and street violence, to abandoned and lonely people, it is often hard not to question the idea of a season of peace and love when alcohol, frustration, avarice, and the belief that one should have the best of times whatever the consequences for others appear to take centre stage.

Homelessness is another condition regularly associated with physical and mental health problems, especially at Christmas. Hospital emergency departments often see a particular increase in such individuals attending with both real and fabricated ailments, often just to get themselves off the streets for an evening. Moreover, while the media's tendency to focus on issues such as the plight of the homeless at Christmas can be understood as a means of normalizing this situation while often proffering Dickensian Christmas charity as the appropriate response (Devereux, 2021), understanding the context is essential. Homeless individuals often feel doubly ostracized during the festive season as the society around them is busy preparing for this predominantly home-based celebration while they prepare to survive the forthcoming months of darkness, cold, and increasing personal danger. As such, even those for whom mental health issues did not initially play a prominent role in their homelessness.[12] Christmas is when such problems can arise and come to the fore (Yeiser, 2021).

A further contributing factor to increased levels of homelessness and a need for help, often medical, over Christmas, as well as a further consequence of the additional pressures people frequently feel during the season, is domestic violence or abuse. Incidents of such violence and abuse traditionally rise over

Christmas (Oppenheim, 2021) and, as Claire Verney (2021) observes, reported seasonal occurrences almost doubled between 2019 and 2020 in the UK, reaching around 369,000 cases. While this increase can partly be explained by the impact of the COVID-19 pandemic during these years, as Verney (2021) further notes, we also have to look to the excuse the stresses of Christmas often unjustly provide its perpetrators, alongside what is often a lack of an escape route for its victims. This can be due not only to the home-centric ideals of Christmas, which mean that family and friends are often hunkered down and less interested in what is taking place outside their immediate sphere but is also a consequence of many organizations that might otherwise have provided support or a haven for the abused, such as schools, workplaces, and GP surgeries, being either closed or operating with minimal staffing (Oppenheim, 2021).

Moreover, as one might expect, health and social care issues place a particular strain on those organizations, both statutory and voluntary, charged with addressing them. Women's refuges, for example, often find themselves under increased pressure during the season as they serve to shelter not only women who are victims of domestic abuse but their children as well. At Christmas, not only can this mean trying to provide a safe environment but also something of the magic of the season, with small gifts and meals provided wherever possible, depending on public generosity and support (Balloo, 2020).

For organizations dedicated to helping the homeless while much of their work can revolve around raising awareness and running funding campaigns over Christmas in an attempt to tap into the charitable discourse of the season,[13] it can also mean a vast organizational effort to directly help the homeless to find shelter, food, and companionship over the holiday when few other avenues for support are open to them. In the UK, the charity *Crisis* – originally *Crisis at Christmas* – is renowned for providing all these for the homeless across London. With its first 'Open Christmas' event held in 1971, it now mobilizes over 11,000 volunteers to help run its London centres, while volunteers across the UK help support those without a home over the holiday period. Similarly, in other regions of the UK, as well as worldwide, church and civic organizations focus on Christmas both as a time for political campaigning as well as a time of direct support and local interventions.[14]

Policing Christmas

While not always associated with positive interventions for those forced to live on the streets, another organization that frequently finds itself stretched and experiencing the worst that the season can bring is the police. In the UK, the additional demands generated by the season often start to be felt by forces up and down the country weeks before Christmas itself as campaigns to deter or apprehend those who consume alcohol or illegal drugs and then drive start to take shape. Even in December 2020, a relatively quiet year due to the ongoing impact of COVID-19 restrictions, it was still reported, for example, that police forces across the country stopped around 50,317 vehicles and undertook 42,613 screening breath tests and 6,217 screening drug tests, resulting in 6,730 motorists being caught drink or drug driving during the period.[15]

One officer I spoke to informally about working over the season noted that while Christmas Day could be relatively quiet in some respects, some areas of activity could be particularly demanding. Apart from public order disturbances associated with revellers on Christmas and especially New Year's Eve, perhaps unsurprisingly given what I have already said, attending to domestic violence incidents is a significant source of police activity over Christmas. Some UK forces, such as Merseyside Police, now utilize specialist domestic abuse detectives who are available during the Christmas and New Year period to accompany patrol officers to incidents in the family home,[16] something which is considered particularly necessary at a time of the year when tensions are high and younger family members are more likely to be witnesses. As one Derbyshire officer reports online:

> [I] was attending a domestic where a family had a load of frozen food on their worktops. They were obviously putting more effort than normal into cooking the dinner, but an argument had broken out and the step-dad had stamped on some of the presents in anger. When we arrived, the kids were sat on the floor, upset, but not affected by a police presence at all, this was 'the norm' for them.
>
> *(Reason, 2019)*

Domestic burglaries and, increasingly, electronic fraud also require additional police attention during this time of the year. With darker evenings and the likelihood of expensive consumer goods, pre-packaged and stored in a single place, being found in the home, police reports of burglaries traditionally increase over December with, for example, a seasonal spike of 11% recorded in Birmingham, the UK's second-largest city, during Christmas 2021 (Storer, 2021). Online fraud is another growing concern as levels of online shopping have grown as Christmas consumers appear ever more eager to purchase an online bargain while not necessarily being aware of the risks (Hache and Ryder, 2011). According to the UK's National Fraud and Cyber Reporting Centre, in 2019, fraudsters successfully conned over £13.5 million out of online shoppers, a 20% increase on the previous year,[17] a figure rising to £15 million in 2020 (Topham, 2021), and one that is expected to grow in years to come.

While many of the challenges faced by the police at Christmas, and not only in the UK but globally, stem from seasonal increases in the kinds of serious social and criminal activities considered above, others, while of a less severe nature, can also prove to be almost as stressful. Particularly in an age of social media, police activities at Christmas open themselves up to greater critical scrutiny than at any other time of the year. A Christmas tree located outside a police station in London, for example, achieved national, if not global, notoriety due to its more than lacklustre appearance and the fact that the metal barriers surrounding it gave the impression of it having been 'kettled' by officers (Al-Othman, 2015). More recently, in Germany, police officers were filmed arresting a man dressed as Santa Claus, purportedly for failing to produce ID while participating in a demonstration against proposals for compulsory COVID-19 vaccinations in the country. The video quickly went viral, with reports even appearing in the pages of *Newsweek* magazine (Kaonga, 2021), with mockery and abuse expressed in equal measure towards the police by those opposed to state-led attempts to curb the virus and those upset by the 'manhandling' of this paragon of seasonal virtue.

Whatever the future holds for Christmas, however, and I suspect it will essentially be more of the same, the pressure it puts on our natural environment, our health and well-being and those organization that endeavour to protect and sustain us is unlikely to dissipate. As I have already observed, Christmas has become almost impossible to resist or be drawn into in one way or another. It might be, of course, that as the influence of Christianity declines in the West (Coren, 2022) that the season's Saturnalian tendencies will come even more to the fore, but if that is the case, then one can only perhaps wonder as to the kind of impact it will have on those areas of concern I have referred to above. That is, might it become even more environmentally disastrous and personally damaging as our seasonal hedonism colludes with the imperatives of a world in which we are constantly told to organize for a season during which, as Bernard Shaw once bemoaned:

We must be gluttonous because it is Christmas. We must be drunken because it is Christmas. We must be insincerely generous; we must buy things that nobody wants, and give them to people we don't like; we must go to absurd entertainments, that make even our little children satirical; we must writhe under venal officiousness from legions of freebooters, all because it is Christmas.

(Shaw, 1973: 119)

Contesting an Organized Christmas

Despite such challenges to everything from the natural environment to individual well-being and from being something to be embraced to something often simply endured, Christmas continues to exert a massive hold on the popular imagination. With images of peace, plenty and the joys of hearth and home, along with its promise of a magical time spent with friends, family, and loved ones, it continues to enchant vast swathes of the global population as they work, save, and strive to have the best Christmas ever. However, as Bennett (1981:72) acknowledges, to sustain this seasonal illusion, it is vital that 'the formal means and mechanisms' by which the ideal of Christmas is manufactured often remain obscured from the mass of those who observe it. Hence, while we enjoy its spectacles and delights, we are discouraged from looking behind the curtain lest, as with waiting up for Santa Claus, the truth spoils the magic forever, and we are forced to grow up before our time.

Nevertheless, at the risk of finding myself on the naughty list, I have spent much of this and the preceding chapters considering these very means and mechanisms. In doing so, I have tried to reveal a nexus where not only forms of organization intertwine but also where the relationship of business to society and those practices by which individuals form and sustain their own seasonal identities as producers, consumers, and members of civil society are perhaps less opaque. In doing so, to return to the story of the magic key I alluded to in the introduction, I have argued that Christmas is 'hard work' on many levels, be it that involved in making the season happen or in becoming the ideal Christmas subject: one who not only shops and celebrates but whose labour, both visible and indeed invisible, cements the whole event together.

I have also hinted and, at times, taken full tilt at what I consider the more damaging consequences of Christmas for how we might live. For while I have tried to avoid taking sides in those debates that identify Christmas as something that has fallen from grace, or that position it in respect of simplistic binaries such as holy or secular, Christian or pagan, or even naughty or nice, this has not always been possible. From its complicity in sustaining power amongst elite social classes and institutions, through its ideological celebration of both individually and environmentally damaging over-consumption, to the exploitation of a global workforce and the stresses it places on both our everyday lives and those organizations charged with protecting and caring for us, Christmas perpetuates many damaging social pathologies. Moreover, while it would be naive to claim that such unwholesome consequences are always a direct result of the organizational character of the season, there is undoubtedly something of what in Weberian sociology might be termed an elective affinity between them (Weber, 1976). For not only do both the rationality of organization, and Christmas, demonstrate a genealogical legacy, with each born of a drive to exert control over both the natural and human environment, but they have also come of age together, each displaying a sympathetic upholding of many of the other's practices and principles as they seek to bring their own version of order and regularity to the world.

Not that this suggests some conscious or perfect alignment of shared values and practices between them. For even when mediated through economic forms of organization such as capitalism or social structures such as patriarchy, Christmas retains an often allotropic quality exiting simultaneously as the cultural embodiment of profoundly human and even spiritual values of love, life, and spontaneity as well as of the relentless instrumentality of economic production, consumption, destruction, and disposal. As such, in addition to reproducing and reinforcing organizational ideas and practices, Christmas can also visibly problematize them be it through the hedonistic excesses of the office party, the sacrifice of time and energy for the pleasure of others, or even those often profoundly irrational passions that can generate potentially subversive forms of disorder and conflict at Christmas. And, while, as I have observed, these can bring with them their own risks, they can also expose, if only temporarily, the inconsistencies and contradictions of those potentially damaging systems of thought and practice that the season ordinarily appears to legitimize.

All this said, however, one thing that cannot be easily escaped is that to have any hope of achieving all that Christmas offers, and indeed demands of us, we remain dependent on systems and technologies that are central to the activities of a global marketplace. This is a marketplace that, despite seasonal claims to the contrary, operates on relations of equivalency and identity based not on the use or emotional value of a gift or service but on an abstract value measured in currency and often exclusiveness. As we have seen, there is little about Christmas that cannot be bought and sold for profit. Not that this is, as I have argued elsewhere, an exclusively contemporary phenomenon. Winter festivals have always involved some degree of organization and featured economic transactions of one form or another. Nonetheless, there is something intrinsically modern about how the Anglo-American Christmas is embedded in an order of social and economic organization that is highly rationalized in its ideals and its indebtedness to the values and practices of consumer capitalism (Rycenga, 2008). This is an indebtedness that, in turn, forces celebrants into pursuing extremes of personal and financial organization to be able to meet its demands and the expectations it generates, while driving a multitude of organizational forms to devise ever more sophisticated means by which this might be obscured from sight.

In a similar vein, the seemingly easy alignment between the espoused ethical values of Christmas, such as the virtue of generosity, and more destructive practices, such as those of mass consumption, require large quantities of work so that this festive facade stays in place. The songs, stories, advertising, and the rest of the symbolic assault launched every year by those whom Bella (1992: 191) describes as the 'pushers' of the Christmas culture industry are organizationally intensive pursuits designed to convince us that to reproduce Christmas through gifting, eating, and drinking and, most importantly, by ignoring the cost to world around us, is how to truly embrace the spirit of the season. To spend often more than we can afford while taking more than we need is reconfigured into a virtue rather than a vice whereby, at 'least four of the seven deadly sins against which Christianity once railed now seen by some to be venerated in Christmas celebrations: avarice, gluttony, lust, and envy' (Belk, 1993: 75).

Furthermore, as Dickens's *Carol* reminds us, for all its progress and purported wealth creation this version of seasonal modernity can come at a heavy price. Despite being an exemplary adherent of the Protestant virtues of hard work and frugality, not only is Scrooge himself at risk of losing his humanity but the political settlement that sustains those forces of socio-economic organization through which he achieved his wealth is also threatened by the social pressures they have unleashed. For while clothed in redemptive zeal, Dickens's message is still, 'spend your money now! Have a good time today and don't worry about tomorrow' (McCaffrey, cited Davis, 1990: 223) and, in doing so, help ensure the continuation of an economic and social order that itself produces the very need for short-term remedial acts such as charity at Christmas (Storey, 2008), something that is as true today as it ever was.

Now I am not suggesting that all or indeed any of these critical insights are in themselves particularly new. Christmas is far from without its existing critics, many of whom have appeared within the pages of this book. Nonetheless, the majority of these have tended to be largely academic, restricting the force of their argument to the pages of scholarly articles or obscure books – such as this – whose readerships rarely extend beyond a small circle of like-minded souls and fellow travellers. There does exist, however a few who have taken their predominantly political objections to the season into the public sphere in a more accessible manner. Some, for example, offer small remedies for the season's worst excesses such as more sustainably shopping and celebrating more inclusively (Losada, 2022). Others, however, take a more politicized position with organizations such as *Adbusters*, who run campaigns such as 'Buy Nothing Christmas' and, more recently, 'Buy Nothing Day' every year on Black Friday to discourage excessive Christmas consumption, a campaign that has now spread worldwide.[18] In doing so, they highlight how a culturally ubiquitous dependency on consumption and the destruction that goes with it has become almost identical to the values of generosity and communal celebration that might otherwise underpin a truly rejuvenating midwinter festival.[19]

Possibly one of the best-known such anti-Christmas campaigns focusing on a similar message attacking the detrimental environmental, individual, and social costs of excessive consumption is run by New York-based performance group, *Reverend Billy and the Church of Stop Shopping*. Led by actor and activist William Talen, they have become infamous, especially on social media, for, amongst other things, guerrilla protests at stores and shopping malls over Christmas. Describing Christmas as 'toxicity with great advertising', Talen presents the argument publicly that Christmas, while ostensively premised on the celebration of love and generosity, is actually characterized by a disregard for others as our infatuation with consumerism destroys the world for everyone (Talen, 2019), including those whom we profess to care for.

Nevertheless, to reiterate the point, whatever the force and insight of such protests, there is little sign that Christmas's global popularity, especially its Anglo-American celebration, is likely to succumb to such assaults anytime soon. On the contrary, while Christmas spending will undoubtedly respond in kind to the troughs and peaks of economic trends and global uncertainties, its preeminent position as a time of consumption and extravagance is likely to be something we can expect to see for many years to come. Nor, therefore, will the focus on planning, organizing, and execution that characterizes so many people's domestic celebrations be likely to disappear either. Indeed, if one thing distnguishes Christmas, it is its resilience and ability to absorb the challenges and shocks of its time despite the contradictions that beset it. Even war and poverty, as much as love and affluence, have, at one time or another, been rationalized, packaged, and ultimately sold as integral to the magic of the season, one from which there is seemingly no escape.

Hope for Christmas?

Given such a critical and somewhat pessimistic tone, it may appear rather disingenuous to refer to hope and Christmas in the same sentence. After all, the proposition that Christmas is implicated in sustaining relations of power and the organization of particular attitudes, beliefs, and practices that, in one way or another, underwrite dominant and potentially destructive interests in society has formed an important and guiding theme throughout this book. However, this should not be taken to mean that I consider Christmas to be solely repressive or, indeed, oppressive. One cannot view power so reductively. For instance, as I argued in Chapter 1, early pagan mid-winter festivals effectively promoted social organization and integration. Faced with the threats and privations of the winter months, they reaffirmed social obligation and interdependency, which, in turn, reconstituted an active social subject and helped ensure the survival of the community.

This is not the same as claiming that all power is exercised positively or benevolently, of course. On the contrary, power can operate in structurally pathological ways, producing docile or aspirationally limited subjects (Foucault, 1979) who often act quite willingly, against their best interests. Today, for example, the ideal Christmas subject, while often formed in a similar manner, appears orientated much more towards reproducing a relatively narrow model of family life and the pursuit of a perfect Christmas through excessive acts of environmentally, and, to take Waldfogel (1993, 2009) seriously, economically destructive consumption. Similarly, as was observed in Chapter 6, seasonal magazines can be understood as active in discursively promoting narrow and restricted forms of gendered identities where women, in particular, are limited to being homemakers and domestic managers, an identity or state of subjectivity that is subsequently performed and reproduced during the season and beyond.

At the same time, as we have seen, Christmas is a complex and contradictory event. On the one hand, considering the machinations of political and religious elites, the global exploitation of both natural and human resources, and the activities of a Christmas culture industry that peddles the illusion of a unique or magical time of year based on a narrowly idealized image of the consuming festive subject, it appears to offer little in the way of the good life. Nevertheless, on the other, as Stephen Law (2003: 67) observes, Christmas often seems to go out of its way to remind us of our responsibilities towards each other and that 'there is more to life than simply accumulating wealth and possessions'. For whatever the reality of the current outcome, infused and inescapable within the Christmas message is a call to explore other ways of relating to each other; ways that transcend the strictures of an often narrowly oriented organizational rationality and that might genuinely resonate with something that, for argument's sake at least, we can call the true spirit of Christmas. This is a utopian spirit, but one that continues to tug against the narrow imperatives of the Anglo-American Christmas and that harks back to those ancient myths and stories of collective endurance, generosity, and the anticipation and celebration of renewed life. And it is here, where these two forces meet, or so I would argue, that an idea of hope might still be found.

Bloch and the Cultural Surplus

Ernst Bloch (1986a) was a radical German philosopher who significantly influenced Adorno and other Frankfurt scholars through his work, largely during the first half of the twentieth century. However, while he shared much of their emphatic distaste for mass culture, especially that of an American variety, as Vince Geoghegan (1996) has observed, Bloch resisted the idea that culture could be reduced simply to a medium of economic domination. In contrast to the pessimistic philosophy associated with many of the members of the Frankfurt School, Bloch's strain of critical theory retained a belief that no matter how ideological cultural artefacts or practices might appear, or how wedded they were to serving and protecting dominant interests, they also contained what he considered to be a utopian or transgressive content. One underpinned by what Bloch viewed as a continuing 'dream of a better life' (Bloch, 1986a: 156) that individuals might still recognize and act upon.

As cultural critic Frederic Jameson (1979) observes, what Bloch recognizes, therefore, is that ideologies – ideas circulating in society that are traditionally understood to serve the limited interests of certain groups or institutions – must contain what he considers to be a utopian element. That is, something which people desire and hope for otherwise such ideologies would not offer anything or appeal to those whose compliance they demand. Adopting an essentially Hegelian view of humankind as 'not yet finished' (Bloch, 1976: 8) and therefore open to progressive ideas, Bloch looks in particular to myths and fairy tales as repositories of such unrealized possibilities and ideas; possibilities that make themselves known through stories and adventures that tell of different worlds and that offer hope for a 'not yet', but possibly better future.

And although Bloch's emphasis is on European folklore, one can still utilize this method to examine various facets of modern culture, prompting them to expose their own potential for advancement through what Bloch calls a 'cultural surplus' (Bloch, 1986a: 154); a surplus that consists of progressive principles and aspirations that, while essential for the continuous propagation of prevailing ideologies throughout history, also maintain alternative ways of envisioning the world and its future.

Furthermore, if, like Bloch, we are interested in exploring folklore and stories as sources of hope and inspiration for envisioning alternative ways of shaping our world, it would be difficult to argue that Christmas does not offer such a source. Despite embodying the contradictions and challenges of a culture that prioritizes the efficient attainment of ends – be they economic, political, or even simply having the 'perfect' Christmas – over the intrinsic value of those ends, the Anglo-American celebration nevertheless retains a suggestion of hope for a more compassionate world, even as it justifies its worst excesses. As we have observed, beyond the superficial sentimentality, consumerism, and social pressures that come with the holiday, it may also give us sight of a more balanced way of organizing our collective existence.

From ancient carols that remind us of our shared vulnerability and responsibility to one another, to contemporary stories that transport us from the realm of self-absorption to the warmth and comfort of a season that illuminates the diverse array of emotions and aspirations that we may feel but fail to recognize in others (Bloch, 1986b: 966), Christmas offers a glimpse of a more open and compassionate approach to our relationships with each other and the world we inhabit. With its messages of goodwill and tales of redemption that arise from openness, generosity, and kindness, the holiday evokes a world in which sentiments and even gifts manifest the mutual and essential connections we share, rather than a calculated attempt to outdo others in consumption. Although rooted in idealized depictions of past seasons, such a Christmas belongs to Bloch's (1986a) concept of the 'not yet', a world that perhaps awaits us just beyond the horizon on a clear winter's night.

In the end, it is this quality that gives Dickens's tale such immense power and explains why, like so many others who are drawn to the spirit of Christmas,

I find myself returning to it time and again. Despite its self-interested defence of the prevailing social order, albeit through the guise of the values of generosity and goodwill, it is a story that ultimately hinges on the enduring importance of such values. Regardless of its imperfections, it compels the reader to contemplate dominant forms of social and economic organization, challenging the disparities and injustices that arise from them, and in so doing, it evokes the legacy of more radical ideals and possibilities. Therefore, while it is true that the most persistent legacy of *A Christmas Carol* is its emphasis on the need for middle-class philanthropy, it also insists that its actual practice is grounded in more ancient seasonal notions of reciprocity and the obligation we have to care for and support one another, recognizing our mutual interdependence and, particularly at this time of year, heightened vulnerability.

Approaching Christmas in this way raises questions and opens up the possibility of reimagining the organization of the holiday as something less transactional and more substantive. By rediscovering older ideals about the need to come together in mid-winter to acknowledge our mutual reliance on each other, it may, as echoed by the Santa Claus performers I interviewed, offer a real chance to 'give something back' and to embody the values of compassion and generosity that are so often espoused but rarely realized during the holiday season. However, this generosity cannot be measured solely by the amount one spends on gifts or participates in rituals of exchange. Rather, it should be reclaimed as the core of a truly intersubjective celebration, where giving is a way of being with others in the world, based on recognizing each other's unique but interconnected status and interdependence (Diprose, 2002).

A different perspective on Christmas could transcend the mere exchange of gifts and time between individuals. Instead, it could be rooted in older ideals of mutual interdependence and vulnerability, where acts of generosity and compassion are not just espoused but realized. This transformation would necessitate recognizing the intricacies and fragility of our existence and fostering an environment conducive to mutual growth and genuine fulfillment. Such an approach would not diminish the importance of organizing Christmas as a celebration; but would seek to embrace alternative avenues of pursuing it, becoming a collective acknowledgment of life amidst a season of decay and an uncertain future, mirroring the earth's renewal as another year begins.

This would be neither exploitative nor sentimental, but rather characteristic of a Christmas that mediates not only individual wants and desires, but our mutual interdependence. Like Santa Claus, it would not judge or take advantage of our need for recognition but instead serve as a foundation for a more meaningful and fulfilling Christmas worthy of the name.

Not that it is my intention to provide a definitive blueprint for what a transformed Christmas would look like in terms of its organizational practices. Such an endeavour goes beyond the scope of this book. Moreover, the likelihood of ever realizing such a vision seems remote given the current balance of power and the pervasive demands and expectations associated with the holiday. To achieve such a transformation would require a fundamental shift in the economic, cultural, and individual pressures that have come to define Christmas.

Nonetheless, even in the face of such obstacles, it may yet be worthwhile to hold onto the dream of a more compassionate and generous Christmas, not as a final destination, perhaps, but as a glimmer of hope and a reminder of the true spirit – or possibly three – of the season. This may yet give Christmas a renewed sense of purpose and meaning, not only for those who seek a deeper understanding of the holiday but for anyone who aspires to more redemptive ways of managing, organizing, and living their everyday lives both at Christmas and throughout the year. Lives that, as Dickens (2006: 12) reminds us, need not be defined solely by self-interest, but rather by a recollection of the fact that we really are but 'fellow-passengers to the grave, and not another race of creatures bound on other journeys'.

Notes

1 www.un.org/en/actnow/facts-and-figures
2 www.unep.org/explore-topics/climate-action/facts-about-climate-emergency
3 www.gov.uk/government/news/a-greener-christmas-is-the-best-present-for-the-environment
4 https://weareearthcollective.com/6-facts-about-christmas-waste-amp-what-you-can-do-to-help-show-the-planet-some-kindness-this-christmas/
5 www.york.ac.uk/news-and-events/news/2007/carbon-christmas/
6 https://wayback.archive-it.org/9650/20200402070851/http://p3-raw.greenpeace.org/africa/en/News/news/A-Greener-Christmas/
7 www.youtube.com/watch?v=wr2LCTdIzd4
8 https://t.co/YL0GIvfRuq
9 www.all-creatures.org/articles/ar-thetrue-factsheet.pdf
10 www.youtube.com/watch?v=ePPmOgdV8BQ
11 www.mind.org.uk/information-support/tips-for-everyday-living/christmas-and-mental-health/
12 According to the Mental Health Foundation, around 26% of homeless people in the UK cite mental health issues as a reason for their homelessness. www.mentalhealth.org.uk/explore-mental-health/mental-health-statistics/homelessness-statistics
13 See, for example, the 2021 Christmas campaign by UK housing and homeless charity Shelter, and their hard-hitting seasonal video, www.youtube.com/watch?v=u08qmwGl90E&t=2s
14 For example, this local project in the City of Bristol, UK – www.youtube.com/watch?v=xPcOXVLiXzk&t=1s
15 https://news.npcc.police.uk/releases/forces-to-crack-down-on-drink-and-drug-driving-this-christmas
16 www.merseyside.police.uk/news/merseyside/news/2021/december/support-for-domestic-abuse-victims-at-christmas/

17 www.actionfraud.police.uk/news/action-fraud-launches-new-campaign-to-fight-back-against-fraud-this-christmas
18 www.buynothingday.co.uk
19 www.adbusters.org/submissions/what-does-an-anti-capitalist-christmas-look-like

References

Al-Othman, H. (2015) 'Lewisham Police Christmas Tree Labelled "Most Depressing in UK"'. *Evening Standard*, Wednesday December 9.

Australian Conservation Foundation (2005) *The Hidden Cost of Christmas: The Environmental Impact of Australian Christmas Spending*. Carlton: Australian Conservation Foundation.

Balloo, S. (2020) 'Reality for Children Spending Christmas in a Women's Refuge After Fleeing Domestic Abuse'. *Birmingham Live*, November 29. Available at: www.birminghammail.co.uk/news/midlands-news/reality-children-spending-christmas-womens-19339902

Belk, R. (1993) 'Materialism and the Making of the Modern American Christmas'. In, D. Miller (ed.) *Unwrapping Christmas*. Oxford: Oxford University Press. Pp. 75–104.

Bella, L. (1992) *The Christmas Imperative: Leisure, Family, and Women's Work*. Halifax: Fernwood Publishing.

Bennett, T. (1981) 'Christmas and Ideology'. In, *Popular Culture: Themes and Issues 1*. Milton Keynes: Open University Press. Pp. 49–74.

Berger, P.L. (1967) *The Sacred Canopy: Elements of a Sociology of Religion*. New York, NY: Anchor Books.

Bloch, E. (1976) 'Dialectics and Hope'. *New German Critique* 9: 3–10.

Bloch, E. (1986a) *The Principle of Hope, Volume One* (trans. N. Plaice, S. Plaice and P. Knight). Oxford: Basil Blackwell.

Bloch, E. (1986b) *The Principle of Hope, Volume Three* (trans. N. Plaice, S. Plaice and P. Knight). Oxford: Basil Blackwell.

Bové, A-T. and Swartz, S. (2016) *Starting at the Source: Sustainability in Supply Chains*. Available at: www.mckinsey.com/capabilities/sustainability/our-insights/starting-at-the-source-sustainability-in-supply-chains

Browne, B. (2021) 'Irish Households Create More Than 81,000 Tonnes of Packing Waste Over Christmas'. In, *Independent.ie*, January 2. Available at: www.independent.ie/regionals/corkman/news/irish-households-create-more-than-81000-tonnes-of-packing-waste-over-christmas-39915167.html

Bryant, R.L. (2010) 'Peering into the Abyss: Environment, Research and Absurdity in the 'Age of Stupid'. In, M. Redclift and G. Woodgate (eds) *The International Handbook of Environmental Sociology*. Cheltenham: Edward Elgar. Pp. 179–188.

Burton, N. (2012) 'Is Suicide More Common at Christmas Time?'. *Psychology Today*. Available at: www.psychologytoday.com/gb/blog/hide-and-seek/201212/is-suicide-more-common-christmas-time

Cavanagh, B., Ibrahim, S., Roscoe, A., Bickley, H. et al. (2016) 'The Timing of General Population and Patient Suicide in England, 1997–2012'. *Journal of Affective Disorders* 197: 175–181.

Colbeck, I. (2016) 'Air Pollution Expert: Why Christmas May Be the Most Toxic Day Of The Year'. *The Conversation*, December 21. Available at: https://theconve rsation.com/air-pollution-expert-why-christmas-may-be-the-most-toxic-day-of-the-year-70611

Coren, M. (2022) 'Christians Can't Blame Anyone Else for the Decline in Belief: A Vocal, Intolerant Minority Has Defined Us for Too Long'. *The New Statesman*, November 30. Available at: www.newstatesman.com/quickfire/2022/11/decline-christianity-ons-census-uk-resolve

Cotton, B. (2021) 'Is Christmas Ruining the Environment?'. *Business Leader*, December 8. Available at: www.businessleader.co.uk/is-christmas-ruining-the-environment/

Dale, R., Budimir, S., Probst, T., Stippl, P. and Pieh, C. (2021) 'Mental Health During the COVID-19 Lockdown Over the Christmas Period in Austria and the Effects of Sociodemographic and Lifestyle Factors'. *International Journal of Environmental Research and Public Health* 18: 1–15.

Davis, P. (1990) *The Lives and Times of Ebenezer Scrooge*. New Haven, MA: Yale University Press.

Devereux, E. (2021) 'Not Just for Christmas: News Media Coverage of Homelessness'. In, S.L. Borden (ed.) *The Routledge Companion to Media and Poverty*. Abingdon: Routledge. Pp. 331–339.

Dickens, C. (2006) 'A Christmas Carol in Prose: Being a Ghost Story of Christmas'. In, R. Douglas-Fairhurst (ed.) *A Christmas Carol and Other Christmas Stories*. Oxford: Oxford University Press. Pp. 5–83.

Diprose, R. (2002) *Corporeal Generosity: On Giving with Nietzsche, Merleau-Ponty and Levinas*. Albany, NY: SUNY.

Dobson, M. (2022) 'Christmas Packaging Facts: The Definitive List'. *GWP Group*, December 5. Available at: www.gwp.co.uk/guides/christmas-packaging-facts/

Dodds, L. (2019) 'Unwrapped: Christmas Waste Costs the UK £26 Million'. *Mattress Online*, November 27. Available at: www.mattressonline.co.uk/blog/family/christ mas-waste-unwrapped/

Etzioni, A. (2004) 'Holidays and Rituals: Neglected Seedbeds of Virtue'. In, A. Etzioni and J. Bloom (eds) *We Are What We Celebrate: Understanding Holidays and Rituals*. New York, NY: New York University Press. Pp. 3–40.

Fancourt, D., Bu, F., Mak, H.W., Paul, E. and Steptoe, A. (2022) *Covid-19 Social Study: Results Release 42*. London: Nuffield Foundation. Available at: www.covid socialstudy.org/_files/ugd/064c8b_aa8703947d6f4baa97bbbeca2d127ca4.pdf

Farbotko, C. and Head, L. (2013) 'Gifts, Sustainable Consumption and Giving Up Green Anxieties at Christmas'. *Geoforum* 50: 88–96.

Ferner, R. and Aronson, J.K (2020) 'Harms and the Xmas Factor'. *British Medical Journal*. Available at: www.bmj.com/content/371/bmj.m4067.full

Foucault, M. (1979) *Discipline and Punish: The Birth of the Prison* (trans. A. Sheridan). London: Penguin.

Geoghegan, V. (1996) *Ernst Bloch*. London: Routledge.

Hache, A.C.B. and Ryder, N. (2011) 'Tis The Season to (Be Jolly?) Wise-Up to Online Fraudsters. Criminals on the Web Lurking to Scam Shoppers This Christmas: A Critical Analysis of the United Kingdom's Legislative Provisions and Policies to Tackle Online Fraud'. *Information & Communications Technology Law* 20(1): 35–56.

Hall, M. (2021) 'Christmas Waste Facts – It's Not Very Jolly'. *Business Waste.co.uk*. www.businesswaste.co.uk/christmas-waste-facts-its-not-very-jolly/

Hancock, P., Tyler, M. and Godiva, M. (2021) 'Thursday Night and a Sing-along "Sung Alone": The Experiences of a Self-employed Performer During the Pandemic'. *Work, Employment and Society* 35(6): 1155–1166.

Hillard, J.R., Holland, J.M. and Ramm, D. (1981) 'Christmas and Psychopathology: Data from a Psychiatric Emergency Room Population'. *Archives of General Psychiatry* 38(12): 1377–1381.

Horrigan, L., Lawrence, R. S. And Walker, P. (2002) 'How Sustainable Agriculture Can Address the Environmental and Human Health Harms of Industrial Agriculture'. *Environmental Health Perspectives* 110(5): 445–456.

Insley, J. (2010) 'Three Pets Abandoned Every Hour Over Christmas – RSPCA'. *The Guardian*, December 31. Available at: www.theguardian.com/money/2010/dec/31/three-pets-abandoned-christmas-rspca

Islam, S., Uwadiae, N. and Hayter, J.P. (2016) 'Assault-Related Facial Injuries During the Season of Goodwill'. *Oral Surgery, Oral Medicine, Oral Pathology and Oral Radiology* 121(6): 139–42.

Jameson, F. (1979) 'Reification and Utopia in Mass Culture'. *Social Text* 1: 130–148.

Jessop, A. (2022) 'Christmas Pollution: Why is it Important to Have An Eco-Friendly Christmas?'. *Commercial Waste*. Available at: https://commercialwaste.trade/the-true-cost-of-christmas/

Kaonga, G. (2021) 'Santa Claus Detained by Police at Christmas Market in Viral Video'. *Newsweek*. Tuesday September 2022.

Kay, A. (2019) *Twas the Nightshift Before Christmas*. London: Picador.

Kuehnel, T. (2016) 'Time to Rethink the Turkey: What Christmas Really Costs Us'. *The Vegan Society*, December 23. Available at: www.vegansociety.com/news/blog/time-rethink-turkey-what-christmas-really-costs-us

Law, S. (2003) *The Xmas Files: The Philosophy of Christmas*. London: Weidenfeld & Nicolson.

Losada, I. (2022) 'Tis The Season For Cheap Tat and Bad Food. Or – Why Not Try a truly Jolly Green Christmas?'. *The Guardian*, Wednesday, December 21.

Marsden, R. (2017) *A Very British Christmas: Twelve Days of Discomfort and Joy*. Harper Collins: London.

Miller, D. (1993) 'A Theory of Christmas'. In, D. Miller (ed.) *Unwrapping Christmas*. Oxford: Oxford University Press. Pp. 3–37.

Mohammad, M.A., Karlsson, S., Haddad, J., Cederberg, B., Jernberg, T., Lindahl, B. et al. (2018) 'Christmas, National Holidays, Sport Events, and Time Factors as Triggers of Acute Myocardial Infarction: SWEDEHEART observational study 1998–2013'. *British Medical Journal*. 363: k4811.

Morris, T. (2015) *The Hidden Dangers of a Victorian Christmas*. Available at: www.thomas-morris.uk/hidden-dangers-christmas/

NHS Choices (2012) *Keep Safe this Christmas*. London: NHS.

Nolsoe, E. (2019) 'How Does Christmas Impact People's Mental Health?'. *YouGov*, December 18. Available at: https://yougov.co.uk/topics/health/articles-reports/2019/12/18/christmas-harms-mental-health-quarter-brits

O'Brien, M. (2008) *A Crisis of Waste: Understanding the Rubbish Society*. London: Routledge.

Office for National Statistics (2022) Coronavirus, Spending Habits and Spending Plans Over Christmas, UK: January 2022. Available at: www.ons.gov.uk/peopl epopulationandcommunity/healthandsocialcare/healthandwellbeing/articles/ coronavirusspendinghabitsandsocialisingplansoverchristmasuk/january2022

Oppenheim, M. (2021) 'Women's Charities Fear an Increase in Domestic Abuse This Christmas'. *The Independent*, November 21. Available at: www.independent.co.uk/ news/uk/home-news/domestic-abuse-christmas-stresses-b1956631.html

Palmer-Sutton, N. (2014) 'Save Santa's Home | Integrated Campaign' *Creativepool*. Available at: https://creativepool.com/NatSutton/projects/save-santas-home-for-gre enpeace

Peachey, K. (2022) 'Cost of Living: Charity Warns Christmas Debt Could Take Years to Repay'. *BBC News*, February 26. Available at: www.bbc.co.uk/news/business-64235996

Phillips, D., Barker, G.E. and Brewer, K.M. (2010) 'Christmas and New Year as Risk Factors for Death'. *Social Science of Medicine* 71(8): 1463–1471.

Powys, L. (2010) *Christmas Lore and Legend: Yuletide Essays*. Sherborne: The Sundial Press.

Reason, N. (2019) 'Officers of the Christmas Shift'. December 12. Available at: www.der byshire.police.uk/news/derbyshire/news/campaigns/2019/december/officers-of-the-christmas-shift/

Rycenga, J. (2008) 'Religious Controversies Over Christmas'. In, S. Whiteley (ed.) *Christmas, Ideology and Popular Culture*. Edinburgh: Edinburgh University Press. Pp. 71–87.

Shaw, B. (1973) *Music in London 1890–94: Criticisms Contributed Week by Week to the World, Volume III*. New York, NY: Vienna House.

Storer, R. (2021) 'Burglaries Rise Over Christmas in West Midlands and Most Go Unsolved'. *Birmingham Live*, December 31. Available at: www.birminghammail. co.uk/black-country/burglaries-rise-over-christmas-west-22615946

Storey, J. (2008) 'The Invention of the English Christmas'. In, S. Whiteley (ed.) *Christmas, Ideology and Popular Culture*. Edinburgh: Edinburgh University Press. Pp. 17–31.

Talen, W. (2019) 'Christmas Is Toxicity with Great Advertising'. *Medium*, December 27. Available at: https://medium.com/@revbillytalen/christmas-is-toxicity-with-great-advertising-cd92ca6875d7

Topham, G. (2021) 'Police and Banks Tell Shoppers to Be Vigilant for Black Friday Scams'. *The Guardian*, Monday November 22.

Urry, J. (1990) *The Tourist Gaze: Leisure and Travel in Contemporary Societies*. London: Sage.

Verney, C. (2021) 'Why the Increase in Domestic Violence Over Christmas?'. *DV-ACT*. Available at: www.dvact.org/post/why-does-domestic-violence-increase-over-christmas

Waldfogel, J. (1993) 'The Deadweight Loss of Christmas'. *The American Economic Review* 83(5): 1328–1336.

Waldfogel, J. (2009) *Scroogenomics: Why You Shouldn't Buy Presents for the Holidays*. Princeton, NJ: Princeton University Press.

Weber, M. (1976) *The Protestant Ethic and the Spirit of Capitalism*. London: Allen & Unwin.

Wild, U., Shaw, D.M. and Erren, T.C. (2021) 'Avoiding a Crisis at Christmas: A Systematic Review of Adverse Health Effects or "Chrishaps" Caused by Traditional Hazard Sources and COVID-19. *Australian and New Zealand Journal of Public Health* 46(1): 32–35.

Yeiser, B. (2021) 'My Homeless Christmas: During the Holiday Season, I Look Back on Christmases I Spent Outside, Alone'. *Psychology Today*, December 4. Available at: www.psychologytoday.com/gb/blog/recovery-road/202112/my-homeless-christmas

INDEX

Printed in the United States
by Baker & Taylor Publisher Services